Supporting Traumatized Children and Teenagers

by the same author

Grief in Children
A Handbook for Adults
2nd Edition
Foreword by Professor William Yule
ISBN 978 1 84310 612 8

Grief in Young Children
A Handbook for Adults
Foreword by Professor William Yule
ISBN 978 1 84310 650 0

Effective Grief and Bereavement Support
The Role of Family, Friends, Colleagues, Schools and Support Professionals
Kari Dyregrov and Atle Dyregrov
Foreword by Magne Raundalen
ISBN 978 1 84310 667 8

of related interest

Children and Adolescents in Trauma
Creative Therapeutic Approaches
Chris Nicholson, Michael Irwin and Kedar N. Dwivedi
Foreword by Peter Wilson
ISBN 978 1 84310 437 7
Community, Culture and Change Series

A Child's Journey to Recovery
Assessment and Planning with Traumatized Children
Patrick Tomlinson and Terry Philpot
Foreword by Mary Walsh
ISBN 978 1 84310 330 1
Delivering Recovery Series

Living Alongside a Child's Recovery
Therapeutic Parenting with Traumatized Children
Billy Pughe and Terry Philpot
Foreword by Mary Walsh
ISBN 978 1 84310 328 8
Delivering Recovery Series

Introduction to Counselling Survivors of Interpersonal Trauma
Christiane Sanderson
ISBN 978 1 84310 962 4

Safeguarding Children Living with Trauma and Family Violence
Evidence-Based Assessment, Analysis and Planning Interventions
Arnon Bentovim, Anthony Cox, Liz Bingley-Miller and Stephen Pizzey
Foreword by Brigid Daniel
ISBN 978 1 84310 938 9
Best Practice in Working with Children Series

Supporting Traumatized Children and Teenagers

A Guide to Providing Understanding and Help

Atle Dyregrov

Jessica Kingsley *Publishers*
London and Philadelphia

First published in 1997 in Norwegian by
Fagbokforlaget, Bergen, Norway, as *Barn og Traumer*

This edition first published in English in 2010
by Jessica Kingsley Publishers
116 Pentonville Road
London N1 9JB, UK
and
400 Market Street, Suite 400
Philadelphia, PA 19106, USA

www.jkp.com

Copyright © Atle Dyregrov 1997
Translation copyright © Diane Oatley 2010

This translation has been published with the financial support of NORLA

Library of Congress Cataloging in Publication Data
Dyregrov, Atle.
  [Barn og Traumer. English]
  Supporting traumatized children and teenagers : a guide to
providing understanding and help / Atle Dyregrov.
    p. ; cm.
  Includes bibliographical references and index.
  ISBN 978-1-84905-034-0 (alk. paper)
  1. Child psychotherapy. 2. Adolescent psychotherapy. I. Title.
  [DNLM: 1. Stress Disorders, Traumatic. 2. Adolescent. 3. Child. WM 172 D998s 2010a]
  RJ504.D9713 2010
  618.92'8914--dc22

                          2010004297

British Library Cataloguing in Publication Data
A CIP catalogue record for this book is available from the British Library

ISBN 978 1 84905 034 0

Printed and bound in Great Britain by
MPG Books Group

Contents

Preface   9

1   What is Trauma?   11

2   Children's Reactions During and After Traumatic
     Events   15
     Immediate reactions   *15*
     The after-effects of traumas   *21*
     The long-term effects of traumas   *34*
     Post-Traumatic Stress Disorder (PTSD)   *42*

3   Some Important Aspects of Trauma   50
     Trauma and different life stages   *50*
     Traumatic reminders   *53*
     Interactions with others – parents' reactions, attachment and the home
     environment   *55*
     Children who live with domestic violence   *58*
     Trauma and memory   *61*

4   Girls and Boys – Alike or Different?   67
     Gender differences in the context of trauma   *67*

5   The Significance of Friends Following a Trauma   73
     The significance of friends in the lives of children   *73*
     Friends and traumas   *74*
     Encouraging contact with friends   *77*

6   What Promotes Risk and What Protects?   79
     Coping with traumatic events   *79*
     What influences children's reactions to trauma?   *81*
     When does the child need more help?   *83*
     Factors that contribute to resilience in children   *89*
     Assessment of the need for help   *90*

7 Help for Children After Traumas   **95**
Early intervention   *95*
Different intervention methods for helping children   *101*
Help methods   *118*

8 Groups for Children Following Trauma   **128**
The purpose of gathering in a group setting   *128*
Debriefing groups for children   *132*

9 Post-Traumatic Therapy   **143**
What works?   *143*
Commencement of therapy   *148*
Post-traumatic therapy – different methods   *152*
Therapy for avoidance reactions   *167*
Help for 'existential' problems and feelings of guilt   *183*
Therapy after cumulative traumas   *191*

10 Traumas and the School   **198**
Traumas and school performance   *198*
Handling trauma and grief in the school   *203*
Schools and violence   *207*
Schools and suicide   *214*

11 Being a Helper   **220**
Why is work with traumatized children so exhausting?   *220*
Reactions among those who help traumatized children   *221*
Help for helpers   *223*
Conclusion   *229*

Appendix 1
Post-Traumatic Problems: Help for Preschool
and Early School-Age Children (4–7 years)   231

Appendix 2
Post-Traumatic Problems: Help for School-Age Children   233

Subject Index   235

Author Index   239

List of Figures, Tables and Boxes

Figures

Figure 2.1 Immediate reactions 15
Figure 7.1 Being witness to a grandfather's death 113
Figure 9.1 Example of a computer mixing board 157

Tables

Table 3.1 Traumatic reminders 53
Table 4.1 How do you think adults can help children and young
people who are grieving? 68
Table 6.1 Risk profile 87
Table 9.1 Changing views of a traumatic event 181

Boxes

Box 4.1 Help for boys and men 71
Box 6.1 Risk factors 84
Box 7.1 Immediate intervention for children after traumas 95
Box 7.2 Early help for children after traumas 98
Box 7.3 Help measures 102
Box 7.4 Discussions with children and young people 119
Box 8.1 Addressing a traumatic event in a group 132
Box 8.2 Simple advice for the day the trauma occurred 133
Box 8.3 Small event-related groups for older children and adolescents 136
Box 9.1 Simple advice for establishing good contact 150
Box 10.1 Risk signs of PTSD among friends after a suicide 216

Preface

Up until very recently, the general assumption has been that children are affected by traumatic events only to a limited extent. The expression 'out of sight, out of mind' was presumed to be a reflection of a child's reality. If adults only avoided speaking about what had happened, the child would forget and grow out of any problems. This attitude remains prevalent, and adults will frequently deny children access to information, to participation in rituals or to knowledge about how adults are feeling.

Although children should have the right to forget and be permitted to decide for themselves how much they wish to speak about painful topics, we know that 'protection' from the realities of life can hurt more than help them.

This book is intended as a helpful tool for adults, both specialists and lay people, in their meetings with children who have experienced traumas, or as a form of preparation for such situations. Some parts of the text may seem obvious to those who already have a lot of knowledge, while other parts may be difficult for those who do not have experience of working with traumatized children. When interventions are described, the emphasis has been on including a number of concrete methods that can alleviate the impact of trauma. These are found predominantly in the therapy chapter (Chapter 9). Many of these methods can be used as self-help methods, without it being necessary for adults to have the expertise of trained therapists in order to be able to help children in using them. I have attempted to cover the field in such a way as to make it possible for many to benefit from the presentation. I hope I have been successful in this endeavour.

Although a single author is listed as responsible for this book, it is of course a product of collaboration and discussions with others working within the field. First and foremost, colleagues at the Center for Crisis

Psychology have been of great significance in my work on the book. The many discussions, and in particular the unique climate of mutual respect and professional inspiration found at the Center, have provided insight and energy for the writing process. Although all my colleagues have been important, Magne Raundalen must be singled out. His generosity and intellectual breadth have held a unique importance for my work with traumatized children in general and with this book in particular.

Professor Emeritus William Yule in London and his colleagues have given me valuable support over the course of many years. Although they are not responsible for what I have written in this book, the many conversations and discussions we have had, and everything that they have taught me, have influenced the presentation.

My dear wife has made extremely valuable contributions towards understanding the reactions of children and adults in confrontation with a potentially traumatizing death, in addition to the warm support she has provided on the home front. Without the added benefits of her professional experience in this field, the writing process would have been too great a burden to bear. My children and grandchild have also provided me with the energy for new projects.

I am also extremely thankful that we have received funding from Denmark for 'Grief center — a research project funded by the Egmont Fund'. This makes possible increased knowledge and improved assistance for the many children who experience traumatic death.

1

What is Trauma?

Words such as 'crisis', 'catastrophe' and 'trauma' have become a part of our daily vocabulary, although in our usage of these words we do not always necessarily have an awareness of their actual meaning. Most people associate such words with sudden readjustments, dramatic events and psychological stress and strain. The word 'crisis' is perhaps the least potent, because some crises do not occur suddenly or dramatically, but instead develop gradually or in connection with transitional phases in life. In the latter case, the crisis is called 'a developmental crisis'. But the word 'crisis' is most frequently used in reference to changes that occur suddenly and unexpectedly, without allowing time for any particular emotional preparation. The words 'catastrophe' and 'trauma' are used almost exclusively in reference to sudden and dramatic events. Catastrophes signify large-scale events that have an impact on many people, such as accidents where a large number of people are injured or killed. But individual accidents and events are just as catastrophic for those who are affected – these are sometimes called 'private catastrophes'.

This book is about trauma. Within the field of medicine, the word 'trauma' is most commonly used to describe bone fracture injuries. Usage of the term has gradually evolved to refer to overwhelming psychological strain. Psychological traumas will almost always entail a crisis situation, although a crisis situation is not necessarily always a traumatic situation. We know that many incidents, in spite of their being extreme in nature, do not necessarily inflict long-term reactions in those who experience them. The expression 'potentially traumatic events' is therefore the correct term. This is, however, such a cumbersome expression that I have chosen instead to use the word 'trauma' for these events too, fully aware that not everyone will subsequently suffer long-term problems. The expression 'psychological trauma', or 'trauma', as it is used in this book, refers to overwhelming, uncontrollable incidents entailing an extraordinary psychological strain for the child or young person exposed to them. Usually such incidents arise suddenly, and unexpectedly, but some are repeated in a manner that is more or less identical (maltreatment, sexual abuse, etc.) without the child having any possibility to prevent this. Such incidents often lead to the child feeling helpless and vulnerable.

What is traumatic for a child depends on a number of factors. The situation or context in which the incident occurs is of significance; for example, should a bomb explode in London, this would be experienced differently from the way it would be in Gaza. If a child experiences a threatening experience while accompanied by parents who react calmly, the incident can be experienced as simply stressful, while those who are not in the presence of their parents, or whose parents are extremely anxious, can experience the situation as traumatic. The significance that the child attributes to the event, the child's developmental stage, temperament and previous developmental history are other contributing factors that determine the extent to which the situation is traumatic for a child. Children who are prepared in advance for a medical procedure, for instance, or for hospitalisation, can master such experiences well, while children who are unprepared can experience the situation as clearly traumatic. It is therefore not the case that a given situation in itself can be clearly said to be traumatic or not for a child: the child's interpretation of [...] factors in the situation contribute to determining [...]

[...] psychiatrist Leonore Terr (1991) distinguished [...] types of traumatic situations. She called one of [...] his involves individual events such as an accident, [...]ality, violence, rape or another kind of dramatic, [...] cond type of trauma she called 'type II trauma', [...] where people live through a series of traumatic [...] buse, maltreatment or war. It has also been shown [...] eatments, associated with some serious illnesses, [...]ost-traumatic reactions (Kazak *et al.* 2007). Type [...]ult if children witness violence and abuse in the [...] hether or not this leads to a splitting up of the [...] d that exposure to bullying during childhood can [...] reactions in children, although little systematic investigation has been carried out on this subject.

[handwritten note: Type I and Type 2 Trauma]

Children need not personally be the victims of dangerous or frightening events in order to be traumatized: being a witness to frightening events, such as the death or serious injury of others, can also result in post-traumatic reactions. In particular, witnessing violence against a parent is a traumatic experience for many children. Saigh (1991) has also shown that hearing about a serious threat that affects the child's immediate family or friends can traumatize children. Research on world events, such as the terrorist attacks on 11 September 2001, has shown that children's indirect exposure through television and the internet can also lead to an increase in post-traumatic symptoms among those who are not affected personally and who are far away from the site of the disaster (Lengua *et al.* 2005, 2007).

Children who experience potentially traumatic situations do not necessarily develop long-term post-traumatic problems. If the living conditions in their environment are good, if they have good internal resources and a good caring environment, very many children cope well both during and after traumatic events. A number of children, on the other hand, develop problems or symptoms that collectively fall under the definition of Post-Traumatic Stress Disorder (PTSD), which will be described in further detail in Chapter 2. A traumatic situation can of course also result in after-effects other than PTSD, such as strong feelings of guilt, phobias, depression or behavioural problems.

The type, scope and duration of post-traumatic reactions will to a large degree depend upon whether the child experiences an isolated event, or is exposed to a series of traumatic events. An isolated event does not involve the same degree of change in the psychological make-up as do repeated events (cumulative traumas). With a good caring environment to provide support in working through what has taken place, an isolated incident can be more easily confronted, expressed and integrated into the child's emotional life than is the case with long-term, repetitive trauma situations.

If children live under the constant bombardment of traumatic events, different emotional mechanisms will be activated to help them live with or defend themselves against what is happening. As a defence against the intense inner feelings that are produced, children who experience such cumulative traumas will often employ denial, rejection and repression of their own emotional reactions. In addition, children can employ so-called dissociation, which means that a division is automatically created between feelings, behaviour and thoughts. Dissociation is an effective mechanism for protection against psychological pain, and once it has first been implemented is often employed with increasing frequency over time.

> A girl who experienced living in constant conflict due to domestic violence in her home relates that to survive she imagined that she was at the movies, and watching everything from the outside. This permitted her to be a kind of observer of it all without being obliged to react emotionally.

Such dissociation provides distance from the event, but it can also be accompanied by the sense of not being whole as a human being. In adulthood, those who have employed dissociation frequently as children may find that they continue to protect themselves from feelings in the same manner. Children who have experienced sexual abuse can describe how they employed 'self-hypnosis' in a manner that enabled them to avoid feeling pain in the situation. Regardless of which mechanisms children employ to master such a situation, the result of long-term traumatization appears to be an increasing emotional constriction, whereby they gradually lose the ability to register their feelings. Diseth (2005), who has presented a good overview of dissociation in children, maintains that a high percentage of patients within child and adolescent psychiatry show dissociation symptoms, and that many of these are mistakenly diagnosed with a number of other disorders. The dissociation reactions to a large extent reflect the relatively large number of children who experience psychological or physical maltreatment and sexual abuse.

References

Diseth, T.H. (2005) 'Dissociation in children and adolescents as reaction to trauma – an overview of conceptual issues and neurobiological factors.' *Nordic Journal of Psychiatry 59*, 79–91.

Kazak, A.E., Rourke, M.T., Alderfer, M.A., Pai, A., Reilly, A.F. and Meadows, A.T. (2007) 'Evidence-based assessment, intervention and psychosocial care in paediatric oncology. A blueprint for comprehensive services across treatment.' *Journal of Pediatric Psychology 32*, 1099–1110.

Lengua, L.J., Long, A.C. and Meltzoff, A.N. (2007) 'Pre-attack stress-load, appraisals, and coping in children's responses to the 9/11 terrorist attacks.' *Journal of Child Psychology and Psychiatry 47*, 1219–1227.

Lengua, L.J., Long, A.C., Smith, K.I. and Meltzoff, A.N. (2005) 'Pre-attack symptomatology and temperament as predictors of children's responses to the September 11 terrorist attacks.' *Journal of Child Psychology and Psychiatry 46*, 631–645.

Saigh, P.A. (1991) 'The development of posttraumatic stress disorder following four different types of traumatization.' *Behavior Research and Therapy 29*, 213–216.

Terr, L.C. (1991) 'Childhood traumas: an outline and overview.' *American Journal of Psychiatry 148*, 10–20.

2

Children's Reactions During and After Traumatic Events

Immediate reactions

Figure 2.1 depicts some of the mechanisms that are activated when children and adults experience traumatic situations.

Physical

- Mobilization of the body
  - Adrenaline
  - Nor-adrenaline

  ↓

- Physical mobilization
  - Rapid reaction
  - Ready to handle danger

  ↓

- Block/reduce pain

Mental

- Mobilization of the mind
  - Previous experience and knowledge available
  - Increased sensory awareness
  - Focused attention
  - Strong memory formation
  - Rapid processing of information

- Emotional suppresion

Figure 2.1 Immediate reactions

These are mechanisms that nature equips us with, mechanisms that cause a rapid mobilization in response to danger. These mechanisms have evolved over the course of thousands of years, in eras with living conditions very different from those of the current era. The mechanisms are activated when we experience different kinds of threats. While our knowledge about the physical mobilization is well documented, we have less knowledge about the emotional mobilization (Dyregrov, Solomon and Bassøe 2000). Clinical experience and knowledge acquired from regions engaged in warfare indicate that these mechanisms begin to function even in relatively young children, but naturally it is difficult to acquire reports from preschool age children.

When we are exposed to something that we experience as a serious threat, both physical and emotional survival mechanisms are activated that help us in the situation. On the physical level, a mobilization of the body occurs that enables us to react quickly (with flight or a fight for survival) and increase our muscular strength. This equips us to address the danger. If a child is inflicted with a serious physical injury, these survival mechanisms can diminish or block out pain, thus enabling the child to warn others or reach home before being overwhelmed by pain. A rapid response can lead to children running from danger or increasing their chances of survival in other ways. On the emotional level, a corresponding mobilization occurs. If the child has previously experienced or learned something that can be used to handle the new situation, this experience will be activated. This can occur automatically in the form of what we call intuition, or by the child remembering something heard from their parents or at school, or picked up from television, the newspaper, etc.

> A boy was home alone when a fire broke out in a pot on the stove. He reacted spontaneously and correctly by putting a lid on the pot and extinguishing the fire. Afterwards he explained that he had heard a friend explaining this solution. In the situation he knew immediately what he should do.

The brain searches through 'the experience bank' for relevant experiences. It goes without saying that a child's experience bank is smaller than an adult's and therefore children can frequently make an incorrect assessment or not know what to do.

When the brain has registered the dangerous situation, the sensory input will be intensified, so that information from the surroundings can be absorbed quickly and clearly for use in an evaluation of what must be done. A good example of this mechanism is when children are home alone and think that they hear a sound. They become frightened and believe that somebody may be trying to break into the apartment or house. Immediately they become attentive to every sound that occurs, but sounds can often be misinterpreted and they then become convinced that someone is trying to break in. In such a situation, children are extremely sensitive to all auditory signals.

In a traumatic situation, a heightened sensitivity in the sensory channels helps children to take in information. This occurs in order to determine how the situation is to be handled. At the same time, the children's attention is focused on what they perceive as being the most important aspect of the situation at hand. In a threatening situation, children will be extremely focused on the perpetrator's eyes and any weapons or threatening movements that this person makes. Such survival responses enable children to 'read' the situation more easily and act accordingly.

Denholm (1995) tells an incredible story of how an 11-year-old girl survived an attack by a puma. She utilized what she had learned from a first-aid course to stop the bleeding from a head wound, and to stay calm while waiting for help she concentrated on repeating to herself some pages from her maths book. In this way she was able to prevent herself from becoming 'hysterical'. The puma attacked her several times during the four-hour period before she was rescued. She needed medical treatment for more than six months afterwards. Her account shows clearly how well the emotional survival mechanisms can function in a traumatic situation. She maintained control and stayed focused on surviving, while personally treating her wounds throughout, even though the danger of attack was still present.

Recall or memory functions change in a traumatic situation so that some things are remembered well while other things are forgotten. After a traumatic situation children may speak of how they can remember certain aspects of the incident in great detail and with great intensity, while other aspects can be easily overlooked or experienced as having been forgotten. The focused attention results in some aspects being 'imprinted' more deeply than others, and combined with the intensified sensory input this results in strong memory formation. Such strong memory has survival value for both children and adults. When we are able to recall dangerous situations accurately and quickly, we can more easily identify a threat if we should be confronted with it again later ('once burned twice shy'). The price that we pay for the improved ability to detect danger is a painful revisiting of the sensory impressions absorbed at the time. However, in repeated traumatic situations, such as with domestic violence, the opposite will apply because a denial of what is taking place will be the most expedient response. Forgetting and remembering in connection with traumatic situations will be addressed in further detail later on in this book (see Chapter 3).

Many children state that during the traumatic episode they thought of an incredible number of things during a short period of time. This reflects the fact that the brain processes a large volume of information in a few seconds. When this occurs, it is also a reflection of how time is experienced differently from usual, such as when an eternity of time passes while waiting for help or for information about a loved one.

> A ten-year-old girl sat beside her grandfather who had just been seriously injured, while her grandmother went to call for help. When the psychologist later asked her to tell him about how it was to wait, she answered that 'it took forever' before her grandmother came back. She also told of how she thought about an incredible number of things while she sat and waited. She was then asked to go out onto the street and wave to the ambulance when it arrived (to show the way). She waved and the ambulance personnel waved back and drove right past. Afterwards they told her that children often waved to them so they had not understood that she had wanted to show them where they should stop. While she waited for the ambulance to turn around and come back, she felt as if time was standing still. Afterwards she thought that perhaps things would have turned out better for her grandfather had she managed to stop the ambulance right away.

Some children speak of how everything seems to be happening in slow motion in such situations. If their reaction is 'delayed', they can mistakenly come to blame themselves later on: 'I reacted so slowly that I could have been killed.' The consequence of large volumes of information being processed on the emotional level over a short period of time is that it leads children to believe that just as much time as it would normally take to think of so many things (to process a corresponding amount of information) must have passed. In a sense we gain time in a crisis situation when we are able to think rapidly. Such an extension of time can increase our likelihood of survival. If someone experiences a traumatic situation that extends over a long time period, such as a kidnapping or plane hijacking, the opposite experience can arise. One can then subjectively speaking have the sense of less time having passed than is actually the case (Terr 1983). Here another type of coping mechanism is activated, which reflects expedient mechanisms that we utilize in response to extended periods of stress.

Perhaps one of the most important immediate reactions is that feelings can be pushed aside. In this way the emotional system frees up all of its capacity to handle the external threatening situation. This means that a number of people have emotional reactions after the danger has passed. How frequently this occurs in children is something we know little about. Probably more children than adults react with fear and other emotions during the trauma situation itself. Disconnection from emotional reactions is often followed by a feeling of shock and unreality, particularly in older children. It is difficult to determine the age at which this reaction first arises, because younger children use different words and expressions from those of adults, and infants lack the necessary language skills to express their emotions.

From the age of ten, however, children describe their reactions as adults do, with words such as 'dream', 'like something I have seen on the telly', 'as completely unreal', etc. Here are a number of statements made by a group of young people who experienced having a friend killed in a dramatic car accident:

- 'It was like it wouldn't sink in. I didn't believe it.'
- 'I couldn't believe that it was true.'
- 'I did not believe my own ears.'
- 'I did not have any particular emotional reactions right away, I did not believe it could be true.'
- 'I could not believe that it was true; losing him was inconceivable.'

Such reactions can be dissociative, in other words be characterized by daydreaming, escaping into an imaginary realm, etc. In situations involving chronic traumatization this can serve to diminish pain and anxiety; a child who experienced sexual abuse, for example, drew a picture of her body under a cloud, while her head was above the layer of clouds. While the reaction of unreality enables one to keep one's reactions at a distance in an acute situation requiring action, a repeated employment of such reactions, as in the case of repetitive trauma, can easily lead to the formation of unsuitable patterns that continue even after the external situation has changed.

The shock can be quickly followed by reactions: 'First I think that I was in shock and was maybe a bit apathetic. Then the tears came and the anger and the feelings of injustice and powerlessness.'

This is typical for many; the reactions begin to surface when the initial shock starts wearing off. If children are in more chronic danger situations, however, their reactions can be put 'on hold' for a long time.

If children are in dangerous situations and do not know how others are doing, they can experience extreme anxiety for the safety and well-being of their loved ones. But this usually occurs after they feel that they are personally out of danger (Pynoos and Nader 1989).

Some children respond with rage, protest and a kind of emotional rampage, while others react with paralysis. The paralysis is often a reflection of an overloading of the brain's capacity. When there is too much to address, the brain's ability to handle information breaks down. If a child's life is at risk, the child will of course experience intense feelings of fear, but if the situation is resolved quickly, the events may have taken place so rapidly that this response will first occur only after the incident.

Children can also behave in ways that may appear to be extremely irrational to an outside observer, while they can be logical from the perspective of the individual child. Such 'irrational' actions can often be a reflection of children's lack of knowledge about what they should do, as a result of not having received sufficient guidelines from adults about how best to respond. When after a fire children are found deceased or unconscious in a closet or under a bed, this need not represent irrational behaviour but in fact an attempt to protect themselves from danger. Incorrect actions on the part of children in crisis situations can be prevented through measures such as better information and guidelines from adults regarding what they should do when hazardous situations arise.

Children can, like adults, resort to familiar actions in a traumatic situation in an effort to create a familiar and secure situation in a reality that is suddenly collapsing all around them. For example, children who have just had a dramatic experience may immediately afterwards ask whether they may go out and play, or they may continue with activities as if nothing has happened. Adults can of course experience this as a provocation, in the event for instance that they have just learned that a family member has died, while it can be extremely helpful for the children because it provides a kind of security and restores some stability to their existence.

Very young children are dependent upon adults' management of a traumatic situation. They will turn to adults for protection and to reduce fear. Young children are equipped with alarm signals (crying, screaming, etc.), which call for adults' attention and protection. When the signals do not summon a response, children can react with resignation and apathy.

The after-effects of traumas

When children have experienced a traumatic situation, they will usually display a number of normal post-traumatic reactions, which adults can find disturbing but which need not mean that the children have developed serious problems. These post-traumatic reactions are a reflection of the fact that our emotional systems need time to process what has happened, so that one can gradually integrate the occurrence into the thought structures used to organize or understand the world and other human beings. Some of the most common post-traumatic reactions among children are:

- vulnerability, fear and anxiety
- strong intrusive memories
- sleep disturbances
- feelings of guilt or self-reproach
- avoidance behaviour
- concentration difficulties
- anger
- sadness
- bodily reactions
- regression
- play and 're-enacting' the incident
- problems with social contact
- changes in meaning and values.

Vulnerability, anxiety and fear are expressions of the insecurity that has entered into a child's existence. Starting from birth children gradually develop an experience of security and safety in existence, through daily interactions with adult caregivers. This implies that as they mature, they will believe that things happen to others and not to them. They are consequently able to keep the unhappiness of others at a distance. A traumatic event upsets this balance and results in their feeling a much greater sense of vulnerability and fear that the same thing is going to happen again, or that other terrible things are going to occur. The child thus goes from living in a relatively safe world to being dramatically confronted with the fact that terrible things can happen without warning.

> A teenage girl was the victim of erotic advances from an adult man. Afterwards she was afraid not only of strange men but also of men whom she knew and had no reason to fear. She became vigilant and avoided all contact with them. At home she wanted to keep the light on and the door open when she went to bed at night.

After a break-in or violence perpetrated by strangers, children can become over-concerned about safety at home, demand additional locks on the doors and windows or insist on having the curtains drawn. If parents, most frequently mothers, have been subjected to violence, children can become extremely protective of them. They want to keep them within sight and can expend a lot of energy thinking about ways to protect them. Children who have experienced a fire, or that something caught fire, can be over-sensitive to the smell of smoke, crackling sounds, or a fire in a stove or fireplace. Young children will exhibit their anxiety by:

- wanting to play in the same room where adults are
- protesting about separations
- wanting the light on or the door open, or protesting when it is time to go to bed
- wanting to sleep in their parents' bed.

If children experience a number of traumatic events in close succession, the sense of vulnerability and anticipated disaster can be particularly enhanced. In such a case they can constantly and over a long period of time expect that another terrible incident is going to occur. In a long-term perspective, something will often happen, naturally enough, which will then confirm what they feared and were anticipating. In the worst case, this can lead to personality changes that can have an impact on their behaviour for the rest of their lives.

> A 15-year-old boy related that when his mother died it was a confirmation of something he had feared for a long time. Several years before this his parents had got a divorce, and, two years before his mother passed away, a grandmother died: 'After this I just waited for what would come next.'

Children who experience 'near miss' situations can also become more vulnerable in the period following a traumatic incident, but they seldom experience the same specific fear in response to signals recalling the event as do those who are directly involved. An example of this is the case of 13 girls who wanted to take a trip on a cruise ship, but failed to secure tickets. Some of their friends, however, did. The ship was wrecked and sank, and the 13 girls developed clearly increased anxiety afterwards. However, they did not report more specific fears of things associated with ships than did a control group (Yule, Udwin and Murdoch 1990).

An increased sense of vulnerability involves a state of constant preparedness arising from an expectation that something is going to happen. This is reflected by a nervous system that is often overactive and by children investing a lot of emotional energy in keeping 'the radar' on, in order to detect new signs of danger. At the same time, this danger preparedness will cause bodily tensions and muscular pains, particularly around the neck and shoulders. Digestive problems and headaches are also common reactions.

Increased fear in children is first and foremost connected with things that remind them of an event. The greater the similarity to the trauma, the greater the reaction of fear. Everything that reminds them of the incident can awaken fearful reactions in children, whether this is something they see, hear, smell, touch, or taste. Such traumatic reminders can be found in their surroundings or come from within. A few examples will best illustrate this.

- Ove witnessed his friend being hit by a car. Afterwards he had a strong reaction whenever he saw cars that were of the same make as the one that had hit his friend, he felt fearful when he heard the sound of sirens, he could not bear to watch hospital scenes on the

TV and he was terrified if someone was running along the side of the road when he was sitting in the car while his parents were driving.

- Siv reacted to the scent of a particular deodorant. She had been exposed to sexual violation and the attacker had smelled of this deodorant. A friend of the family who used the same deodorant was the key to finding out which scent this was, because for a long time after the event Siv did not know which odour caused her reaction.

- Kari was as a young adolescent molested by a stranger and her reactions involved frequent abdominal pains. She later had a sense of increased fear every time she had a stomach ache, such as in connection with her period.

Although fear is triggered predominantly by things directly associated with a traumatic incident, it can also be elicited by conversations and symbolic stimuli, such as songs and music played at a funeral, or the same day of the week or the anniversary of the day when the incident occurred.

Eva had a strong reaction every Thursday evening around 7–8 pm. She eventually came to understand this pattern and explained that it was at exactly this time that she had received word that one of her closest friends had died in an accident.

Many children relive what took place in the form of strong intrusive memories that surface in the mind during the period following the incident. First and foremost these memories are connected with visual, auditory and olfactory impressions, but the other sensory channels can also be involved. Some children relate that they relive everything that happened or that they get a feeling of the same thing happening again, while others relate that fragments from the episode surface in their thoughts. It is more common for younger children to experience such a reliving exclusively in response to an individual sound, odour, or image that they associate with the threat or injury, while older children and adolescents can relive the incident in its entirety. Children more than adults rely upon external things to trigger memories, but during adolescence such external 'triggers' are less essential and the memories more frequently enter the thoughts uninvited.

Traumatic incidents often involve strong sense impressions and these are central in the reliving of the incident. Because sense impressions can be 'unpleasant', it can also be difficult to communicate them to others: both friends and family members can exhibit discomfort when listening to descriptions of such things. The result of this is that most often the worst aspects of an incident are those that are spoken about the least. The sensory memories can therefore remain partially unprocessed.

Children experience having little control over the memories that flow into their thoughts when they least want them. It is common for the memories to surface when children are not busy with other things, such as after they have gone to bed. They feel helpless to stop them. Such memories appear even in extremely young children and, even before children develop language, the memory images can be strongly imprinted. When the memories are formed before the child has developed sufficient language skills with which to communicate them, the chances are great that the memories will continue as sensory memories that became apparent in bodily reactions, behaviour, or through more indirect forms of expression. Some children communicate their memories once they acquire the linguistic skills to do so. Young children's replaying of what occurred in behavioural or action sequences is called 'behavioural memories' (Terr 1988). Such behavioural memories can reflect that a child has not reached a developmental stage where the incident can be expressed in a more abstract form (symbolically, linguistically, etc.) but is instead demonstrated in a concrete form adapted to the child's developmental stage.

A number of studies, which we and others have carried out, have shown that such intrusive memories can continue for a long period of time (such as a number of years) in children who have absorbed strong sensory impressions (Dyregrov, Gjestad and Raundalen 2002; Nader et al. 1993; Sack et al. 1993). Many of these children suffer from these symptoms without telling adults about them.

As mentioned earlier, this memory material often surfaces when a child has gone to bed at night, so that it can result in sleep disturbances, particularly difficulties in falling asleep. Because the memories incite fear with subsequent bodily activation, a vicious cycle can be started and some children acquire relatively serious sleep disorders. Frequently the memory material also enters into a child's dreams and causes nightmares where the child either re-experiences what happened or has other dreams of catastrophes where terrible things happen; insomnia can occur as a result.

> Carl, a six-year-old boy, told his parents that a ghost came to get him when he was sleeping. It had huge, penetrating eyes and wanted to eat him up. Carl had experienced the police entering his home in full 'battle dress' to warn his family about a dangerous situation in the neighbourhood.

Guilt and self-reproach in a number of different forms are found in children following traumatic incidents. In particular, younger children can experience feeling guilty of having contributed to what occurred, even when this appears to be completely irrational in the eyes of adults.

> An 11-year-old girl states that she remembers very well when she was 7 years old and her mother tried to commit suicide. She says: 'I thought that it was my fault because I hadn't cleaned my room.'

This girl's statement also shows how children with increased maturity and greater mental capacity can reassess and change their perception of an incident that took place a number of years before. Throughout childhood and adolescence, children will reflect on traumatic situations that they have experienced in light of the altered capacity that comes with increased age and maturity.

Children can feel a sense of guilt about not having said or done something in relation to a critical event, or they can blame themselves for something that they have said, done, or thought. In some situations they feel a true sense of guilt because they think that they may have contributed to causing the traumatic incident, such as by playing with matches before a fire, or disturbing a parent who was driving just before an accident occurred. If parents are the victims of violence, children can feel guilty about not having intervened and stopped the incident. After such situations some children can develop a fervent interest in learning self-defence techniques such as karate or judo.

Perceived guilt is not unusual when children are present when something terrible takes place. During childhood they often connect events that occur in close proximity, whether in time or space, in such a way that they feel responsible for what occurred.

If children are subjected to, or witness, an assault in the home, they can also feel guilty if, for example, they identify with the person who carried out the attack (the aggressor). Sometimes they assume guilt in order to maintain a more positive image of the aggressor.

> Linda had a father who used subtle manipulations to get her to feel sorry for him, such as by depicting himself as pitiful, crying and saying that there was no hope for him, etc. The message of all of the signals was that Linda was the only one who could help him feel better. Finally she would be the one who would go into his room in the evening before the sexual abuse occurred, which resulted in her struggling with serious feelings of guilt and self-reproach. She also struggled with feelings of shame for this, something that improved when she gained an understanding that the reason for her going in to him was to get it over with, because she otherwise experienced the waiting period beforehand as extremely stressful. She could not prevent the abuse from happening, but she could take control of the timing.

In sexual abuse situations the feelings of guilt can be further aggravated if children or adolescents experience sexual arousal or receive some type of material reward.

Children can often feel survival guilt when they survive an accident in which friends or family members die.

> Tine was in her early teens when she survived an accident in which several family members died. She could not understand why she had been permitted to survive while others died, and she experienced this as a heavy burden to carry. It was difficult for her to allow herself to be happy about being alive: all her energy went towards thinking about how unfair it was that she had escaped.

The self-reproach can be extremely intense and, in the worst cases, bring about a diminished future perspective as the children expect to be punished for what they thought, did, said, or brought about.

When different stimuli constantly provoke emotional and bodily responses, it is natural for children to try and stay away or protect themselves from these. Such avoidance reactions find expression in the avoidance of situations, places, persons, conversations, or activities that resemble, are parallel to, or are reminiscent of what caused the trauma. For example, if children have survived a transport accident, they may be reluctant to board a car, train, aeroplane, boat, etc. because this awakens strong reactions of fear. The fear can be so strong that it becomes phobic in nature, and can intervene in children's future lives in a negative way by imposing limitations on their ability to take part in certain activities. A number of children appear to avoid memories and thoughts by staying constantly active. Others have an opposite reaction and keep seeking to return to the incident. They relate what happened again and again, sometimes to strangers, in a manner that indicates that they are almost compulsively taking control of their anxiety in this way. Younger children can compulsively repeat certain play sequences that either directly or indirectly relate to what happened. Some young people seek out dangerous situations to prove to themselves that they are safe now. For example, young rape victims can attempt to build up their sense of security by seeking out dark areas at night. Demanding sports activities such as mountain climbing, river paddling or high-risk automobile and boat driving can be attempts to control or test out life or death situations. Such behaviour will naturally increase the risk of experiencing new traumatic events.

Once children reach school age it is easy to detect the concentration problems that traumas can bring about. Children who are younger than school age can demonstrate this through restlessness or being easily distracted, and they can have difficulties sitting and playing for uninterrupted periods of time after a trauma. School children may find it hard to concentrate on their homework and schoolwork. Often this is a consequence of uninvited thoughts and memories entering their minds, particularly when they are to perform thought sequences that require concentration. School problems that arise in connection with traumatic incidents will be described in Chapter 10. As adults, however, we should be aware that children can defend themselves against intrusive thoughts by initiating activity, because it helps to create a distraction from painful responses or memories. This can of course create problems both at home and at school. Sometimes children who acquire Post-Traumatic Stress Disorder (PTSD) are mistakenly diagnosed with Attention-Deficit Hyperactivity Disorder (ADHD), often called hyperactivity.

It is not unusual for anger to be demonstrated as a consequence of a traumatic incident. This can be anger that is directed towards those deemed responsible for what happened, or it can be directed towards the child's immediate family members because they are convenient targets. Sometimes the anger is directed inward, because children blame themselves adamantly for what happened. If children sleep poorly, invest a lot of emotional energy in handling things that remind them of the incident and on ensuring that it does not happen again, they are expending so much emotional energy that they become tired and irritable. The irritability can be expressed in an explosive fashion.

> Cato experienced a dramatic incident as a five-year-old. His mother relates how his temperament, which had been forceful before this happened, afterwards became volatile. He had attacks of rage that were so violent that he had to be cooled off with a cold flannel against his forehead. His mother was also worried about the fact that he took his anger out on his little sister.

Young children with little control over their anger can destroy games or develop problems interacting with their age group in kindergarten because they constantly find themselves in conflicts with others. Unprocessed revenge fantasies can later affect their ability to keep aggression in check (impulse control). In the worst cases, unprocessed anger can affect moral development and lead to violence. This risk is greatest in connection with repeated violence within a family, where a child can learn violent patterns in addition to the revenge fantasies that become established. Children who are exposed to war and military violence demonstrate more extroverted behaviour and aggression, probably stemming from the feelings of frustration and helplessness that can arise in this situation (Qouta et al. 2008).

Many traumatic events involve different types of loss for a child. This is particularly the case if one or more of the child's loved ones die, but also if the child loses possessions through fire, flood, etc. In addition to this comes personal loss, such as loss of control, loss of self-esteem, loss of predictability and security in existence, etc. The many losses can lead to the child having feelings of sadness, longing and yearning. Not infrequently children demonstrate this by bursting into tears more readily when they meet with adversity, see something sad on the telly, etc. Children are seldom sad for long periods of time, but they can experience strong emotional outbursts in reaction to situations where a loss is particularly highlighted. This can be when they go to bed in the evening, at school when it is Mother's Day or Father's Day, or when something else occurs that reminds them of the person or things that they have lost. I have elsewhere described children's grief reactions in greater detail (Dyregrov 2008a, b).

A number of children experience bodily reactions such as muscle aches, dizziness and headaches. This can be a reflection of constant tension in the body in anticipation of something else bad happening, with an accumulation of tension in the body as a result. A stomach ache is the most common. Some children develop an upset stomach while others experience constant nausea. If in the traumatic situation the child reacted with violent trembling or nausea, anything that recalls the trauma subsequently can trigger similar reactions. Such reactions are triggered easily by the sense of smell, such as the sensation of the lingering presence of an odour in the nose. The child can also become more tired and more vulnerable to infection.

Through our work with other cultures, we have received reports of children who have epileptogenic seizures following traumatic situations such as acts of war. Some develop epilepsy as a result of head injuries they have incurred during the war, while others react with psychologically triggered seizures, so-called psychogenic attacks. In some cases I have observed similar seizures in Norwegian children.

> A girl fainted several times a week in the schoolyard and was in great haste driven to the emergency room and sometimes on to the hospital. She was examined in all imaginable ways but no organic basis for the epilepsy-like seizures was found. In therapy it was disclosed that she had been raped several years earlier. As she was gradually able to put into words both what had happened and various aspects of her emotions and thoughts about it, the seizures first diminished in frequency and then eventually disappeared completely. When she later saw the rapist again, a stranger, the seizures returned and then quickly diminished again.

Regression or a return to a previous developmental stage, is often found in young children. They can begin bedwetting again, they can become more childish in their behaviour, revert to use of 'baby talk', demand help when eating, start sucking their thumb, or want to bring a security blanket or stuffed animal or doll with them everywhere they go. Regression is usually transitory and age-appropriate behaviour is resumed when the child begins to feel more secure.

Play about what happened, often in the manner of a re-enactment (repetition) of the event(s) is common, particularly with preschool age children. They can play such games at kindergarten or at home – for example, a child who has experienced a car accident may play with cars that collide.

> After a plane crash where both a preschool teacher and her child (who attended the kindergarten) were killed, the parents related at a parents' meeting that the children 'played' the accident at home. The plane crash and the funeral constituted part of their play for a period of time and made processing of the incident possible. Strangely enough, the children refrained from playing these games at kindergarten until the staff had had the chance to process the incident and were capable of 'accepting' the game.

Conversation and social contact with friends, parents and others can sometimes be impeded. This is particularly the case with adolescents. Friends can be perceived as dumb, immature and lacking in understanding: 'Nobody understands what I have experienced.' The comments of friends can be experienced as hurtful, resulting in social withdrawal.

Contact with parents can also become more difficult. Some children do not want to speak with their parents about what has happened because they notice that it makes their parents uneasy. Others feel that parents do not want to speak about it, that they avoid the subject, say 'Don't think about it, think about something positive' or indicate that the children are supposed to try to forget. Stallard and Law (1994) write about how after a minibus accident where nine adolescents miraculously survived when the vehicle drove off the road, none of the young people felt that their parents understood the impact that this incident had had on them or how long the after-effects continued.

Some children find that they spend more time than they did before the incident thinking about the meaning of existence, and about how unfair it was that this should happen to them. This is first and foremost the case with school-age children, especially as they approach adolescence. But even very young children can express deep thoughts about life's truths.

> Marianne, who was three and a half years old, was talking with her girlfriend after Marianne's father died in a tragic car accident and she stated: 'It is so unfair that daddy died before

grandmother.' This is advanced language use and advanced thought on the part of a precocious preschool child. On one of the first days following the death she had a high fever, without any other signs of illness. She then shocked her mother so profoundly that she called the psychologist around midnight. What Marianne said was: 'Do you know why I am ill, mommy?' 'No.' 'It is because daddy died.'

The need to search for meaning and a cause is great, and many children are interested in omens, in signs that were given before the incident in question that can provide some kind of explanation. For the child, 'finding' such warnings can help to make the world once again more predictable. The idea is: 'If we receive warnings, then such terrible things don't happen without our being able to know about them in advance.' This brings a kind of control into existence again, and more order and calm to chaotic thoughts. It is important to recognize that many things happen that we cannot explain. It is far too easy to quickly rationalize or give a logical explanation for the things children relate. As adults we must make ourselves more open to children's thoughts and not immediately attempt to provide a rational explanation for something we can never fully know for sure.

On the same night that his father died in an accident, Bill had been awakened by a thumping sound in the house at two o'clock in the morning and gone out onto the stairway and called for his father. He asked the psychologist: 'Do you think that he died at the same time while I was out and calling for him?'

Such signs or warnings are to be taken seriously, not just given nice, adult explanations. The boy was told that a thumping sound in the house is considered to be a warning of death in coastal regions in Norway (at least in the western part of Norway) and that I had heard next-of-kin say the same before. We also agreed to contact the police in order to learn what they had found out about the time of death. The police were able to establish that the death occurred at a later point in time but it was, all the same, still a warning.

The endeavour to understand 'why' and 'why me?', and other aspects relating to causes and meaning, are necessary mental activities in terms of developing, restructuring, or creating new 'schemas', also called models of or assumptions about the world. The schema reflects the frames we use to interpret and understand what happens to us. We have schemas for 'certainty and uncertainty', 'justice and injustice', etc. Traumatic incidents can lead us to alter the assumptions or schemas we use to interpret our surroundings and ourselves, and it can take a long time to readjust these schemas after a traumatic incident. After the tsunami in Southeast Asia in 2004, there were many Norwegian survivors who were young people and whose perception of the world changed, but this is certainly not the case for everyone (Stormyren and Jensen 2008).

Simultaneously, traumatic incidents will often lead to our subsequently acquiring different views about what is important and what is trivial. Again this is age-dependent, and usually connected with adolescence. Often intimate, interpersonal things will be experienced as more important than material things:

- 'Now I know how much I love them.'

- 'Now I have learned to appreciate my parents in a way that is completely different from before.'

- 'I can't stand to spend time on unessential things.'

The last quote expresses a desire to spend time differently. Many young people emphasize the need to live in the present and make the most of every day. Several experience increased maturity and strength. They have become more experienced, more self-assured, they may have learned how to speak more openly about difficult things and they know how to help others who are having a difficult time. They may find that it is easier to distinguish what is important from what is not. But it is obvious that the increased life intensity is often a costly experience, which is paid for with increased vulnerability and anxiety, in addition to critical attitudes towards others in their age group. In a study done on Norwegian families who had experienced the tsunami in 2004, Lindgaard, Iglebaek and Jensen (2009) point out that families who have had common traumatic experiences can develop both improved family functioning and reinforced family ties, or the opposite: they can experience more conflict and weakened ties. Early offers of help that focus on sharing the experience and a joint construction of the story (the narrative) can help to create a context (meaning) out of what happened and lead to different experiences being expected and accepted.

The long-term effects of traumas

Research carried out in recent years has shown that traumas in childhood can have a negative impact on a number of aspects of a child's development. It is of course first and foremost cumulative traumas that produce such long-term changes, but some of these have also been observed following isolated incidents. Traumatic incidents can have an impact on:

- personality, character development
- assumptions about the world and one's existence including expectation of another catastrophe and pessimism about the future
- relationships with other people
- moral development
- biological development
- regulation of emotions
- self-perception, self-confidence
- coping ability
- learning capacity
- choice of profession, vocational functions
- future capacity as a parent.

When so many negative consequences are identified, it is important to recognize that most people nonetheless experience a relatively normal development even though they have been exposed to traumatic situations. If a child experiences an isolated traumatic event, but is surrounded by a supportive network of family and friends, and receives the opportunity to process what has happened, as a rule the most negative consequences will be avoided and a natural healing will take place. These long-term after-effects will nonetheless be explored further here because many children grow up in situations where they experience repeated traumatic events, and because many others who seek asylum after having escaped from a war situation have experienced a series of traumatic incidents.

When a child, over an extended period of time, is constantly obliged to repress their emotional reactions in order to survive in a world that is unpredictable and frightening, this will leave traces in the child's personality. Children can become frightened, vigilant and less able to trust in other human beings. They can develop enhanced aggression preparedness, become emotionally constricted and in adulthood subject their own children to harshness similar to that which they personally experienced throughout the course of a traumatic upbringing. There is a great deal of research that has shown how children who are subjected to sexual trauma or abuse are over-represented among those who develop psychological problems later in life, often with deviant personality traits that make them more predisposed to psychological illness (Harris, Putnam and Fairbank 2004). Cognitive problems, including diminished memory, have also been identified (Valentino *et al.* 2008), along with diminished self-confidence (Kim and Cicchetti 2006).

Assumptions about the world and one's existence can also change. Some children develop pessimistic attitudes in terms of their belief that they can influence their own situation, and they will encounter adversity later in life without having any confidence that they can do something to improve their circumstances. Assumptions about the world, themselves and others can be characterized by pessimism and scepticism. It has been established that many children who experience traumatic events, including isolated incidents, can also acquire a sense of foreshortened future, and develop a belief that things will turn out badly for them in life or that they will die young.

> Lise experienced that her father betrayed her completely while she was growing up, following a divorce. The first time that she understood this it was extremely traumatic. She waited and waited for him to come and pick her up. She sat by the window and kept watch for him, and refused to come when her mother wanted her to move away from the window. She remained there until she fell asleep in exhaustion and despair many hours later. This was the first of many betrayals that she experienced. When later someone attempted to molest her, her comment about this in a therapy session was: 'That's just how it is with me.' Her belief that the future would be any different was not particularly strong.

Some children attempt to live their lives as if every day were their last and attempt to squeeze as much as 'possible into the day today'. They refuse to postpone anything until tomorrow that they can experience today.

Many of those who experience repetitive trauma during childhood have been exposed to sexual abuse or physical maltreatment. Frequently they become cautious about forming ties with other people, out of the fear of being hurt, disappointed, or rejected. Many adults who were traumatized as children can struggle with problems in forming close relationships, on both the emotional and physical level.

> A woman relates how she has problems when her husband touches her. She pulls away, feels disgust and must struggle with bodily reactions that she does not wholly understand. This is in spite of the fact that she has given birth to several children. But, as she says, it was easier during pregnancy because it was easier then for her to keep him at a distance. In therapy it emerges that she was sexually abused for a period during childhood. Until this was disclosed in therapy, she had not thought about the connection between the abuse and her discomfort over being touched. It is clear that when her husband touches her body this triggers bodily aversion mechanisms and feelings of discomfort, a learned response from when, as a child, she was abused over an extended period of time.

Traumatic events can also affect the establishment of or formation of friendships. Withdrawal, emotional rigidity and a lack of impulse control can create problems in interaction with friends, while the rapid maturing process many traumatized children and young people experience can create distance in friendships. Younger children can show less flexibility when playing: they do not dare to venture away from adults, or they behave in a threatening manner so they frighten off others in their age group. Collectively these factors can lead to social isolation and insufficient social learning. The need that some children have to re-enact incidents through play, where they as the commanders want other children to assume subordinate or assigned positions or roles in the game, can also create problems in relation to friends or children of the same age.

As a means of protecting themselves from isolation and loneliness, young people may seek out and strongly identify with a group of friends because it provides a feeling of closeness and belonging.

> Karin (15) suddenly lost her father. Her father was the parent to whom she was most closely attached. She worked on her schoolwork because she knew that he thought it was important. She did not personally want to work so hard, but she knew that he would be disappointed if her grades were poor. When

he died she lost all motivation, was absent from school more and more frequently and, no matter what her mother said, this development continued. She began spending her time with a gang of young people who had also dropped out of school, and who lived together on the outskirts of a tough, drug-infested community. Here she found a sense of belonging, and many others who had also 'lost' a parent (through divorce, foster home placement, etc.), and she felt a kind of closeness to them that she was not able to feel in relation to her 'old' friends. In addition, she thought that she could help them as her father had always taught her to do.

If children grow up in homes full of violence and abuse, or survive a war, this can influence their understanding of what is right and wrong, and wipe out boundaries between acceptable and unacceptable behaviour. It is therefore not difficult to understand that there are those who have experienced repetitive traumatization who end up in situations where they come into conflict with the criminal justice system. Many of those who commit serious acts of violence turn out to have had a childhood full of traumatic events. This does not excuse what they have done but it can be a factor in explaining such acts.

In the past decade, research has revealed that traumatic situations during childhood can have an influence on and alter biological development (De Bellis 2001, 2006; Gunnar and Quevedo 2007; van der Kolk 2003). Because such incidents can have an impact on the production of important physiological substances (including hormones such as cortisol), under or overproduction of such substances can result in permanent physiological changes. This can in turn cause the nervous system to respond differently from usual in some children. In fact, it has been speculated as to whether traumatic situations can bring about the early onset of puberty.

Gunnar and Quevedo (2007) have summarized the research done in this area and conclude that frequent activation of neurobiological stress responses, where there is an absence of good support for a child, can cause permanent changes in the neurological basis for emotional and cognitive processes, particularly when the stress occurs during sensitive periods in the child's development. The formation of new neural connections occurs at a rapid pace during the first years of life, with different areas undergoing different types of development at different times. Traumatic experiences during different periods critical to a child's development can therefore have different outcomes from child to child. It is nonetheless important to remember that not all functions are fully developed in the first years – for instance, several of the important executive systems in the brain undergo development during the teenage years (see Chapter 3).

The consequences of such early chronic stress can be an inhibition of the brain's development (neurogenesis), disruption of the neuronal plasticity and so-called neurotoxicity. Social relations play a critical role in the regulation of physiological stress reactions, and protect the brain from the potentially damaging influences of hormones and other substances triggered by stress reactions. It goes without saying that it is therefore extremely important to ensure that children do not live in stress and illness-producing surroundings, that their caregivers become particularly important sources of support, and that measures should be quickly implemented if such circumstances are discovered. Gunnar and Quevedo (2007) point out that structural changes in the brain are not irreversible: they can be turned around by positive surroundings and proper stimulation. Programmes that emphasize early intervention and work on strengthening attachment, among other things through the use of home visits, have shown good results (see Egeland 2009 and Stern 2006).

An extremely important developmental task for children lies in learning to regulate their feelings. This involves modifying and adapting their feelings to the situations they encounter. They must learn a language to describe these feelings, methods to keep them within the framework of what they can tolerate at any one time, and how to interpret the signals that they receive from their body and from other people with respect to the feelings they experience. Traumatic situations can disturb this development and lead to the development of exaggerated defence mechanisms against strong feelings. Some children are not able to bring their feelings under control and strong reactions are triggered far too easily. Those who use dissociation a great deal as a means of protecting themselves against repetitive traumatization during childhood, can in adulthood struggle with serious personality disorders. Most of those who suffer from such disorders have been exposed to long-term sexual abuse or physical maltreatment during childhood (van der Hart, Nijenhuis and Steele 2006). When parents lack positive emotional involvement, appear to be emotionally constricted and are unavailable to interact with young children, the children experience more dissociation (Dutra *et al.* 2009).

The early loss of a caregiver with whom a child can communicate discomfort or negative feelings, or receive comfort and care from, increases the risk of problems later in life. Children who live with domestic violence will have both one parent who is threatening and frightening and another whose capacity to care can be clearly debilitated. Dutra and others (2009) have used the expression 'hidden trauma' about the experiences of young children who live with emotionally unavailable parents. When they live in such a situation over a long period of time, this can lead to their becoming extremely vulnerable to stressors. Following successful therapy, children's altered emotional regulation has been followed by neural changes in a positive direction (Lewis *et al.* 2008).

Children's self-perception can also be influenced in such a way that their self-confidence is damaged. Repetitive traumas can influence, to a large extent, their self-perception and their perception of their value as human beings.

> A girl, who had experienced both being sexually molested and the loss of a close family member during her childhood, told of how she had a very strong experience of not being worth anything. Her self-contempt was communicated by constant statements on her part about how dumb she was, how she only deserved for stupid things to happen to her, etc.

Children and young people with such a background do not expect to be loved and can easily become victims of what is known as self-fulfilling prophecies; in other words, they believe and say negative things to themselves so frequently that they eventually come true. If they are helpless in terms of stopping ongoing traumatization in the home, this can develop into a more long-term debilitated faith in their ability to manage things, along with damaged self-confidence and diminished exploration of their environment as a result.

But children's self-confidence and belief in their own coping abilities can be strengthened if they handle a traumatic situation in a good way and receive praise and support from adults for their conduct. Because children will continue to integrate what has happened over time, this coping potential can become apparent in reality long after the incident has occurred. It is a privilege to witness a young person who with a broad smile states: 'I must have been good to have managed throughout all of this. Now I know that I can handle things.' Children can experience maturation and growth in relation to what is significant in life, such as increased intimacy with people they care about, a clearer experience of what is important and what is unimportant, or an increased sense of the intensity of being alive. Confidence in their ability to handle difficult situations, and knowledge about how they can help a friend who is having a hard time, are other positive consequences.

Children's ability to cope can be weakened or strengthened accordingly, depending upon their own manner of handling the situation, the network they have around them for help and support, and the intensity of the traumatic incident that they have experienced.

Children's capacity for learning can be diminished as a result of reduced attention span and ability to concentrate. When a lot of emotional energy is 'tied up' in avoiding everything that reminds them of what they have experienced, these problems can persist over time. The impact of a traumatic situation on schoolwork will be described in greater detail in a later chapter (see Chapter 10).

Another possible long-term consequence of trauma is that the event(s) can contribute to influencing the choice of vocation that is made later, and also job performance. A number of people who have been traumatized as children later elect to enter health or public safety professions (health and child care personnel, police, fire department, etc.) that allow them to take control over illness, death or other critical situations and, as such, permit them to reverse the helplessness they felt as children.

> A nurse told of how she decided to become a nurse after she was hospitalized at an early age and her grandmother, who was visiting, said she was just going to step out for a minute to buy some sweets and did not return until two days later. This situation was so traumatic that she later decided to become a nurse so that she could prevent others from experiencing the same type of situation.

The choice of profession often occurs more or less subconsciously, so that some people will only become aware of how their past has contributed to steering them towards their profession when they have begun to carry out this occupation or even later (if ever). Some may discover that they function well during their professional training and education, but that relatively strong reactions are activated when they find themselves in situations that remind them of the trauma that they experienced in childhood.

> A girl was studying for a healthcare profession and did well for the first year of her training. However, she had a strong reaction when in the second year she was outplaced in a hospital ward where several years before she had experienced the death of a family member following a sudden injury. She became terrified of injuring the patients, and decided to discontinue her education. Therapeutic help gave her better insight into both her choice of profession and her reaction, but she adhered to her decision to change her career to something other than the healthcare profession.

One area that we have less knowledge about is how cumulative traumas during childhood have an impact on subsequent capacity to be a parent. We know that there is a clear over-representation (a larger number) of parents who have personally been abused sexually or physically who repeat such patterns in interaction with their own children (Holt, Buckley and Whelan 2008). But there is less knowledge about, for instance, the impact a dramatic death during childhood can have in relation to anxiety later in life. Will parents who experienced this as children more easily become overprotective and fearful that something will happen to their own children?

> A woman who lost her mother when she was a child told of how, in the raising of her own children, she had constantly emphasized that they had to be independent. In many ways she had raised them to manage on their own, regardless of what might happen. In a session she nods in assent when I speculate about whether she had raised them so that they could manage on their own in the event that she passed away while they were children, as had been her experience.

We also know that traumas can increase the risk of depression in adults, which in turn clearly has an impact on their interactions with children, and over time can contribute to reduced capacity as a parent.

Although single-event traumas do not usually have lifelong repercussions, many of their effects can last a lifetime if the child does not receive adequate help. It is therefore extremely important that parents, teachers and other adults have good knowledge about trauma reactions and how to help children following traumatic events.

Post-Traumatic Stress Disorder (PTSD)

A few decades ago, the assumption was that, if children reacted to traumatic situations, their reactions were short-term. This assumption derived from adults' desire for this to be the case, the fact that few systematic studies of children had been carried out, and that most of the findings of the studies available had been based on statements made by parents and not on conversations with children personally. Over the years, a range of systematic studies have demonstrated that children can develop PTSD in a form parallel to that found in adults.

The expression 'post-traumatic stress disorder' (PTSD) is a diagnostic category used in psychiatry to describe a specific grouping of post-traumatic problems (a syndrome). Because the expression is used relatively often and children who develop such problems require professional help, a more detailed description of the disorder will be given here. In order to be able to say that children have PTSD, a number of criteria must be met. They must have experienced (either personally or been a witness to or confronted with) an event that involved actual or threatened death or serious injury, or a threat to the physical integrity of self or others. They need to have reacted with intense fear, helplessness, or horror. Children may demonstrate this through disorganized or agitated behaviour. In addition, their subsequent reactions must continue for at least one month and to such an extent that their ability to function socially or at school is debilitated.

The after-effects that a child must experience in order to be defined as having PTSD include, first, persistent re-experiencing of the event in one (or more) of the following ways:

- recurrent and intrusive distressing recollections of the event, including images, thoughts and perceptions
- engagement in repetitive play in which themes or aspects of the trauma are expressed
- recurrent distressing dreams about the event, sometimes without recognizable content
- acting or feeling as if the traumatic event is recurring.

In young children trauma-specific re-enactment may occur; they may experience intense psychological distress when exposed to internal or external cues that symbolize or resemble an aspect of the traumatic event, or physiological activation to these same cues.

The second type of reaction is persistent avoidance of stimuli associated with the trauma, and numbing of general responsiveness. Here children are required to demonstrate three of the following problems:

- avoidance of associated thoughts, feelings or conversations associated with the trauma
- avoidance of activities, places or people that arouse recollections of the trauma
- inability to recall important aspects of the situation
- marked diminished interest or participation in important activities
- feelings of detachment or estrangement from others
- a restricted range of affects
- a sense of foreshortened future.

The last of the symptom groups involves a persistent activation of the nervous system that was not present before the trauma. Here children must demonstrate at least two of the following:

- difficulty falling or staying asleep
- irritability or outbursts of anger
- difficulty concentrating
- hypervigilance
- exaggerated startle response.

The criteria listed here have been taken from the much-utilized Diagnostic and Statistical Manual of Mental Disorders (DSM IV) published by the American Psychiatric Association (1994). The World Health Organization (WHO) has a separate system where the emphasis is more on the intrusive memories: they do not view avoidance reactions and a limited range of emotions as being equally essential to a PTSD diagnosis.

Many will recognize the factors that are mentioned under PTSD as being the common post-traumatic reactions described earlier. That is because it is not the *type* of reaction, but more the duration, scope and combination of problems that enables us to say whether or not a child is suffering from PTSD.

It goes without saying that it is difficult to register or gain insight into a number of these symptoms in young children. Separate criteria have therefore been developed for preschool children where, among other things, children's compulsive re-playing of parts of the trauma and nightmares are included. These criteria are based more on observations than on things children have said (Scheeringa and Zeanah 1995; Scheeringa *et al.* 2003). Young children are only required to demonstrate one symptom of avoidance and it is not a requirement that they demonstrate any reactions at the time of the event (Scheeringa *et al.* 2005). This type of specification enables us to map out the problems of young children.

Even though a great deal of research has been done focusing on PTSD and children in recent years, one should know that the categories mentioned here were developed first and foremost for adults. Among children it is more difficult to detect and measure avoidance and emotional constriction. Attentive parents and other adults can nonetheless notice whether a child avoids special places, activities, conversations, or themes while playing, or other things that can be reminders of the event. Children's withdrawal from ordinary activity or their complaints that others, including parents, do not understand them can provide an indication that they are struggling with avoidance reactions as part of PTSD. Unfortunately, parents often interpret children's failure to mention the trauma as a sign that they have put the event behind them.

Some of the factors that are included under 'the definition' of PTSD are there as a consequence of knowledge drawn from studies on children. This applies for instance to the item 'foreshortened future'. Leonore Terr (1979, 1983) showed that 25 out of a group of 27 children lost their faith in the future after they had been kidnapped and held locked up in a buried trailer for about 24 hours. This was not only the case for the period immediately afterwards, but also in a follow-up study several years after the kidnapping had taken place. When repetition games in children are included as a means of reliving the event, this represents an acknowledgement that the repetition of what happened in play can reflect another, more childish type of reliving than that which appears in the form of images and memories in the mind.

It is possible to gauge or assess whether a child has such a PTSD in different ways. Information can be gathered from parents, teachers (including preschool teachers) and other individuals who are significant in the child's life. Usually a structured interview that is carried out with the parents present provides sound information. When the child reaches school age, a simple questionnaire can also be used, which provides an assessment of how many symptoms the child has, based on the criteria outlined earlier. With the help of psycho-physiological data (heart rate, skin response, etc.), psychobiological measurements (saliva secretion, etc.) and other methods, such as word association tests, it is possible to form a picture of the child's problems. Systematically gauging or assessing children's problems with respect to the areas mentioned is important in order to determine the breadth of the problems that they are struggling with, and in particular to adjust and adapt assistance and treatment. Assessment tools will be discussed in Chapter 6.

Because adults themselves can be traumatized, or because they underestimate children's reactions and experiences of a situation, many prominent professionals in this field consider it important to talk to children directly (Meiser-Stedman *et al.* 2007). It is only then that one can form an accurate image of any issues a child may be struggling with.

As adults, however, we must distinguish between what are normal post-traumatic reactions in a child, reactions that will gradually subside with time and reactions that have become 'stuck', either in the form of PTSD or chronic and blocked grief reactions. It is precisely because the same reactions that are normal in the first time period after a trauma are also included as reactions in PTSD that it is so difficult to know when a child needs professional help. In Chapter 6 some concrete advice is therefore given regarding when it can be necessary to contact healthcare professionals to acquire help for children.

The prevalence of PTSD

The prevalence of PTSD in the entire population of children and young people has usually been around 10 per cent in epidemiological studies (Elklit 2002; Giaconia *et al.* 1995; Kessler *et al.* 1995). The most commonly reported traumatic experiences that lead to PTSD are being a witness to or hearing about the injury or death of others, or personally experiencing an injury or accident. If one looks at groups of children who have experienced specific events, the rates vary greatly, in part due to use of different methodology and in part because events vary in many dimensions. In a review of studies following natural disasters, La Greca and Prinstein (2002) found relatively severe PTSD symptoms among

30–50 per cent, while 5–10 per cent of the children met all the criteria for the PTSD diagnosis. Among children who are exposed to horrific events, extremely high rates of post-traumatic problems are found, as with Pynoos and others (1993) who found 90 per cent in young people following an earthquake in Armenia, or as we found (Dyregrov *et al.* 2002) among children following the massacres in Rwanda in 1994.

In different studies of children who have experienced traffic accidents, the PTSD rates have varied from 29 per cent after 4 weeks, 36 per cent after 6 weeks, 6–25 per cent after 12–15 weeks to 14 per cent 9 months after the accident (Stallard, Salter and Velleman 2004).

Studies of the rate of PTSD in children who experience war vary from 25–70 per cent, depending upon the degree of exposure and type of war. Following sexual assault, the rates also vary greatly; in fact, studies show a divergence from 0–90 per cent (see Salmon and Bryant 2002), but usually the rates are high. While around 20 per cent of all girls under the age of 18 have experienced sexual assault, around 8 per cent of boys have experienced it (Pereda *et al.* 2009). Similar rates are found for children who witness domestic violence or who are personally subjected to violence (the two often go hand in hand). Violence by friends, including bullying, is also associated with post-traumatic stress, as is exposure to violence in the community (Mynard, Joseph and Alexander 2000; Luthar and Goldstein 2004). Those who experience cumulative traumas naturally exhibit more trauma symptoms than those who experience isolated incidents (Suliman *et al.* 2009).

A large number of children experience traumatic events without developing PTSD. In fact, the PTSD rates are lower in children than in adults, something that can be a reflection of the fact that the DSM-IV criteria have been developed for adults (Copeland *et al.* 2007). Children have greater difficulties describing symptoms of avoidance because this requires that they report something that they are successfully denying. It has been documented that this can result in an under-reporting of symptoms. (Scheeringa *et al.* 2006).

References

American Psychiatric Association (APA) (1994) *Diagnostic and Statistical Manual of Mental Disorders* (DSM IV). Arlington, VA: APA.

Copeland, W.E., Keeler, G., Angold, A. and Costello, E.J. (2007) 'Traumatic events and posttraumatic stress in childhood.' *Archives of General Psychiatry 64*, 577–584.

De Bellis, M.D. (2001) 'Developmental traumatology: the psychobiological development of maltreated children and its implications for research, treatment, and policy.' *Development and Psychopathology 13*, 539–564.

De Bellis, M.D. (2006) 'The psychobiology of neglect.' *Child Maltreatment 10*, 150–172.

Denholm, C.J. (1995) 'Survival from a wild animal attack: a case study analysis of adolescent coping.' *Maternal-Child Nursing Journal 23*, 26–34.

Dutra, L., Bureau, J-F., Holmes, B., Lyubchik, A. and Lyons-Ruth, K. (2009) 'Quality of early care and childhood trauma.' *Journal of Nervous and Mental Disease 197*, 383–390.

Dyregrov, A. (2008a) *Grief in Children. A Handbook for Adults.* 2nd edition. London: Jessica Kingsley Publishers.

Dyregrov, A. (2008b) *Grief in Young Children. A Handbook for Adults.* London: Jessica Kingsley Publishers.

Dyregrov, A., Gjestad, R. and Raundalen, M. (2002) 'Children exposed to warfare. A longitudinal study.' *Journal of Traumatic Stress 15*, 59–68.

Dyregrov, A., Solomon, R.M. and Bassøe, C.F. (2000) 'Mental mobilization in critical incident stress situations.' *International Journal of Emergency Mental Health 2*, 73–81.

Egeland, B. (2009) 'Taking stock: childhood emotional maltreatment and developmental psychopathology.' *Child Abuse and Neglect 33*, 22–26.

Elklit, A. (2002) 'Victimization and PTSD in a Danish national youth probability sample.' *Journal of the American Academy of Child and Adolescent Psychiatry 41*, 174–181.

Giaconia, R.M., Reinherz, H.Z., Silverman, A.B., Pakiz, B., Frost, A.K. and Cohen, E. (1995) 'Traumas and posttraumatic stress disorder in a community population of older adolescents.' *Journal of the American Academy of Child and Adolescent Psychiatry 34*, 1369–1380.

Gunnar, M. and Quevedo, K. (2007) 'The neurobiology of stress and development.' *Annual Review of Psychology 58*, 145–173.

Harris, W.W., Putman, F.W. and Fairbank, J.A. (2004) 'Mobilizing trauma resources for children.' Paper presented in part at the meeting of the Johnson and Johnson Pediatric Institute: Shaping the Future of Children's Health, San Juan, Puerto Rico, 12–16 February.

Holt, S., Buckley, H. and Whelan, S. (2008) 'The impact of exposure to domestic violence on children and young people: a review of the literature.' *Child Abuse and Neglect 32*, 797–810.

Kessler, R.C., Sonnega, A., Bromet, E., Hughes, M. and Nelson, C.B. (1995) 'Posttraumatic stress disorder in the National Comorbidity Survey.' *Archives of General Psychiatry 52*, 1048–1060.

Kim, J. and Cicchetti, D. (2006) 'Longitudinal trajectories of self-system processes and depressive symptoms among maltreated and nonmaltreated children.' *Child Development 77*, 624–639.

La Greca, A.M. and Prinstein, M.J. (2002) 'Hurricanes and Earthquakes.' In A.M. La Greca, W.K. Silverman, E.M. Vernberg and M.C. Roberts (eds) *Helping Children Cope with Disasters and Terrorism.* Washington: American Psychological Association.

Lewis, M.D., Granic, I., Lamm, C., Zelazo, P.D. *et al.* (2008) 'Changes in the neural bases of emotion regulation associated with clinical improvement in children with behaviour problems.' *Development and Psychopathology 20*, 913–939.

Lindgaard, C.V., Iglebaek, T. and Jensen, T.K. (2009) 'Changes in family function in the aftermath of a natural disaster: the 2004 tsunami in southeast Asia.' *Journal of Loss and Trauma 14*, 101–116.

Luthar, S.S. and Goldstein, A. (2004) 'Children's exposure to community violence: implications for understanding risk and resilience.' *Journal of Clinical Child and Adolescent Psychology 33*, 499–505.

Meiser-Stedman, R., Smith, P., Glucksman, E., Yule, W. and Dalgleish, T. (2007) 'Parent and child agreement for acute stress disorder, posttraumatic stress disorder and other psychopathology.' *Journal of Abnormal Child Psychology 35*, 191–201.

Mynard, H., Joseph, S. and Alexander, J. (2000) 'Peer-victimisation and posttraumatic stress in adolescents.' *Personality and Individual Differences 29*, 815–821.

Nader, K., Pynoos, R.S., Fairbanks, L.A., Al-Ajeel, M. and Al-Asfour, A. (1993) 'A preliminary study of PTSD and grief among the children of Kuwait following the Gulf crisis.' *British Journal of Clinical Psychology 32*, 407–416.

Pereda, N., Guilera, G., Forns, M. and Gomez-Benito, J. (2009) 'The prevalence of child sexual abuse in community and student samples: a meta-analysis.' *Clinical Psychology Review 29*, 328–338.

Pynoos, R.S. and Nader, K. (1989) 'Children's memory and proximity to violence.' *Journal of the American Academy of Child and Adolescent Psychiatry 28*, 236–241.

Pynoos, R.S., Goenjian, A., Tashjian, M., Karakashian, M. *et al.* (1993) 'Post-traumatic stress reactions in children after the 1988 Armenian earthquake.' *British Journal of Psychiatry 163*, 239–247.

Qouta, S., Punamaki, R.L., Miller, T. and El-Sarraj, E. (2008) 'Does war beget child aggression? Military violence, gender, age and aggressive behavior in two Palestinian samples.' *Aggressive Behavior 34*, 231–244.

Sack, W.H., Clarke, G., Him, C., Dickason, D. *et al.* (1993) 'A 6-year follow-up study of Cambodian refugee adolescents traumatized as children.' *Journal of the American Academy of Child and Adolescent Psychiatry 32*, 431–437.

Salmon, K. and Bryant, R.A. (2002) 'Posttraumatic stress disorder in children: the influence of developmental factors.' *Clinical Psychological Review 22*, 163–188.

Scheeringa, M.S. and Zeanah, C.H. (1995) 'Symptom expression and trauma variables in children under 48 months of age.' *Infant Mental Health Journal 16*, 259–270.

Scheeringa, M.S., Zeanah, C.H., Myers, L. and Putnam, F.W. (2003) 'New findings on alternative criteria for PTSD in preschool children.' *Journal of American Academy of Child and Adolescent Psychiatry 42*, 561–570.

Scheeringa, M.S., Zeanah, C.H., Myers, L. and Putnam, F.W. (2005) 'Predictive validity in a prospective follow-up of PTSD in preschool children.' *Journal of American Academy of Child and Adolescent Psychiatry 44*, 899–906.

Scheeringa, M.S., Wright, M.J., Hunt, C.H. and Zeanah, C.H. (2006) 'Factors affecting the diagnosis and prediction of PTSD symptomatology in children and adolescents.' *American Journal of Psychiatry 163*, 644–651.

Stallard, P. and Law, F. (1994) 'The psychological effects of traumas on children.' *Children and Society 8*, 89–97.

Stallard, P., Salter, E. and Velleman, R. (2004) 'Posttraumatic stress disorder following road traffic accidents. A second prospective study.' *European Child and Adolescent Psychiatry 13*, 172–178.

Stern, D. (2006) 'Introduction to the special issue on early preventive intervention and home visiting.' *Infant Mental Health Journal 27*, 1–4.

Stormyren, S. and Jensen, K.T. (2008) 'Verdensanskuelser etter en katastrofe.' *Tidsskrift for Norsk Psykologforening 45*, 1498–1506.

Suliman, S., Mkabile, S.G., Fincham, D.S., Ahmed, R., Stein, D.J. and Seedat, S. (2009) 'Cumulative effect of multiple trauma on symptoms of posttraumatic stress disorder, anxiety, and depression in adolescents.' *Comprehensive Psychiatry 50*, 121–127.

Terr, L.C. (1979) 'Children of Chowchilla. A study of psychic terror.' *The Psychoanalytic Study of the Child 34*, 547–623.

Terr, L.C. (1983) 'Chowchilla revisited: The effect of psychic trauma four years after a schoolbus kidnapping.' *American Journal of Psychiatry 140*, 1543–1550.

Terr, L.C. (1988) 'What happens to early memories of trauma? A study of twenty children under age five at the time of documented traumatic events.' *Journal of the American Academy of Child and Adolescent Psychiatry 27*, 96–104.

Valentino, K., Rogosch, F.A., Cicchetti, D. and Toth, S.L. (2008) 'Memory, maternal representations, and internalizing symptomatology among abused, neglected, and nonmaltreated children.' *Child Development 79*, 705–719.

van der Hart, O., Nijenhuis, E.R.S. and Steele, K. (2006) *The Haunted Self.* New York: Norton Professional Books.

van der Kolk, B.A. (2003) 'The neurobiology of childhood trauma and abuse.' *Child Adolescent Psychiatric Clinics 12*, 293–317.

Yule, W., Udwin, O. and Murdoch, K. (1990) 'The "Jupiter" sinking: effects on children's fears, depression and anxiety.' *Journal of Child Psychology and Psychiatry 31*, 1051–1061.

3

Some Important Aspects of Trauma

Trauma and different life stages

Children develop at different rates but all children must complete a series of developmental tasks during the period from the age of preschool to adulthood. Traumas can affect this development in a range of areas.

At preschool age children learn to differentiate between different types of emotional states, something that continues into school age, to culminate later in a deeper understanding of the origins of feelings and their consequences in adolescence and early adulthood. Traumatic situations affect tolerance for experiencing and differentiating between emotions. Traumas can influence the ability to feel compassion or empathy, and to tolerate and express strong emotions. Fear and anxiety can result in children being less daring to venture far away from their security bases (usually their parents) and they can become anxious about their attachment, depending upon how available the adults are for them. Learning how to regulate emotions is wholly dependent upon the adult caregivers. The child implements interaction sequences, and adults must respond and be sensitive to the child's signals in order for the child to derive the full benefits of this contact in terms of development and learning. If parents of young children are traumatized or depressed, this can have an impact on this interaction. Children's internal models of how others are and will meet them are strongly shaped by their relationships to the most important people in their early, immediate environment.

Young children are protected by their inability to see the long-term consequences of a traumatic situation, and they can also to a lesser degree understand an acute danger. As long as parents stay calm, young children can remain quite untroubled. Simultaneously, young children have less experience with which to interpret an event, a greater tendency towards magical thought and misconceptions, and they are less capable of transforming what has happened, using their imagination. In addition to this, young children are those who are spoken to the least, who receive the least concrete information to counteract ungrounded fears, and who are most easily overlooked following traumatic events.

School children understand more of what is happening during traumatic events, so it is easier for them to imagine that such things can reoccur. Increased understanding opens up the fear of reoccurrence or that other things can happen, which is in turn confirmed by things that they see on television, read about in the newspaper or speak about with friends. At the same time, school children are able to influence a situation: they can do something or choose not to do anything. This gives them more control, but also potentially thoughts of how they should have avoided or could have prevented what happened, and, as such, a greater tendency for self-reproach than is the case for preschool age children. School children to a greater extent also manage to verbalize feelings and are not dependent upon demonstrating feelings through actions. They can both reflect upon and put into words thoughts and feelings. Such cognitive development makes it easier to regulate feelings and with increased age children can also evaluate their own feelings – in other words, they are able to think about feelings. This is something that appears to be difficult for traumatized children. They have problems thinking about feelings, and to avoid thinking about or having contact with their emotions they will often initiate activities.

School children can redo the event in their thoughts by reversing the sequence of events, saving those involved, etc. The coping repertoire increases in keeping with the capacity to assume responsibility – for example, for not having done something when father beat mother until she was black and blue. School children also become more interested in the sequence of events, of who is guilty and how injust it was that this took place. Increased maturity with regard to thought processes offers the opportunity for a deeper understanding, but also for more anxiety about everything that could happen. The increased significance of friends can also make it more difficult to show emotions or speak about thoughts, out of the fear of being viewed as special or experienced as different.

Young people have a pattern of reactions that in many ways resembles that of adults. In recent years we have understood that many of the executive systems in the brain – those systems that help us to plan far into the future, restrain behavioural responses and regulate our behaviour – are developed in adolescence and early adulthood (Giedd 2008). This provides a greater emotional flexibility and the possibility for emotional regulation in social situations. Young people understand to a large extent the significance of what they have experienced and they can reason their way to positive and negative sides of their own conduct in the situation. They can be extremely judgemental of themselves and of their reactions, and impose unreasonable demands with regard to what they should or should not have done. They experience extremely intense emotions, but frequently have problems expressing them and can easily defend themselves against this intensity by attempting to repress their reactions or by finding a dramatic expression for them. Simultaneously, they often have a child's soul trapped in an adult's body. Their emotional intensity can have a childish quality, while their thoughts can reflect a more 'adult' thought system. It is therefore perhaps not so strange that many young people struggle terribly in coming to terms with traumatic events when these occur during an otherwise turbulent period of adolescence.

A number of young people will begin assuming adult roles, mature quickly and cease taking part in the things that others in their age group find interesting. This maturity spurt can have the effect of removing and isolating them from their friends but many manage, over time, to utilize the knowledge in a positive manner, in relation to others. Unfortunately, a number of young people will utilize self-destructive behaviour to distract themselves from anxiety and painful memories. Some also appear to become 'dependent' upon intense stimuli, in order to feel that they are alive, and can seek out high-risk activities as a means of achieving this. Increased alcohol consumption, as a means of relieving tension and numbing feelings of privation, is a response found among young people, but we find few systematic studies done on this. This is a known problem among adults following traumatic situations (see Breslau, Davis and Schultz 2003) and exposure to sexual abuse and domestic violence are also risk factors in terms of substance abuse in young people (Kilpatrick et al. 2000).

The maturing of thought processes, providing the possibility for more abstract thought and more complex reasoning, can lead to older children and adolescents blaming themselves less but also to posing stricter requirements with regard to what they should have done to change or prevent the situation.

Traumatic events must be understood and processed in light of the life stage the child is passing through. An event which a child experiences as a 7-year-old can be viewed in an entirely different light when the child is 11, or later when 14. A childhood characterized by violence during the preschool period provides a poorer basis for handling new traumatic events later in childhood.

Traumatic reminders

Children who have lived through a trauma will often wander through a memory landscape filled with reminders of what happened.

Table 3.1 Traumatic reminders

External	Internal
• Stimuli associated with the event (vision, hearing, smell, touch, taste).	• Recurring thoughts.
• Symbolic stimuli.	• Intrusive memories.
• Conversations about the event.	• Repetition fantasies.
• Cyclic reminders – important dates, holidays, seasons.	• Emotional states.
• New crisis situations.	• Bodily sensations and bodily positions.

In Table 3.1, a number of reminders are mentioned that can easily trigger thoughts, and emotional and bodily reactions. A number of the external stimuli that trigger such thoughts and reactions have already been discussed. Everything from a scar or cut from an accident, to smoke that is a reminder of a fire someone experienced, can trigger memories and provoke reactions. In a child's everyday life, at home, at school, in kindergarten or other places, there can be situations or things that easily trigger reactions, often without adults having any awareness of this.

A boy who had been in a traffic accident had a strong reaction every time he heard the sound of brakes squealing outside the school. At that moment his thoughts immediately returned to the traffic accident that he had survived, and the images and memories from this incident would be replayed in his mind. In the classroom he would go into his own world and have difficulties following the thread of what was taking place in class. Because the school was located in an area with heavy traffic, this occurred frequently.

Symbolic stimuli that are associated with what took place, such as fairy tales, and especially television programmes, can also cause reactions. Red letter days, such as those associated with seasons, anniversaries and holidays, can provoke a strong reaction in a child, sometimes even without the child having any real awareness of what day it actually is.

There is less awareness about internal factors that can easily awaken thoughts about an experience than there is about external factors. As long as the memory material is unprocessed, thoughts and memories will often return. If the child was not present, such as if a father dies in a work-related accident, fantasized versions of what actually happened can be a disturbing factor. It is also the case that if the child should come into the same state of mind or emotional condition as during or after the traumatic event, this can awaken the traumatic memories. It can be helpful to compare this to an image of a spider's web, where the traumatic events are woven together by emotional threads. If you start moving some of the threads in one area, vibrations will reverberate throughout all the threads of the entire web.

Bodily sensations and positions that the body assumes can also spontaneously awaken memories of what happened. For example, a child who has been obliged to assume a specific body position during sexual abuse, torture or even a medical examination, can have a powerful reaction in situations where they must once again assume the same position. If they felt a sensation of intense fear in the stomach during the traumatic situation, similar sensations in the stomach can trigger memory images from the original trauma.

Last but not least, new crisis situations can quickly activate thoughts about things one has experienced previously.

A young woman who was raped as an adult was asked what her first thought was when she was attacked. She replied that it was not a thought but an image that appeared. She saw immediately an image of herself as a little girl (around 3–4 years old) when she witnessed her father taking her mother in a stranglehold before her older brother managed to come to the mother's rescue.

Situations that involve a threat to our own life or the lives of loved ones appear to be stored in a memory network with associations to other similar situations, so that a new situation can release thoughts, emotions and bodily reactions from previous experiences. If such events are stored in the memory in an unprocessed form, it appears that children to a very large degree can experience similar situations as if they are experiencing the same thing all over again.

Interactions with others – parents' reactions, attachment and the home environment

The reactions of parents have already been mentioned as being of importance in terms of how children react. It is particularly difficult for young children if the parents or adults who have the daily responsibility for the children are traumatized. During early childhood, young children are dependent upon a finely regulated interaction with their closest caregivers, most frequently the mother. The interaction is mutually regulated and interwoven and both the mother and child are constantly adjusting their communication in response to signals from the other. Even 6-week-old babies will attempt to gain the attention of an inattentive caregiver through a series of actions and sounds. As children's repertoires expand, they become more efficient at achieving interaction with a social partner, while also being able to understand more of the partner's intentions. Mothers (parents) with securely attached children are more sensitive, warm and give a better response to children's signals than do mothers of children with an insecure attachment. The mother's sensitivity also shows a connection with the child's cognitive development (Evans and Porter 2009).

Existing research has so far concentrated on mothers, because they usually have the primary contact with infants. As an example, it has been shown that the neurological (autonomous) development of 6-month-old children of depressed mothers is delayed (Field 1995). Depressed mothers spend less time watching their infants, touching them and talking 'with' them. In the interaction fewer smiles (positive faces) and more negative facial expressions are registered in the mothers. The children respond by vocalizing less, they have a lower activity level, smile less (fewer positive facial expressions) and they also show more negative facial expressions in interaction with their mothers. The children appear to imitate the mothers' emotional state (Field 1995). Short-term depressions do not appear to have long-term effects, while a depression that is more than six months in duration appears to have a clearly negative impact on the child. In the case of depression it appears as if the mother's insensitivity to the child's signals stems from her being over-preoccupied with her own situation. The good news here is that simple counselling has positive effects on the interaction between children and parents.

By encouraging depressed mothers to give their children massages for 15 minutes on 12 different days over a six-week period, Field (1995) was able to show a positive development in the children's behaviour. By training mothers to be sensitive to children's signals (interaction coaching), such as by teaching them to notice when the child is under- or over-stimulated, the negative consequences could be reduced. A simple recommendation to parents that they massage their infants appears also to have positive effects (Field 1995). Non-depressed parents and those who work in kindergartens can compensate for the negative effects of one of the parents being 'run-down'. The same positive effects with regard to a decline in depression and anxiety were found in mothers who massaged their prematurely born child for eight minutes before being released from the hospital (Feijó et al. 2006).

Parents lacking the energy to stimulate a child during infancy are absent during a period when children are forming their most important attachments, when they learn important techniques for regulating their emotions, and when the development of both the self and important behavioural patterns is taking place. The studies mentioned here were carried out on the children of depressed mothers and we cannot immediately apply the results to children of parents who have experienced trauma. Clinical experience does nonetheless indicate that there are many similarities between traumatized and depressed parents, and that many parents become depressed following a trauma. Parents in both groups can become over-consumed by what has happened and not 'see' their own children. In addition to depression, parents can also develop chronic grief problems. In some families, parents are subjected to chronic traumatization (e.g. mothers who are physically abused) so that the child suffers. Research has also shown that PTSD in one parent can disrupt family relationships and lead to problems for other family members (McFarlane, Policansky and Irwin 1987; Meiser-Stedman et al. 2006; Proctor et al. 2007).

In some traumatic situations, the roles are turned upside down. This happens when parents are incapable of handling the situation, become hysterical or paralysed, and the child is either a passive witness to this or personally takes responsibility and the initiative. The situation can result in the parents' behaviour and reactions becoming a greater source of strain than the traumatic situation itself.

> A 12-year-old girl experienced that her father fell dramatically ill during a holiday trip. The mother collapsed and the girl had to take over by contacting the guide to call for help. After they came home she continued in the role as the parent of her own mother. She became so dominant that other family members grew worried and contacted our centre on their behalf so that the core family could receive help.

Inactivity or overactivity on the part of the parents in a dangerous situation can also be experienced as extremely threatening by the child, and can be the cause of intense reactions after the event. It is of course difficult to reassume ordinary roles after such a role reversal. The problems can be further compounded if the parents have a guilty conscience or are ashamed of their behaviour, and either will not talk about what happened or swear the children to secrecy to prevent others from finding out about it.

A failure to recognize the child's experience on the part of the parents can be a problem for children, even if the parents' conduct has been adequate. Some parents become so uneasy or afraid when they think about the event that they want to deny how bad it was, or they repress it. In such situations, they often resist speaking about it. Parents can also derive clear benefits from neglecting to communicate about what the child has experienced. This is particularly the case in situations where the child has witnessed violence. It has been found that parents seriously underestimate how badly off children are in such situations (Martinez and Richters 1993). Whether this applies to violence in the neighbourhood or in the family, an admission of this means that parents must recognize their own helplessness with regard to protecting their children from such exposure. The type of under-communication referred to here also implies that the parents will to a lesser degree acquire the help that their children need or overlook opportunities to help them. This illustrates how important it is that we speak to children personally, to acquire the most complete picture possible of what they experience and how they react to these experiences.

Open communication about traumatic events is clearly associated with greater resilience and a better overall situation for children following a trauma (see Dyregrov 2001). Openness does not just mean talking about the information that the child needs to understand an event, but also emotional openness: the parents' ability to communicate about feelings (Lutz, Hock and Kang 2007). Children and young people who experience a lack of support from their parents exhibit a higher level of symptoms (Bokszczanin 2008). If children experience serious exposure in a traumatic situation and their parents simultaneously become controlling and over-protective of them, this is associated with particularly high levels of PTSD (Bokszczanin 2008).

It is important to understand that the parents' behaviour has the greatest significance for young children. Here the reactions are most 'contagious', because children are dependent upon adults to interpret and understand the situation. While the presence of symptoms in infants is best foretold by the reactions of the parents, it is the traumatic event that best predicts the symptoms of older children and adolescents (Green *et al.* 1991). But although older children and adolescents are less dependent upon their parents for the interpretation of an event, it is clear that the home environment (openness and support) also has great significance with regard to how this group masters a trauma.

Children who live with domestic violence

A great many children are witnesses to domestic violence. Four questionnaires distributed among adults reported that between 11–20 per cent recalled having seen violence between their parents (partners) as a child (for a summary, see Wolak and Finkelhor 1998). In addition, many children are personally victims of physical and verbal maltreatment, sexual abuse and neglect. There is substantial documentation now for the long-term, sometimes lifelong, negative consequences that this can have. Such cumulative traumas have a more profound impact on the human psyche and, because they continue over time, can result in permanent changes in a number of different areas, such as the regulation of emotions, theories about the world, relations to others, etc.

Verbal aggression on the part of parents is an extremely damaging form of child abuse, which alone can have extremely serious consequences.

But it will often be experienced in combination with other forms of violence (poly-victimization), which can create a negative synergy effect (Teicher et al. 2006). Twin studies show a clear causal connection between child abuse and serious psychopathology (Harris, Putnam and Fairbank 2004). Such children will be predisposed to drop out of school early, to drug abuse and promiscuity, and to the development of depression, poor physical health, not finding a job and PTSD (Harris et al. 2004). Cognitive problems, including memory impairment, have also been proven (Valentino et al. 2008), along with reduced self-esteem (Kim and Cicchetti 2006). It is unfortunately the case that the closer the relationship the child has to the individual responsible for the misdeeds, the longer the time period before those in the child's surroundings gain knowledge of the abuse (Foynes, Freyd and DePrince 2009).

In the past decade researchers have also proven how child abuse and maltreatment has a traumatic effect on the child's biological development (see Chapter 2). Because the exposure to domestic violence is often chronic and not an isolated incident, it can lead to a negative neurobiological adaptation of a central nervous system undergoing development; and, in the worst cases, to more or less permanent structural changes in the brain, along with the impact that violence has on the development of empathy, trust in surroundings, cognitive capacity, etc. (De Bellis 2001, 2006; Perry and Pollard 1998). As if the negative effects mentioned here were not enough, what also occurs is that the violence is passed on to subsequent generations, in that many of those exposed to violence personally develop violent behaviour later in life (Holt, Buckley and Whelan 2008). Research also indicates that changes in the brain in connection with different types of violence-related symptoms are linked to the age of the child when the exposure occurs. During different sensitive periods, the exposure to violence can affect brain structures differently (Andersen et al. 2008).

If young children experience violence from family members, the result can be that they learn not to feel anything and that adults are not to be trusted. They can attempt to become 'independent' of adult contact, often with the result that they develop difficulties in forming ties to other people. Sexual abuse can lead to over-sexualized behaviour, early sexual debut, and is believed potentially to accelerate the onset of puberty and entail an increased risk of subsequent abuse. Early traumas (preschool age) can have a strong impact on the regulation of emotions, independence and the tolerance of intimacy in relation to others.

In homes where abuse takes place, the majority of children develop a so-called insecure attachment, in this case a form known as 'disorganized attachment', something which in turn is a reflection of a parent–child interaction that is characterized by hostility and a low level of reciprocity, engagement and synchronization (Tarabulsy *et al.* 2008). Parents of children who exhibit disorganized attachment often behave in a threatening manner and react atypically to children's signals of discomfort or agitation. They are insensitive and unpredictable in relation to the children's needs, so that the children learn that they cannot rely on the parents for comfort and protection. Children who early in life experience such traumatic strain, and who develop a disorganized attachment, unfortunately receive a poor life foundation. This type of attachment is strongly associated with problems in childhood, adolescence and early adulthood (Tarabulsy *et al.* 2008). Children with disorganized attachment appear to have difficulties handling frightening situations and in regulating their emotions later on (MacDonald *et al.* 2008).

Almqvist and Broberg (2004) documented that a majority of the children at crisis centres struggled with post-traumatic problems and approximately 25 per cent fulfilled the criteria for the diagnosis of PTSD, while a number of others had what is known as sub-syndromal PTSD (many symptoms close to the level for PTSD). They see three different tendencies in the exposed children's symptomatic make-up. First, there are children with relatively clear post-traumatic symptoms; then there is another group that has become more and more fixated on violence, and finally a third group that has developed in such a way that they are focused on taking care of their mothers. Children in this group are helpful and comforting and simultaneously afraid and anxious. Some overlapping between the groups exists. What also characterizes these children is that they have greater difficulties in relationships and exhibit anxious or disorganized attachment behaviour.

There are in particular two factors that consistently, across different studies, appear to foretell or predict psychopathology among children who have been exposed to such traumatic events. One factor is the degree of exposure to a dangerous incident and the other the degree of social support that can be summoned (Pine and Cohen 2002). Children who live in homes where they are exposed to violence, and at the same time must assume too much responsibility in the manner of being charged with stressful caregiving tasks, are at risk of becoming 'parentified' children. Such children can experience problems with social contact, schooling and different psychological problems.

Trauma and memory

Children's memory with regard to traumatic situations has been the subject of a great deal of research interest. A number of adults in therapy have claimed to remember sexual violations they experienced as children without previously having had any awareness of this. This has led to accusations that it is the therapists who have created the memories through their focus on potential abuse. It is wholly possible for a therapist to create such erroneous memories with influence acquired over patients' emotional lives. It is also probable that the abuse may have happened. There is no question at all about the fact that different remembering or forgetting mechanisms can lead to the repression of traumatic events in childhood, either wholly or partially, and over varying periods of time. Studies have confirmed that the memory system can keep traumatic events 'hidden' from us for many years, from childhood to adulthood. Williams (1994) has shown that 38 per cent of a group of women (N=136) who had been sent to the emergency room due to sexual abuse as a child did not report this when they were interviewed 17 years after it had happened. Although it is possible that they simply chose not to mention it, there was a good deal of supplementary information indicating that they did not remember the abuse. She also found that extremely young children remembered less than older children and that those who had a close association with the attacker remembered less than those who did not have a close relationship as such.

Those who experience isolated incidents or type I traumas have more complete and precise memories. Memory displacement happens most frequently when a child is subjected to repeated traumas. In these situations, the child remembers more of a kind of compiled version or script of the event. Children appear to have problems describing details from similar traumatic situations that they experience frequently. This means that their episodic memory is impaired and a more general memory is developed (Price and Connolly 2008). Long-term stress affects parts of the brain that are of key importance for memory. Carrion, Weems and Reiss (2007) have in a longitudinal study shown that abused children with a high level of PTSD symptoms and high cortisol levels display a reduction in the size of the hippocampus over time. The hippocampus plays an important part in memory formation and the regulation of cognitive functions; among other things it controls our ability to create time sequences of events and to connect memories to a context.

Amnesia or loss of memory of parts of or the entire trauma is a result of the difficulties involved in addressing a negative memory that is irreconcilable with other important factors in existence, such as that a father who is so pleasant in the afternoon does such terrible things in the evening. It is nonetheless important to know that most adults remember very little from the time before the age of 4–5 years, and this does not necessarily mean that they have been subjected to something traumatic. Traumatic amnesia is connected with age and the degree of traumatization: the younger the child is when the trauma takes place and the longer the period that the traumatic events persist, the greater the possibility for amnesia (see van der Kolk and Fisler 1994).

Terr (1983) has shown that children can report memory displacement in terms of time. They can remember something that actually occurred after the trauma as if it happened before, which can lead to the child believing that this was an omen or warning. Here we can clearly see how the brain can help us to improve predictability in our unpredictable lives, at the cost of losing an entirely truthful version of an event.

Memory displacements and omissions and mistaken perceptions of what happened and at what point in time are not unusual among children. Certain aspects of the event are remembered with greater clarity, while others are forgotten. When something is missing in a memory, it is not unusual for the brain to fill in the blank. The memory is not static, but rather an active process that can also contain elements of a child's wishes, beliefs and imagination. Pynoos and others (1987) found that children who were close to a threatening situation (a sniper shooting into a schoolyard) remembered being further away than they actually were, while those who were further away (out of danger) remembered being closer to the danger. Memory displacements and omissions can protect the child from unbearable, strong feelings.

> A boy who survived an accident had memories only from the time after he had been brought to safety, even though he was relatively unhurt and had not lost consciousness. Other information from the accident indicates that in order to survive he was obliged to act in a way that had consequences for a family member who died.

Children can also allow imagined actions to become part of their memory of the event. Nader and Pynoos (1991) tell of an 11-year-old girl who remembers standing over her seriously wounded girlfriend (shot in the schoolyard) and saying 'I love you'. The truth was that nobody could get close to the girl due to the dangerous situation. The example shows how the brain can spontaneously expand upon memory traces, here through the imagination, so that we are better prepared to master the period afterwards. In the same way, to reduce a threat, children can deny or omit elements of an event. The examples show how remembering something is more a reconstruction than a mirroring of what we have experienced.

But even though changes occur in the memory for some, it is clear that many children retain extremely precise, often detailed memories. Children who are under 2½–3 years of age when a traumatic event occurs, will seldom be able to provide a coherent, verbal account of the event later. But although children cannot verbally express memories of things that happen at this age, the memories appear to be stored in a pre-verbal, often visual form, which can find expression in play and actions or in the form of bodily memories. Kaplow and others (2006) describe how a girl, who at 19 months old experienced her mother being shot while she was in her arms, was gradually able to make her implicit memories explicit through therapy. This came about after she as an 11-year-old had the memory triggered by an incident with clear parallels to the original event. As an 11-year-old she developed symptoms that strongly resembled those she had displayed as an infant.

Young children can re-enact or play parts of what they have experienced or they can exhibit fear of certain things that were present in the traumatic situation without their being able to speak about the trauma. While a verbal memory requires conscious attention, this is not necessary with behavioural memories. Behavioural memories are based on primary sense impressions, particularly visual memories, which verbal memories are not. Developmentally speaking, this is a reflection of the use of brain structures that mature early (visually based). Structures that involve verbalization require symbolic activity and mature later. Girls seem to be able to speak about memories earlier than boys, something that is probably a reflection of their earlier and more proficient mastery of language.

Also with older children the traumatic memories can be found stored at a non-verbal level. There the meaning can be changed and processed as the child develops. Memories can also become clearer if they are given the form of a narrative. When children are asked to review an event thoroughly and in detail, they are often able to fill in blanks, organize the sequences of what took place, remember details and account for how they experienced the situation (Pynoos and Nader 1989).

Contemporary memory research has shown that young children are dependent upon parents (or other adults) using a narrative or elaborative (as in developing the story) style when speaking to their child, in order to support the child in the memory storage process. A so-called elaborative or developmental style enables better coping over time than if conversation is not permitted or one person has hegemony or dominates the story telling (Bohanek *et al.* 2006; Harley and Reese 1999). Children who speak to adults about an event establish a more integrated, detailed and well-organized representation or memory of the event (Bauer and Saeger Wewerka 1995). This has a therapeutic effect, which helps prevent the memory from becoming intrusive.

References

Almqvist, K. and Broberg, A. (2004) *Barn som bevittnat våld mot mamma.* Gøteborg: Lundby Stadsdelsförvaltning.

Andersen, S.L., Tomada, A., Vincow, E.S., Valente, E., Polcari, A. and Teicher, M.H. (2008) 'Preliminary evidence for sensitive periods in the effect of childhood sexual abuse on regional brain development.' *Journal of Neuropsychiatry and Clinical Neurosciences 20,* 292–301.

Bauer, P.J. and Saeger Wewerka, S. (1995) 'One- to two-year-olds' recall of events: the more expressed, the more impressed.' *Journal of Experimental Child Psychology 59,* 475–496.

Bohanek, J.G., Marin, K.A., Fivush, R. and Duke, M.P. (2006) 'Family narrative interaction and children's sense of self.' *Family Process 45,* 39–54.

Bokszczanin, A. (2008) 'Parental support, family conflict, and overprotectiveness: predicting PTSD symptom levels of adolescents 28 months after a natural disaster.' *Anxiety, Stress and Coping 21,* 325–335.

Breslau, N., Davis, G.C. and Schultz, L.R. (2003) 'Posttraumatic stress disorder and the incidence of nicotine, alcohol, and other drug disorders in persons who have experienced trauma.' *Journal of the American Medical Association 60,* 289–294.

Carrion, V.G., Weems, C.F. and Reiss, A.L. (2007) 'Stress predicts brain changes in children. A pilot longitudinal study on youth stress, posttraumatic stress disorder, and the hippocampus.' *Pediatrics 19,* 509–516.

De Bellis, M.D. (2001) 'Developmental traumatology: the psychobiological development of maltreated children and its implications for research, treatment, and policy.' *Development and Psychopathology 13,* 539–564.

De Bellis, M.D. (2006) 'The psychobiology of neglect.' *Child Maltreatment 10,* 150–172.

Dyregrov, A. (2001) 'Telling the truth or hiding the facts. An evaluation of current strategies for assisting children following adverse events.' *Association for Child Psychology and Psychiatry,* Occasional paper *17,* 25–38.

Evans, C.A. and Porter, C.L. (2009) 'The emergence of mother-infant co-regulation during the first year: links to infants' developmental status and attachment.' *Infant Behavior and Development 32*, 147–158.

Feijó, L., Hernandez-Reif, M., Field, T., Burns, W., Valley-Gray, S. and Simco, E. (2006) 'Mothers' depressed mode and anxiety levels are reduced after massaging their preterm infants.' *Infant Behaviour and Development 29*, 476–480.

Field, T. (1995) 'Infants of depressed mothers.' *Infant Behavior and Development 18*, 1–13.

Foynes, M.M., Freyd, J.J. and DePrince, A.P. (2009) 'Child abuse: betrayal and disclosure.' *Child Abuse and Neglect 33*, 209–217.

Giedd, J.N. (2008) 'The teen brain: insights from neuroimaging.' *Journal of Adolescent Health 42*, 335–343.

Green, B., Korol, M., Lindy, J., Gleser, G. and Kramer, L.A. (1991) 'Children and disaster: age, gender, and parental effects on PTSD symptoms.' *Journal of the American Academy of Child and Adolescent Psychiatry 30*, 945–951.

Harley, K. and Reese, E. (1999) 'Origins of autobiographical memory.' *Developmental Psychology 35*, 1338–1348.

Harris, W.W., Putman, F.W. and Fairbank, J.A. (2004) 'Mobilizing trauma resources for children.' Paper presented in part at the meeting of the Johnson and Johnson Pediatric Institute: Shaping the Future of Children's Health, San Juan, Puerto Rico, 12–16 February.

Holt, S., Buckley, H. and Whelan, S. (2008) 'The impact of exposure to domestic violence on children and young people: a review of the literature'. *Child Abuse and Neglect 32*, 797–810.

Kaplow, J.B., Saxe, G.N., Putnam, F.W., Pynoos, R.S. and Lieberman, A.F. (2006) 'The long-term consequences of early childhood trauma: a case study and discussion.' *Psychiatry 69*, 362–375.

Kilpatrick, D.G., Acierno, R., Saunders, B., Resnick, H.S., Best, C.L. and Schnurr, P.P. (2000) 'Risk factors for adolescent substance abuse and dependence data from a natural sample.' *Journal of Consulting and Clinical Psychology 68*, 19–30.

Kim, J. and Cicchetti, D. (2006) 'Longitudinal trajectories of self-system processes and depressive symptoms among maltreated and nonmaltreated children.' *Child Development 77*, 624–639.

Lutz, W.J., Hock, E. and Kang, M.J. (2007) 'Children's communication about distressing events: the role of emotional openness and psychological attributes of family members.' *American Journal of Orthopsychiatry 77*, 86–94.

MacDonald, H.Z., Beeghly, M., Grant-Knight, W., Augustyn, M., *et al.* (2008) 'Longitudinal association between infant disorganized attachment and childhood posttraumatic stress symptoms.' *Development and Psychopathology 20*, 493–508.

Martinez, P. and Richters, J.E. (1993) 'The NIMH community violence project: II. Children's distress symptoms associated with violence exposure.' *Psychiatry 56*, 22–35.

McFarlane, A., Policansky, S.K. and Irwin, C. (1987) 'A longitudinal study of the psychological morbidity in children due to a natural disaster.' *Psychological Medicine 17*, 727–738.

Meiser-Stedman, R.A., Yule, W., Dalgleish, T., Smith, P. and Glucksman, E. (2006) 'The role of the family in child and adolescent posttraumatic stress following attendance at an emergency department.' *Journal of Pediatric Psychology 31*, 397–402.

Nader, K. and Pynoos, R. (1991) 'Play and Drawing as Tools for Interviewing Traumatized Children.' In C.E. Schaefer, K. Gitlin and A. Sandgrund (eds) *Play, Diagnosis and Assessment.* New York: John Wiley.

Perry, B.D. and Pollard, R. (1998) 'Homeostasis, stress, trauma, and adaption.' *Child and Adolescent Psychiatric Clinics of North America 7*, 33–51.

Pine, D.S. and Cohen, J.A. (2002) 'Trauma in children and adolescents: risk and treatment of psychiatric sequelae.' *Society of Biological Psychiatry 51*, 519–531.

Price, H.L. and Connolly, D.A. (2008) 'Children's recall of emotionally arousing, repeated events: a review and call for further investigation.' *International Journal of Law and Psychiatry 31*, 337–346.

Proctor, L.J., Fauchier, A., Oliver, P.H., Ramos, M.C., Rios, M.A. and Margolin, G. (2007) 'Family context and young children's responses to earthquake.' *Journal of Child Psychology 48*, 941–949.

Pynoos, R.S. and Nader, K. (1989) 'Children's memory and proximity to violence.' *Journal of the American Academy of Child and Adolescent Psychiatry 28*, 236–241.

Pynoos, R.S., Frederick, C., Nader, K., Arroyo, E. *et al.* (1987) 'Life threat and posttraumatic stress in school age children.' *Archives of General Psychiatry 44*, 1057–1063.

Tarabulsy, G.M., St-Laurent, D., Cyr, C., Pascuzzo, K. *et al.* (2008) 'Attachment-based intervention for maltreating families.' *American Journal of Orthopsychiatry 78*, 322–332.

Teicher, M.H., Samson, J.A., Polcari, A. and McGreeney, C.E. (2006) 'Sticks, stones, and hurtful words: relative effects of various forms of childhood maltreatment.' *American Journal of Psychiatry 163*, 993–1000.

Terr, L.C. (1983) 'Chowchilla revisited: the effect of psychic trauma four years after a schoolbus kidnapping.' *American Journal of Psychiatry 140*, 1543–1550.

Valentino, K., Rogosch, F.A., Cicchetti, D. and Toth, S.L. (2008) 'Memory, maternal representations, and internalizing symptomatology among abused, neglected, and nonmaltreated children.' *Child Development 79*, 705–719.

van der Kolk, B.A. and Fisler, R.E. (1994) 'Childhood abuse and neglect and loss of self-regulation.' *Bulletin of the Menninger Clinic 58*, 145–168.

Williams, L.M. (1994) 'Recall of childhood trauma: a prospective study of women's memories of child sexual abuse.' *Journal of Consulting and Clinical Psychology 62*, 1167–1176.

Wolak, J. and Finkelhor, D. (1998) 'Children Exposed to Partner Violence.' In J.L. Jasinski and L.M. Williams (eds) *Partner Violence: A Comprehensive Review of 20 Years of Research* (pp.73–112). Thousand Oaks, CA: Sage Publications.

4

Girls and Boys — Alike or Different?

Gender differences in the context of trauma

Many reports have established that women react with more serious trauma reactions and PTSD than men (for a summary, see Olff *et al.* 2007). Studies of children are not equally unambiguous, but most come to the same conclusions: girls exhibit more reactions than boys. With regard to reactions such as anxiety, depression and other subjective ailments, the studies show that girls usually experience more symptoms and discomfort than boys. But if one investigates behavioural disorders, reported agitation, or conflicts with the surroundings, etc., this levels out to a greater extent. Accordingly, we can say that girls experience mild emotional disturbances while boys display negative effects in the manner of behavioural problems.

With respect to seeking out others to speak to about what has happened, the differences are very clear: this is much more common among girls than among boys. In the follow-up of a group of pupils who had experienced the murder of their teacher, and another group of pupils who had experienced having a classmate killed in a dramatic accident, we found that the girls to a much greater extent sought help and comfort from their friends and their parents than did the boys (Dyregrov *et al.* 1994, 1995). The gender differences follow the same trend also with regard to use of the written word. Girls commonly use many more words than boys to describe their reactions, and they also use more emotionally charged words than boys.

After a boy in the 8th grade was killed in a tragic accident, almost 60 per cent of the girls in the class felt that they would never get over it, while only 20 per cent of the boys responded accordingly. The girls thought to a greater extent than the boys that speaking about the death had been extremely helpful. This was the case both in terms of speaking to friends, where 100 per cent of the girls thought that it had been extremely helpful, versus 64 per cent of the boys, and in terms of speaking with their mother or father, where 73 per cent of the girls and 33 per cent of the boys thought this was extremely helpful. The girls found that on the whole expressing their feelings and/or thoughts about the event by crying, talking or writing about it was a much bigger help than the boys did. However, with respect to how adults could help children and young people following a traumatic death, they were in agreement when asked to assess the statements in Table 4.1.

Table 4.1 How do you think adults can help children and young people who are grieving?

% who acknowledged the reaction:	Girls %	Boys %
• Talk to them.	100	100
• Activate them.	64	40
• Speak about the event as little as possible.	9	18
• Come up with positive things to do together with them.	91	92
• Allow them to participate in rituals (see the deceased, funeral etc.).	100	83
• Let them meet other people in the same situation.	73	64

All the girls and half the boys agreed with the assertion that it was easier to speak to girls about what happened, but few boys (23%) or girls (25%) agreed that the boys had an easier time, and could put things behind them more quickly. In terms of friendship, girls appear to be 'involved': they confide in their girlfriends more than boys confide in their male friends, and it is easier for them to share their innermost

thoughts and feelings. Being in touch with their fe
that they are more aware of them, and experienc
and discomfort, while they also have the ability to
discomfort into words. If the trauma involves th
girls are particularly vulnerable due to a loss of
which they have grown accustomed. Boys conne
to activities and the loss is felt with the greatest
is not there during sports activities or other thing
together.

Boys have an oral tradition that differs from tha
in one another more than boys do, while boys
stories of boys are often focused on action and tl
formalized in a written form such as a diary.

> Rolf lost his brother in an accident. In response to the question
> of whether he had kept a diary, he looked at me as if I were
> from another planet, that I could ask such a thing! It was clear
> that a diary was something for girls. 'But have you written
> anything after the accident?' I asked again. 'Do you mean on
> the computer?' When I asked what he had written he told me
> it was about things that he and his brother had done together.
> And to yet another question about when he took this out, he
> answered: 'When I miss him, it helps me to read about all the
> fun things we did together.'

Following the loss of friends it is predominantly boys who are responsible
for the technical arrangement of memorial pages on the internet, while
girls are more enthusiastic contributors of texts. Another difference that I
have observed is the tendency of boys to give advice, while girls express
understanding more and are less action-oriented. The following letter
was sent to a mother after her son died. One of her son's good friends
had written it. Notice both the narration of the story and the advice at
the end:

> Dear...
>
> I know how you feel; personally I could not hold back the
> tears when I learned that Inge was dead. I felt that I had lost
> a good friend. He took everything seriously, even when it was
> a joke.

Once I was bullied at school. Then Inge came and said, 'Some guys I know are twice as big and twice as strong and can take them.' Then I asked, 'How many are there?' He said 'Ten.' And he said that they would come on Friday. When Friday came and there were no big boys, and I asked him where the boys were he said, 'No, they couldn't come because they were at school.' Then I said that he was just kidding, but no, he was not kidding (he said).

Sincere regards...

P.S. Don't cry so much. Plus if you need any help call this number xxxxxx.

In spite of the gender differences that are emphasized here, there are large individual differences and many boys are more like girls and vice versa.

Pynoos and Nader (1988) did a study on a group of children who had witnessed the rape of their mothers. The girls reported having recurring dreams about being attacked and they became afraid of strangers. The boys also felt more vulnerable but some identified with the rapist. In addition to this, they fantasized about intervening and taking revenge. The authors speculated that the girls were more depressed and fearful than the boys, who for their own part reacted with more behavioural problems, because of differences in how they reacted to traumatic helplessness. Such gender differences can have many causes, but it is believed that they derive from a combination of different role expectations, learning differences and different biological points of departure.

To a limited extent help measures for children and young people have taken into consideration the existence of such gender differences and a good deal of the help offered has used conversation as the most important tool, something which clearly favours girls. Girls have received more training in sharing thoughts and feelings with one another from their friendships with other girls. In fact, studies show (Tannen 1990) that, when boys meet a best friend to have a conversation, even their sitting position is different from girls: boys do not sit across from one another the way girls often do, but side by side, without direct eye contact, with a visual focus on a common external point, rather than on one another. Girls, on the other hand, sit across from one another, as is common in most therapeutic situations.

It is, however, important to recognize that these differences appear to even out more as the two genders acquire more similar learning histories. We also know that some boys are more 'girlish' than many girls, and some girls more 'boyish'. The differences mentioned are perhaps least obvious just after a traumatic event, when both girls and boys have a need to talk about what has happened and to be together with friends. Eventually, as time passes however, the gender differences become more pronounced and the need for gender-adapted help increases. We have begun now to provide more for these gender differences in the follow-up of traumatic situations, so help measures can be adapted to both genders.

In our work with children who have experienced traumatic death, we have developed a number of help methods designed to better reach boys, based on the fact that they use words and conversation less and they have greater difficulties expressing their feelings than girls.

Some of the methods we use are listed in Box 4.1.

Box 4.1 Help for boys and men

- Rituals
- Activity-based 'conversations'
  - Play cards, look in photo albums, etc.
- Fill-in-the-blanks, letter writing, other 'gentle' methods
- Writing on a computer
- Telling stories
- Videos and music
- Use concrete materials
- Visit important places
  - The scene of the event
  - The grave
- Meet helpers (police, rescue and healthcare personnel)
- The structure of the conversation
  - Facts – thoughts – reactions
- Change in sitting position during the conversation
- Development of other expressive skills
- Find own 'expressive language'

This type of more activity-based help meets boys on their own turf, and makes it easier for them to express what they think and feel. While girls have a long tradition of keeping diaries, this is rather unusual among boys. If you instead allow boys to write on a computer and describe what they have done together with a friend who died in an accident, they will find this easier than writing in a diary. The list in Box 4.1 is an attempt to meet boys' needs. It is perhaps also the case that boys can express, using fewer words, the same thoughts and feelings for which girls will use more words. So far there is little to indicate that boys, even with a tradition of using fewer words, struggle more with these events later on. If they need to invest their energy in repressing their reactions, however, this can lead to more problems over time.

Girls struggle more with mild and moderate psychological problems than boys. Perhaps that is the price they pay for being more in touch with their feelings? At the risk of speculating a bit, we can say that boys, by shutting out or repressing their reactions, perhaps live a less problem-filled existence than girls, but they run a health risk if they must expend energy on keeping their emotions at a distance. Girls must struggle with mild nervous complaints; they tend to absorb the unhappiness of others more easily, but are also able to find expression for their experiences and emotions, in words and through other forms of expression, so that the body does not store these up in a manner that becomes a health risk in the long term (see Richards 2004).

References

Dyregrov, A., Gjestad, R., Bie Wikander, A.M. and Vigerust, S. (1995) 'Traumatic grief following the death of a classmate.' Paper presented at the Fourth European Conference on Traumatic Stress, Paris, 7–11 May.

Dyregrov, A., Matthiesen, S.B., Kristoffersen, J.I. and Mitchell, J.T. (1994) 'Gender differences in adolescents' reactions to the murder of their teacher.' *Journal of Adolescent Research 9*, 363–383.

Olff, M., Langeland, W., Draijer, N. and Gersons, B.P.R. (2007) 'Gender differences in Posttraumatic Stress Disorder.' *Psychological Bulletin 133*, 183–204.

Pynoos, R.S. and Nader, K. (1988) 'Children who witness the sexual assault of their mothers.' *Journal of the American Academy of Child and Adolescent Psychiatry 27*, 567–572.

Richards, J.M. (2004) 'The cognitive consequences of concealing feelings.' *Current Directions in Psychological Science 13*, 131–134.

Tannen, D. (1990) 'Gender differences in topical coherence: creating involvement in best friends' talk.' *Discourse Processes 13*, 73–90.

5

The Significance of Friends Following a Trauma

The significance of friends in the lives of children

Children develop their first concept of friendship as early as around the age of 2 and use the word 'friend' when they are 2–3 years old. At preschool age and during the first years of primary school, friendships are formed with children who live close by, and usually of the same gender. There is a high level of reciprocity in the friendships, but even before starting school there can be gender differences.

As children reach a more advanced school age, friends are chosen on the basis of common attitudes, and they develop expectations both with regard to being helped by their friends and of being able to help them if something should happen. Research shows that the friendships of girls are often more intimate, with a larger degree of confidential exchanges of a personal nature, than are the friendships of boys (Rawlins 1992). Boys are more cautious about revealing their inner selves. Boys' friendships develop often as a result of taking part in the same activities and are not as 'personal' as girls' (Rose 2007). Girls experience their friendships as being more supportive, a condition that continues throughout their entire adolescence (de Goede, Branje and Meeus 2009).

It is assumed that girls, through their 'closer' friendships, develop greater expertise about how to understand and support a friend in a crisis than do boys, and that girls feel a sense of caring for a larger sphere of people than boys. Throughout puberty and adolescence, the importance of having a best friend increases for both genders, and lifelong friendships are formed. During this period, a sense of togetherness and intimacy also evolves in the friendships, which are considered significant to the development of identity and closeness with others.

Friends and traumas

In a number of studies we have shown that young people seek out friends for comfort and support following traumatic events (Dyregrov *et al.* 1994; Dyregrov, Bie Wikander and Vigerust 1999). But there are clear gender differences. Girls use their girlfriends as confidants much more than boys, and boys do not tend to seek out as much comfort and support from their parents as girls do. Many young people emphasize that having a friend whom one can confide in is the most important kind of help after a traumatic event. For children in primary school, the parents are certainly still the most important confidants, but it has been shown that as a child approaches adolescence a good friend or girlfriend is the most important.

Difficulties in contact with friends

Although the importance of friendship after traumatic events is emphasized by both boys and girls, these relationships can be fragile and painful. Many young people speak about their friends not fully understanding what they are going through, or about their pulling away. There can be a number of reasons why friends avoid or reduce contact, such as:

- fear of saying or doing the wrong thing
- fear of losing control over own feelings
- not knowing exactly what to say to break the ice
- not wanting to be 'infected'
- believing that the friend wants peace and quiet
- believing that it is best that nothing is said
- desire to maintain a basic sense of security in life
- it is difficult to know for sure how much one can talk about.

While it can feel good to be able to help a friend just after something has happened, it can be more painful to be a confidant over time. Friends are confronted with the fact that such things can happen and therefore with the idea that it could also have happened to them. The desire to re-establish a secure world can lead to friends subconsciously avoiding contact with something or someone who reminds them of their own vulnerability. Experience indicates that friends pull away more quickly if the traumatic event was extremely dramatic or if the friend has experienced a loss or trauma that has not been processed. Research has shown that listening to someone speak about a traumatic event causes increased tension in the listener (Shortt and Pennebaker 1992). Individuals who have a good sense of empathy or compassion are less affected by this than those without such sympathetic insight, something that implies that girls are better equipped to listen to a painful account than boys because girls show more empathy (Rueckert and Naybar 2008).

The contact between a friend and someone who has been through a trauma can easily be damaged if the friend makes comments or statements that are experienced as hurtful or inappropriate.

Examples of such comments are:

- 'It could have been so much worse.'
- 'You must just think about the fact that you are still alive.'
- 'You should have been more careful.'
- 'Time heals all wounds.'
- 'I understand exactly how you are feeling.'
- 'What else can you expect, as careless as you are? It was partly your own fault.'
- 'You must be over it by now.'

Such comments, which diminish what has happened, offer unsuitable advice or encouragement, or accuse the injured person for being responsible for what happened, can all lead to increasing distance within or breaking an important friendship bond. In addition, children and young people can have mistaken ideas about reactions, so they are unable to understand their friend's reactions or are frightened by them, and as such pull away.

Sometimes friends contribute to creating rumours, which is experienced as a betrayal of trust by the injured person, and can cause extremely negative reactions. For this reason, information for the network of friends at an early stage is important.

> Solveig (teenager) was exposed to violence by a friend. There had been media coverage of the event and many rumours began to circulate about what had happened. She contacted a girlfriend, whom she requested inform the other friends. The girlfriend was assigned the task of communicating a) that the boy did not want to accept that their relationship was over; b) what she had done in the situation; and c) that everyone should behave towards her as they had done before.

Teachers and other adults can assist in spreading accurate information to friends.

What type of support do friends want to give and receive?

In a study carried out by Antonsen and Pilø (1995) for the Center for Crisis Psychology, young people were asked about what type of support they would want following the death of a friend. Most of the young people (N=138, grades 7−9) wanted to receive and give help and support characterized by involvement following a crisis situation. This means that they wanted friends and adults to get involved in what had happened by speaking about it, listening and being listened to, crying together, comforting one another, sharing memories and feelings, showing that one cared, and by being understanding and available for one another.

There were however marked gender differences. Significantly more girls than boys wanted to give involved support, while significantly more boys than girls wanted to receive support in avoiding their emotions. Supporting the avoidance of emotions would imply a wish to keep the difficult situation at a distance, distracting the person so they think about other things, speaking about something else, doing things together, cheering the person up, behaving normally and acting as if nothing has happened. The girls prefer support and help that complies with what professionals often recommend, while the boys choose a form of support that professionals associate with increased problems over time: active avoidance. More girls than boys indicate that they want to receive a mixed form of support (both involvement and avoidance) and Antonsen and Pilø (1995) speculate about whether girls have more insight into 'feelings' and thereby can think in a more nuanced manner about their own support needs, such as that needs change over time. It is not known how such strategies affect health in the long term, but adults with responsibility for organizing help should, when initiatives are being planned, use as a basis young people's explicit wishes regarding the type of help they want to receive and give.

Encouraging contact with friends

On the basis of the knowledge that we have about children and young people's wishes to speak to friends, and the fact that during adolescence they seek out support from friends more than from adults, it is important to encourage this type of contact. This can be done in different ways.

Adults can encourage contact with friends by:

- making arrangements to ensure contact
  - arranging gatherings of friends
  - allowing friends to talk together without interruption
- promoting such contact
  - inviting friends
  - asking them to make a phone call, go visiting
- giving information that increases understanding
  - to friends
  - to the injured parties
- talking about how friends can support one another
  - giving examples of what they can do
  - providing information about what helps and what hurts.

As adults we can contribute to contact being maintained with friends by giving friends information about reactions after a traumatic event so they are better equipped to understand the friend they are trying to help. Teachers or other adults can contribute with information about what types of comments can be hurtful and what one can say that is beneficial. We can also prepare those who have suffered the trauma for how friends may react and some of the problems that can arise, so that they can attempt to prevent this. By making arrangements to ensure quick re-establishment of contact between the child (young person) who has suffered the trauma and the friend, this contact can be preserved.

The best help that a friend can give is usually simply to be there for the one who has suffered the trauma and to be attentive and sensitive to the person's needs. By creating a situation characterized by unconditional acceptance, the traumatized person can dare to be wholly him or herself.

Sometimes it can prove helpful to arrange a meeting between young people who have experienced a trauma and their circle of friends so that they can receive information about the incident and how the traumatized young people wish to be met and supported. We have elsewhere described both problems with network support and ways to improve it (Dyregrov and Dyregrov 2008).

References

Antonsen, N.E. and Pilø, A.B. (1995) *Forebyggende arbeid i skolen. Ungdommers tanker om ulike typer støtte ved en venns død*. Hovedoppgave, Det Psykologiske Fakultet, Universitetet i Bergen.

de Goede, I.H.A., Branje, S.J.T. and Meeus, W.H.J. (2009) 'Developmental changes and gender differences in adolescents' perceptions of friendships.' *Journal of Adolescence 32*, 1105–1123.

Dyregrov, A., Bie Wikander, A.M. and Vigerust, S. (1999) 'Sudden death of a classmate and friend. Adolescents' perception of support from their school.' *School Psychology International 20*, 191–208.

Dyregrov, A., Matthiesen, S.B., Kristoffersen, J.I. and Mitchell, J.T. (1994) 'Gender differences in adolescents' reactions to the murder of their teacher.' *Journal of Adolescent Research 9*, 363–383.

Dyregrov, K. and Dyregrov, A. (2008) *Effective Grief and Bereavement Support. The Role of Family, Friends, Colleagues, Schools and Support Professionals*. London: Jessica Kingsley Publishers.

Rawlins, W.K. (1992) *Friendship Matters*. New York: Aldine De Gruyter.

Rose, A.J. (2007) 'Structure, content, and socioemotional correlates of girls' and boys' friendships: recent advances and future directions.' *Merrill-Palmer Quarterly 53*, 489–506.

Rueckert, L. and Naybar, N. (2008) 'Gender differences in empathy: the role of the right hemisphere.' *Brain and Cognition 67*, 162–167.

Shortt, J.W. and Pennebaker, J.W. (1992) 'Talking versus hearing about Holocaust experiences.' *Basic and Applied Social Psychology 13*, 165–179.

6

What Promotes Risk and What Protects?

Coping with traumatic events

Although there are a number of definitions of coping, we can say that, in general, coping is the behaviour or strategies a person uses to meet challenges and to adapt to the requirements of their surroundings. It is possible to rank coping as ranging from adaptive to maladaptive, where maladaptive coping is coping that over time increases the possibilities of negative consequences for a child's development. Usually we use the word coping about factors that promote the handling of or adaptation to a situation, but it is a complicated concept to understand or define, because what can be good for a child in the short term (e.g. an ability to keep pain at a distance) can be damaging in the long term, such as if the coping method diminishes the chances for processing. Accordingly, use of coping methods too early on or too late, too much or too little, or the use of too few coping methods in combination will influence how well a child manages after a potentially traumatic event. Our experience would indicate that it is seldom the use of a single coping method that ensures that everything goes well after a traumatic event, but more the ability to utilize a broad repertoire of strategies to cope with the situation.

Differences in temperament can influence coping behaviour in a positive or negative manner by determining which situations the child views as stressful. Children who have a difficult temperament (i.e., impulsive children) with intense mood swings appear to have more difficulties after experiencing stressful events (see e.g. Wachs 2006) than do those with a 'gentler' disposition. In many ways a number of the post-traumatic reactions that have been described earlier are an attempt to master what happens or has happened. If a child experiences type II traumas (repetition trauma) and they escape by daydreaming or through self-hypnosis or dissociation, this is a means of avoiding pain and 'rescuing' oneself psychologically. Increased anxiety and fear serve as safety mechanisms with a clear survival value, but after individual traumas the continued use of such mechanisms will not be good coping in the long term. For children who live in violent or dangerous surroundings, however, fear and anxiety will continue to be important reaction patterns, as healthy responses to unhealthy circumstances. Guilt also has a coping component because it involves a sifting through of thoughts and behaviour to see if there is something one can learn from what happened, which one can then do differently or better should a similar situation arise again. Intrusive thoughts and memories have a coping component too, because they compel children and young people to confront what has occurred and increase the chances that what happened will be expressed through speech, drawings and play. If we call emotional mechanisms and reactions that increase our chances of surviving a critical situation coping, many common reactions after the event become expressions of children's constructive manner of confronting a traumatic situation.

Children can master life afterwards by spontaneously implementing different strategies to manage daily life better. They can use distraction and busy themselves with activities, they can pray or search for a kind of meaning in what happened, or they can invest a lot of energy in helping others. In the technical terminology for this field, a distinction is often made between active coping, where children actively do things to improve or change a situation or problem, and passive or emotion-focused coping, where they attempt to change their emotional or bodily reactions or the meaning they attribute to a situation. In a study of young people who had suffered the death of a sibling, many mentioned that stress-reducing activities such as playing an instrument, being active, or finding an outlet for accumulated emotions (screaming, crying, etc.) were helpful. Others mentioned the importance of having a religious faith or developing inner strength. Both family and friends were also mentioned as important sources of help (Hogan and DeSantis 1994).

What influences children's reactions to trauma?

It becomes easier to understand that children's reactions to a traumatic event can vary considerably when we take into consideration the many factors that influence a child's reaction. The factors can be broken down into situational factors, factors pertaining to the child, and the caring environment surrounding the child.

Situational factors include the type of warning given about the situation that arose, how much preparation time the child had before the event took place, how difficult it was to understand and address the situation, and, in particular, the intensity of the event to which the child was exposed. The latter factor is about exposure to powerful sensory impressions, including how close the child was to these impressions, the intensity of the impressions and the degree of life endangerment to which the child was exposed. From research on accidents we know that direct exposure to life-threatening and physical injury, and being a witness to the extensive injury or grotesque deaths of others, both show a strong association with the development of post-traumatic problems among children and young people (Dyregrov and Yule 2006; Pynoos 1993; Yule and Williams 1990).

Research on violence has established that the proximity of violence, its duration and the degree of brutality are important risk factors in the same manner as physical force, threats that are expressed during a violent episode, what the child witnesses and the relation to the perpetrator (Kitzmann *et al.* 2003; Pynoos 1993). Exposure to violence in the community is also associated with later problems (Fowler *et al.* 2009). This knowledge tells us that following traumatic events it is important to acquire an understanding of the degree of the child's exposure and reactions over time so that adequate follow-up can be provided.

Children can also be exposed to the behaviour and reactions of parents and other caregivers. From our work with war situations we have experienced that children report more anxiety if parents over-react or display great concern, or when parents are incapable of doing anything whatsoever. When parents are calm and collected in a situation, children's anxiety is diminished, both in the situation itself and afterwards. It is frightening for children to experience that adults are anxious, out of control, confused or disorganized:

The worst thing for me was seeing my parents, whom I have always viewed as calm and in control, break down completely and I had to support them. (16-year-old girl)

It has been established that children who respond with strong emotional reactions a short time after a traumatic event (sadness, anxiety, fear, etc.) also develop more serious post-traumatic problems than those who react less in the acute situation (Lonigan *et al.* 1994; Meiser-Stedman *et al.* 2007). The same holds true for children who believe that they can be hurt again (Salmon, Sinclair and Bryant 2007). This is a reflection of the degree of perceived threat to life, and it is important to take note of this with respect to those who might have a special need for follow-up.

Among the important factors related to or within the child is the child's personality. Research shows that extroverted children appear to handle critical situations better than more introverted children (Amirkan, Risinger and Swickert 1995). It is probable that this bears a connection to the fact that extroverted children are better able to mobilize and utilize support from their surroundings than those who are more introverted. It can also be the result of more optimism and drive in these children. But such personality factors can also comprise risk factors. An extroverted child may have a tendency to seek out other situations that collectively or individually represent a greater exposure to risk.

Children's tolerance to stress varies as well, in part due to inborn traits and dispositions but also as a result of different experiences. Children can learn to master difficult situations such as a fire, and this knowledge can clearly influence their immediate handling of and reaction to a traumatic situation. Children also differ with regard to their coping capacity, which means that they have access to different strategies for mastering both their thoughts and behaviour during and after a trauma, and different emotional capacities for processing what has occurred.

These personal factors also include, of course, the life situation and psychological condition of the child at the time of the event. Children who have previously struggled with or are struggling with psychological problems when a traumatic event occurs, constitute a special risk group (Better and Shannon 1993; Dekovic *et al.* 2008). Children who are anxious before a traumatic situation will be more easily frightened and have their anxiety reinforced, and they will develop PTSD more easily than those who are not anxious (Lonigan *et al.* 1994).

While we can only to a limited extent change situational factors (with the exception of repetition traumas) and only to a certain degree influence personal factors, the opportunity for us to help children lies in the third factor group, the factors that include the caring environment. In certain cases family members are personally responsible for the traumatizing events. This makes the family a risk factor. Psychological problems on the part of the parents, marital problems, domestic violence, unemployment or alcohol and/or drug abuse can increase the chances of traumatization, as well as impede the chances to process what has happened. If the child's parents are struggling psychologically or are traumatized, the child's vulnerability increases, particularly if the child is very young (Massad *et al.* 2009).

Parents who make themselves dependent upon their children for their own support, parents who do not permit children to behave more 'childishly' (regress) for a short period of time after a trauma, and parents who are unable to express feelings openly or to communicate about the trauma can also compound the problems for their children.

Simultaneously, parents and family are the most important sources of support and care. The degree of support from the family and friends is important in terms of how children will manage in the period during and after traumatic situations. Not only will the home and friendship environment be significant, but also the support and help that they receive from staff at kindergarten and in school. Access to professional help and follow-up will also have an impact on the unfolding of trauma reactions over time.

While some of these factors will play a part in influencing the immediate interpretation and handling of the situation, other factors will influence the post-traumatic reactions more. The post-traumatic reactions will also be influenced by the causal understanding the children have and the meaning they attribute to the event(s) over time. The significance that each of the different factors acquires for the traumatized child will also be contingent upon the child's age. As the child grows older, friends, the school and the neighbourhood will gain more importance, as a source of both increased risk and protection.

When does the child need more help?

We can distinguish between risk factors that indicate that we should be particularly attentive to a child who has suffered a trauma, and the reactions or mannerisms that can indicate that they need immediate professional follow-up. A summary is found in Langeland and Olff (2008). The risk factors to be mentioned include those listed in Box 6.1.

Box 6.1 Risk factors

Exposure factors

- Physical injury
- Witness to a grotesque death
- Helplessness in the situation
- Loss of a person close to them
- New trauma or loss experiences

- Violent or unexpected, dramatic death
- Threat to own life or to caregiver's life
- Responsiblity for the event
- Degree of pain
- Many traumatic reminders around them

Characteristics of the child and previous life crises

- Previous anxiety and/or depression
- Unprocessed crises or traumas
- Lack of emotional readiness and preparation
- Avoidance style of coping
- Negative assessment of own reactions

- Introversion
- Rumination
- Gender (girl)
- Genetic predisposition (high physiological reactivity)

Aspects of the caring environment

- Lack of social network
- Lack of communication and openness in the home
- Lack of acceptance of reactions in the family or at school

- Indifferent kindergarten or school environment
- Little contact with friends
- Secondary traumas
- Difficult life situation

These are all factors that have been shown to be associated with a higher incidence of problems in the time period after children have experienced a traumatic situation. However, it is not the case that, if children have experienced one of these factors, they will develop powerful and long-term post-traumatic reactions. These are more to be understood as risk factors that indicate that adults should pay attention to how the children respond in the subsequent period. We do not have precise knowledge about the interaction between all these factors, but we can reasonably assume that, if a child's situation contains a number of these factors, then the risk of long-term problems is great. Risk factors are cumulative. A child can perhaps cope with a few factors, but the greater the number of factors present, the more probable the risk of developmental damage. However, as Rutter (2009) points out, it is important to think not only about characteristics as constituting a form of either risk or protection, but to reveal the processes or mechanisms that constitute a cause, and to determine whether they apply only to vulnerable sub-groups (genetically or socially). A risk factor in one situation can have a protective function in another. Research carried out in recent years has in particular emphasized the importance of cognitive factors, such as children's negative assessment or interpretation of their own reactions and vulnerability (Bryant *et al.* 2007).

The presence of a number of the exposure factors should indicate that from the very start professionals should be brought in to assist the parents, or possibly have direct contact with the child or young person. This is the case for instance with dramatic deaths, where the child witnesses what happens or where there is a strong chance of the child developing fantasies about what took place (such as following a suicide or murder, and dramatic accidents). Children who survive, witness or are told about dramatic events affecting their loved ones or others around them, benefit from early intervention to prevent subsequent long-term symptoms.

Reactions or behaviour that should be cause to consider professional help are:

- the child withdraws from friends and adults
- the child's behaviour changes drastically and persistently
- the child develops phobic reactions
- the child talks about self-harm or committing suicide
- the child reacts with strong self-reproach

- school performance declines
- the post-traumatic reactions are intense and lasting
- the child demonstrates severe denial responses
- the child ruminates constantly over what has happened.

Severe reactions in the period immediately following the event are associated with further problems later on. Some parents become worried if children do not want to talk about what has happened. This can, of course, be a source of concern but it can also reflect that the children need time to approach the pain associated with what they have experienced. For a number of boys this will be a common reaction and constitutes no cause for concern. But if, in addition to not wanting to talk about what has happened, children pull away from friends and adults, keep to themselves too much, sit in their room and avoid taking part in social activities, this is cause for concern. If one also receives word from school that their schoolwork is suffering, their concentration diminished and their performance on the decline, there is cause to contact professionals.

Grief and grief reactions in the form of a sense of loss and longing often persist for a long time and do not represent an immediate cause for concern. Constant anxiety, intrusive images and the presence of other reactions from the list of risk factors, on the other hand, will as a rule diminish during the first few weeks following the incident. Should this not be the case, a referral should be considered. If children develop strong phobic reactions (i.e. if they avoid everything that reminds them of the incident to such an extent that they can no longer, for example, ride in a car if they were in a car accident) it is important to offer professional help at an early stage in order to prevent this from becoming a problem that 'takes hold', with potentially lifelong consequences.

Research among adults has also shown that the immediate denial of emotional reactions described in Chapter 2, which is a common and appropriate reaction in the acute phase, is associated with long-term problems if it is severe and prolonged, so that the person in question is unable to have any contact with their emotional responses. It is then a matter of a dissociative reaction, which entails a tuning out of the emotions in connection with what actually occurred, often resulting in the memory materials finding their way into behaviour or the way of being through other channels. In order to manage to survive in the situation, children who experience cumulative traumas will often utilize a lot of dissociation, which enables them to keep their reactions at a distance. They can become experts at pushing things aside, because then they are not always obliged to feel the psychological (and often physical) pain (see Diseth 2005 for more about dissociation in children).

Children who hint at or admit to suicidal thoughts or plans to kill themselves are of course to be referred to qualified professionals. Children who become over-preoccupied with what has happened, do not manage to find peace in their thoughts, and who brood over the meaning of the event, can also benefit from receiving professional assistance.

In order to facilitate the work of identifying chldren who may be in need of extra help, I have created a risk profile (Table 6.1). Should a child score a series of x's on the 'yes' side, there is cause to consider professional assistance.

Table 6.1 Risk profile

Risk factors	NO	YES
• EXPOSURE		
○ Strong sensory impressions	☐	☐
○ Life threat	☐	☐
○ Strong reactions in family members	☐	☐
○ Physical injury or verbal abuse	☐	☐
○ Worry about a family member	☐	☐
○ Responsibility for what took place	☐	☐
• LOSS		
○ Family member	☐	☐
○ Friend	☐	☐
○ Another person close to them	☐	☐
• BACKGROUND FACTORS		
○ Introverted personality	☐	☐
○ Low tolerance for stress	☐	☐
○ Previous psychological problems and traumas	☐	☐
○ Gender (girl)	☐	☐
• CARING ENVIRONMENT		
○ Low level of family support	☐	☐
○ Low level of support from friends	☐	☐

- ◦ Family problems, insufficient communication and openness in the home; reduced parenting capacity ☐ ☐
- ◦ Interaction problems at school ☐ ☐
- ◦ Experience of secondary traumas ☐ ☐
- REACTIONS
  - ◦ Strong dissociative reaction or strong initial reactions (the first week) ☐ ☐
  - ◦ Drastic change in way of being ☐ ☐
  - ◦ Reactions persist ☐ ☐
  - ◦ School performance declines ☐ ☐

The risk profile is intended to serve as a simple guide with an eye towards gaining an understanding of a child's situation. It must not be viewed as a scientific method.

Complex grief reactions

With respect to children who experience traumas involving the sudden, dramatic loss of loved ones, it can also be fitting to mention some signs of complex grief that can indicate that they are in need of professional assistance:

- chronic reaction patterns
  - ◦ constant weeping, sadness, depression
  - ◦ anger, bitterness, self-destruction
  - ◦ persistent isolation from others
- fear of closeness with others due to a fear of further losses
- inability to express feelings and thoughts about the deceased
- constant rumination over the death, over-preoccupation with the deceased
- oversensitivity for everything having to do with loss and separation
- persistent reduced ability to function at home and at school
- prolonged severe and almost paralysing fear that something is going to happen to loved ones

- persistent strong idealization of the relationship to the deceased
- an insistence that all the possessions of the deceased are to remain untouched, even a long time (>6 months) after the death.

But, once again, it is not the case that the existence of one such factor means that a child needs help, but rather, if the child demonstrates a number of these factors at the same time, that help should be considered. On the basis of research on complex grief reactions in adults, criteria have been developed for a complex grief diagnosis, called Prolonged Grief Disorder (Prigerson, Vanderwerker and Maciejewski 2008). Corresponding research for children, however, has not been conducted.

Factors that contribute to resilience in children

Rutter (1993) has pointed out that protective mechanisms can be divided into four types:

1. those that reduce the risk of being exposed
2. those that reduce the risk of negative chain reactions following exposure
3. those that promote self-confidence and a belief in own ability to influence a situation through the presence of stable and supportive personal relationships or success with things one does, and
4. those that open up positive opportunities.

Resilience is something that is developed over time in a caring environment. Physical or sexual abuse at an early age prevents a child from developing the competence that forms the foundation for healthy resilience. Resilience in children is closely connected to the organization of the home environment, the parents' capacity to take care of and stimulate the child, and their ability to create an environment where the child develops a secure attachment (in contrast to an anxiety-ridden, insecure or disorganized attachment) to its caregivers. A secure attachment in early childhood is an important protective factor that is promoted through considerate and emotionally sensitive caregiving (Egeland, Carlson and Sroufe 1993). It is believed that through interaction with sensitive parents or other caregivers children develop a good self-image, a feeling of self-worth and a capacity for coping in relation to their surroundings. Such caregiving qualities are believed to protect them in the event of subsequent traumatic events.

In many ways it is possible to say that the opposite signs in relation to the risk factors discussed earlier represent factors that will contribute to the child managing well.

Among the factors that can be mentioned as being positive are:

- a personality that solicits the help and caring of others
- self-confidence, independence
- humour
- faith in own ability to manage things, ability to take responsibility
- positive social orientation (extrovert)
- good intellectual ability, realistic, flexible
- ability to understand what is happening
- good support from family and friends, popular with others
- close relationship to one or more adults
- the desire to cope
- good problem-solving abilities
- history of having had success in mastering different situations.

Not all these factors have an exclusively protective effect – for example, intellectual ability in certain cases can mean that a child is more sensitive and attentive to what is happening or could happen, and thereby more vulnerable to certain types of stress.

Children will often continue with ordinary activities, such as play, sports, or spending time with friends, shortly after having experienced traumatic situations. In such situations positive emotional experiences are created. Such experiences and the condition that they produce in the body appear to have an astounding capacity to calm us down and support coping and promote healthy resilience. Positive emotions increase the range of our coping repertoire and make our thoughts more flexible, while simultaneously relieving physiological activation (Tugade and Fredrickson 2006).

Assessment of the need for help

Earlier different risk and protective factors were described. When faced with a child who has been subjected to one or more traumatic events, one should attempt to clarify the following:

- What happened?
- When and where did it happen?
- How did the child or young person react?
- What is the personal significance of the event for the child or young person? (requires a conversation or interview)
- What type of support is available for the child?
- How many risk factors exist? (use Risk profile [Chapter 6, pp.87–88])
- Which protective factors and coping resources can be stimulated or further developed?
- Who is already involved to help? (avoid uncoordinated and parallel measures)

Early assessment is helpful in terms of creating a coordinated and proper follow-up a short time after the event or when knowledge of the trauma is acquired (such as subsequent to child abuse and sexual abuse). Use of systematic assessment tools, such as a questionnaire (e.g. Children's Impact of Event Scale, see Smith *et al.* 2003) and clinical interviews, requires both a certain age and level of maturity in the child, and that professional expertise is utilized. Such tools are often used to identify those who have a need for more follow-up or as a basis for determining where the follow-up initiative is to be implemented. Instruments for the assessment of post-traumatic stress and other post-traumatic reactions can also be found at www.childrenandwar.org.

For more information about such instruments and the assessment of children's trauma reactions, see Nader (2008) and Balaban (2006), and, for a review of the assessment of dissociative reactions in children, see Diseth and Christie (2005). Screening instruments that make possible an early identification of those at risk of developing PTSD have been created in some fields, such as for emergency wards (Ward-Begnoche *et al.* 2006), but the expectation is that these will be further developed. In the area of violence, Finkelhor, Ormrod and Turner (2009) have developed a procedure that with a point of departure in the term 'poly-victimization' can be used by clinicians to identify and give priority to children in a particularly high-risk group.

When has a trauma been fully processed?

Particularly with respect to grief, but also after other crises, it was previously maintained that the event had to be processed through different stages until one reached a final result. In many ways, it has been documented that this is a myth, because some aspects of grief will accompany us to the end of our lives. There are points of similarity in the field of trauma, because both body and soul will always be more vigilant about certain situations, thus enabling us, in a constructive sense, to respond to a corresponding danger if we should encounter it again. Nonetheless, we can say that there are some factors that indicate that a trauma has been processed, so that it need not cast a shadow over the remainder of a child's life. This is the case when:

- the child is able to handle feelings associated with the traumatic memories

- the child can control the memories instead of the memories controlling the child

- the traumatic event has been given a narrative form and transformed into a coherent story with a beginning, middle and end

- self-esteem has been re-established

- the child's important personal relationships have been restored

- the child has developed a system of meaning and beliefs into which the trauma has been incorporated

- the child's reaction to physiological symptoms (activation) is within manageable limits (based on Harvey 1996).

In help measures for traumatized children it is important that they are able to acquire faith in the future and a feeling of continuity in life. As a consequence of the trauma they can also learn to speak openly about painful subjects, learn how they can support others, gain better insight into their own reactions and perhaps develop an improved sense of self-esteem over time.

Post-traumatic growth in children who have experienced traumatic situations has been described in recent years (Cryder *et al.* 2006). It does not appear as if the experience of such growth results in fewer trauma symptoms and only a minority of children experience such growth (Salter and Stallard 2004). It is probable that post-traumatic growth in children is contingent upon good adult caregivers and adult role models.

References

Amirkhan, J.H., Risinger, R.T. and Swickert, R.J. (1995) 'Extraversion: a "hidden" personality factor in coping?' *Journal of Personality 63*, 189–212.

Balaban, V. (2006) 'Psychological assessment of children in disasters and emergencies.' *Disasters 30*, 178–198.

Better, R.W. and Shannon, M.P. (1993) 'Impact of Natural Disasters on Children and Families.' In C.F. Saylor (ed.) *Children and Disasters.* New York: Plenum Press.

Bryant, R.A., Salmon, K., Sinclair, E. and Davidson, P. (2007) 'A prospective study of appraisals in childhood posttraumatic stress disorder.' *Behaviour Research and Therapy 45*, 2502–2507.

Cryder, C.H., Kilmer, R.P., Tedeschi, R.G. and Calhoun, L.G. (2006) 'An exploratory study of posttraumatic growth in children following a natural disaster.' *American Journal of Orthopsychiatry 76*, 65–69.

Dekovic, M., Koning, I.M., Stams, G.J. and Buist, K.L. (2008) 'Factors associated with traumatic symptoms and internalizing problems among adolescents who experienced a traumatic event.' *Anxiety Stress and Coping 21*, 377–386.

Diseth, T.H. (2005) 'Dissociation in children and adolescents as reaction to trauma – an overview of conceptual issues and neurobiological factors.' *Nordic Journal of Psychiatry 59*, 79–91.

Diseth, T.H. and Christie, H.J. (2005) 'Trauma-related dissociative (conversion) disorders in children and adolescents – an overview of assessment tools and treatment principles.' *Nordic Journal of Psychiatry 59*, 278–292.

Dyregrov, A. and Yule, W. (2006) 'A review of PTSD in children. A commissioned review.' *Child and Adolescent Mental Health 11*, 176–184.

Egeland, B., Carlson, E. and Sroufe, L.A. (1993) 'Resilience as process.' *Development and Psychopathology 5*, 517–528.

Finkelhor, D., Ormrod, R.K. and Turner, H.A. (2009) 'Lifetime assessment of poly-victimization in a national sample of children and youth.' *Child Abuse and Neglect 33*, 403–411.

Fowler, P.J., Tompsett, C.J., Braciszewski, J.M., Jacques-Tiura, A.J. and Baltes, B.B. (2009) 'Community violence: A meta-analysis on the effect of exposure and mental health outcomes of children and adolescents.' *Development and Psychopathology 21*, 227–259.

Harvey, M.R. (1996) 'An ecological view of psychological trauma and trauma recovery.' *Journal of Traumatic Stress 9*, 3–23.

Hogan, N.S. and DeSantis, L. (1994) 'Things that help and hinder adolescent sibling bereavement.' *Western Journal of Nursing Research 16*, 132–153.

Kitzmann, K.M., Gaylord, N.K., Holt, A.R. and Kenny, E.D. (2003) 'Child witness to domestic violence: a meta-analytic review.' *Journal of Consulting and Clinical Psychology 71*, 339–352.

Langeland, W. and Olff, M. (2008) 'Psychobiology of posttraumatic stress disorder in pediatric injury patients: a review of the literature.' *Neuroscience and Biobehavioral Reviews 32*, 161–174.

Lonigan, C.J., Shannon, M.P., Taylor, C.M., Finch, A.J. and Sallee, F.R. (1994) 'Children exposed to disaster: II. Risk factors for the development of posttraumatic symptomatology.' *Journal of the American Academy of Child and Adolescent Psychiatry 33*, 94–105.

Massad, S., Nieto, F.J., Palta, M., Smith, M., Clark, R. and Thabet, A-A. (2009) 'Mental health of children in Palestinian kindergartens: resilience and vulnerability.' *Child and Adolescent Mental Health 14*, 89–96.

Meiser-Stedman, R., Smith, P., Glucksman, E., Yule, W. and Dalgleish, T. (2007) 'Parent and child agreement for acute stress disorder, posttraumatic stress disorder and other psychopathology in a prospective study of children and adolescents exposed to single-event trauma.' *Journal of Abnormal Child Psychology 35*, 191–201.

Nader, K. (2008) *Understanding and Assessing Trauma in Children and Adolescents. Measures, Methods and Youths in Context.* New York: Routledge.

Prigerson, H.G., Vanderwerker, L.C. and Maciejewski, P.K. (2008) 'A Case for Inclusion of Prolonged Grief Disorder in DSM-V.' In M.S. Stroebe, R.O. Hansson, H. Schut and W. Stroebe (eds) *Handbook of Bereavement Research and Practice* (pp.165–189). Washington: American Psychological Association.

Pynoos, R.S. (1993) 'Traumatic Stress and Developmental Psychopathology in Children and Adolescents.' In J.M. Oldharn, M.B. Riba and A. Tasman (eds) *Review of Psychiatry, volume 12.* Washington: American Psychiatric Press.

Rutter, M. (1993) 'Resilience: some conceptual considerations.' *Journal of Adolescent Health 14*, 626–631.

Rutter, M. (2009) 'Understanding and testing risk mechanisms for mental disorders.' *Journal of Child Psychology and Psychiatry 50*, 44–52.

Salmon, K., Sinclair, E. and Bryant, R.A. (2007) 'The role of maladaptive appraisals in child acute stress reactions.' *British Journal of Clinical Psychology 46*, 203–210.

Salter, E. and Stallard, P. (2004) 'Posttraumatic growth in child survivors of road traffic accidents.' *Journal of Traumatic Stress 17*, 335–340.

Smith, P., Perrin, S., Dyregrov, A. and Yule, W. (2003) 'Principal components analysis of the impact of event scale with children in war.' *Personality and Individual Differences 34*, 315–322.

Tugade, M.M. and Fredrickson, B.L. (2006) 'Regulation of positive emotions: emotion regulation strategies that promote resilience.' *Journal of Happiness Studies 8*, 311–333.

Wachs, T.D. (2006) 'Contributions of temperament to buffering and sensitization processes in children's development.' *Annals of the New York Academy of Sciences 1094*, 28–39.

Ward-Begnoche, W.L., Aitken, M.E., Liggin, R., Mullins, S.H. *et al.* (2006) 'Emergency department screening for risk for posttraumatic stress disorder among injured children.' *Injury Prevention 12*, 323–326.

Yule, W. and Williams, R.M. (1990) 'Posttraumatic stress reactions in children.' *Journal of Traumatic Stress 3*, 279–295.

7

Help for Children After Traumas

Early intervention

In Box 7.1 a number of important measures are listed that can be carried out to take good care of children immediately after a traumatic event. Some of these measures are most applicable for school-age children while others are age-independent.

Box 7.1 Immediate intervention for children after traumas

- Create a secure, calm situation surrounding the child.
- If the child is separated from loved ones, makes efforts to bring about a reunion as quickly as possible.
- Allow the child to explain what happened; stick to the facts in the conversation.
- Give the child information and facts about the event that contribute to a concrete understanding of the situation.
- Be sure to identify misunderstandings, misconceptions and magical thinking.
- Avoid phrases such as 'I'm sure it will be fine', 'It could have been worse'.
- Allow the child to engage in cognitive tasks that may prevent the formation of negative memories.

> • Work to create openness and directness in the family's internal communication.

Measures carried out immediately to help children following a traumatic event are to be based on what the children have been subjected to, their age and the natural 'helpers' that they have around them. Help must be proactively offered to children and provided early. This need is clearly communicated by parents of children who have experienced traumatic situations such as a sudden death (Dyregrov 2003; Glad *et al.* 2009).

If one or more child needs hospitalization or they arrive at the hospital as next-of-kin, it is important to create a calm and caring situation for those involved. The increased sensitivity to one's surroundings (heightened sensory input) and strong memories that were described in Chapter 2 can lead to negative memories of the help they receive 'becoming ingrained' in the same fashion as the traumatic situation itself. When the child must be removed or moved away from an accident site, away from injury or deceased parents, this can be confusing and frightening for the child. If the child is transported to the hospital, this means being taken away from friends, family and familiar surroundings to a place where everything is unfamiliar and threatening. If an adult or older sibling accompanies the child, this can be very beneficial. If the child is in pain, it is important to alleviate this as quickly as possible. The alleviation of pain, which in turn diminishes bodily activation, can result in limiting the formation of negative memories. If the child has recently formed sensory perceptual memories, research findings indicate that engaging in competing tasks that tap the same brain areas, such as visuospatial tasks if the intense sensory stimulation was visual, may impede the memory formation (Holmes *et al.* 2009).

If nobody is present who knows the child, the child is to be informed that the parents will be contacted immediately so that they can come to the hospital, casualty clinic, or scene of the event as soon as possible. If the child is conscious, a calm explanation of what is going to happen will have a soothing effect. If other members of the child's family are injured, the child should be informed of where they are and how they are doing and told that they will be reunited as soon as possible.

Children are extremely sensitive to non-verbal communication. If, for example, adults know that a mother or father has passed away, but neglect to say anything about this there and then, the child often understands and can harbour resentment towards adults for a long time for not having told the truth.

> I understood it right away but nobody said anything. They didn't think that I knew. (12-year-old boy)

In no other situation is the old adage stating that it is impossible not to communicate more true than in relation to children. Not saying something means that we simultaneously say something, without words, but with facial expressions, intonation, body language, or through frenetic activity or avoidance.

If several children from the same group (e.g. class, sports team, etc.) are hospitalized or affected, efforts should be made to keep the group together if possible. Stallard and Law (1994) write that a girl who was brought to the hospital after a minibus accident neglected to inform the medical personnel about her pains in fear of being isolated from the other survivors, because she had seen this happen with one of the others.

Children and young people who come to the hospital can be overwhelmed by all the equipment around them and by the many medical expressions they hear, in addition to the fact that information about their condition is often given to their parents and not to them. Direct information to children personally can reduce misconceptions, give them a mental understanding of what is happening and establish trust in the healthcare personnel. This can be extremely important in terms of the amount of confidence they will have in healthcare personnel later in life.

> After a trauma Julie struggled with chronic pains for many years. At the hospital she was told that the pains would abate when she reached a certain age. When she reached this age the pains did not diminish. She lost all faith in healthcare personnel and was bitter and reproachful when she spoke about them. In addition, she remembered in great detail and with loathing that she had been obliged to undress her upper body while the entire attending group of physicians (including several medical students) observed her. In early puberty this was a trauma in itself, inflicted upon her by insensitive healthcare personnel.

Adults frequently allow children to witness activity at an accident or disaster site, such as a fire or a large traffic accident, which subjects the child to unnecessary exposure. On the basis of extensive research showing that a higher degree of exposure to traumatic impressions leads to a higher incidence of problems later on, it is important to protect children from unnecessary impressions or to reduce exposure. If possible, children should be prevented from seeing maimed or injured bodies or deceased persons.

> Lise came with her mother to the scene of an accident where several people had drowned. She saw one of the deceased and several months later she developed intense nightmares and daydreams where she could see this person. Going through the nightmares and advice to use her imagination to create a new ending, along with use of trauma therapy (see later) helped her get over these problems.

Children who have lived through a trauma need security around them, something that is best brought about by adults or friends whom they trust. Children can have a need to be physically close, have their back stroked, have someone hold them, or just to sit on the lap of their mother, father or another person whom they love. Simple advice to parents and other adults towards ensuring early normalization of ordinary routines at home should be given as soon as possible. Some specific suggestions are listed in Box 7.2.

Box 7.2 Early help for children after traumas

- Go through what happened to ensure clarity and understanding.
- Address thoughts they had during and after the event. Praise them for what they have managed to do.
- If children have absorbed strong sensory impressions, expression can be found for these in words, play, etc.
- Implement a quick re-establishment of routines in kindergarten, school and at home.
- Give information that normalizes reactions – let children also know that they need not have any reactions to be normal.

- Give advice to children and parents that emphasizes informing and mobilizing kindergarten and school staff to support the children.
- If any new facts about what happened come to light, these should be passed on to the children.
- If any of the children's loved ones are hospitalized, early contact and a meeting with the ward staff should be stressed.
- Give advice about self-help strategies, including how children can handle traumatic memories and reminders.
- Encourage early contact with friends.

Even young children (from age 3–4 years) benefit from going through what happened, as a helpful means of creating a comprehensive understanding of what occurred and as a support for subsequent recollection. Simultaneously, this helps to clarify and counteract misunderstandings and prevent the construction of fantasies. Children must be helped to tell or express themselves in their own way. How to go about carrying out a detailed review of what happened will be presented later on in this book. In this case, the idea is that a considerate adult can help a child with the first conversation and review of what happened.

Children need security and structure around them after a traumatic situation. This is achieved if parents manage to maintain the routines that they are accustomed to from their daily life, such as mealtimes, bedtimes, reading sessions and other things. When we uphold routines, this serves to create continuity in children's lives and provides assurance that, even if the world has become chaotic due to what has taken place, there is nonetheless stability in much of their existence.

After a traumatic event one can ensure early on that children are not creating fantasies based on their not having understood what actually happened.

> Trond was 4 years old when he witnessed his brother being killed in a traffic accident. He saw his little brother get run over and in a conversation more than ten years later he states that at the time he believed that they took his brother to the hospital to put a hose through his mouth and blow air into him so that he could become 'big' again. He believed that he was flattened out when he was run over and that he could be

blown up in the same way as he had seen being done with an air mattress.

The example shows how important it is that adults do not calmly assume that the explanation and facts children have received are sufficient to ensure a correct understanding of what has happened. We must work actively to comprehend their understanding of the situation, an understanding that can often deviate a lot from what adults believe children think. We gain an insight into children's versions through the questions they ask us, the drawings they create, or by carefully asking them about what they believe and think about what happened.

Unfortunately children can be subjected to pressure from parents or other adults to ignore what they experienced or understood. This happens when parents give misleading explanations, commands, threats, or simply are silent. This is of course most common in the case of domestic violence but it can also arise following other types of events.

> Olav was 9 years old when his little brother died of crib death. He was not in the room when his brother was found but he heard his parents' screams, the door slamming, his father driving away at full speed, etc. It was not until the evening that he learned what had happened. Before that he did not dare to ask. Since the day that it happened he has never spoken with his parents about what took place. As a young adult he says, 'It is not the child's job to start such a discussion, now is it?' It is no wonder that he does not have an easy time trusting others.

The objective of the guidelines that are summarized earlier in this chapter is precisely to contribute to children receiving information, understanding the information and seeking out more information. In their understanding of what has happened, children lay the foundation for the perception of the traumatic event that they will carry with them throughout the rest of their life. Simultaneously, we know that the thoughts that they have about what happened and why it happened contribute to determining the feelings that result. Far too often children base their understanding on insufficient facts and the result is that illogical, somewhat frightening fantasies can easily take hold, with the long-term negative development this can entail. Clear, simple, non-censured factual information helps a child to create a realistic picture of what has occurred. An elaborative conversation style where, by way of open questions, parents can talk about important events in children's lives, is important for their autobiographical memory and ability to integrate events into a story about what happened (Reese and Newcombe 2007).

At the same time, as mentioned earlier, it is difficult for adults to uphold the openness and directness that is desirable in communication, because talking about what has happened can be so painful and awaken so many difficult feelings in adults as well. It is therefore of significance that those who counsel parents in an acute situation and over time include the child's perspective and the child's need to be informed, so that children are permitted to seek out information and are also given information after the initial period following the event. A family discussion at an early stage, during which child healthcare personnel can help family members to achieve good family communication and dynamics (i.e., open, sincere and direct communication) is expedient, but it is unfortunately seldom possible due to limited resources and knowledge within the public health service.

There is a difficult balance to be arrived at here. Facts and conversation are not to be imposed on children: they achieve mastery in their own way and will for long periods of time choose to hold what has happened at a distance and out of their thoughts. Accordingly, while on the one hand we shall not compel children to be constantly thinking about what has occurred, on the other hand we cannot allow the incident to go unmentioned in conversations with adults.

Different intervention methods for helping children

There is a series of different help measures that can be implemented in relation to individual children or groups of children who have experienced a traumatic situation. Some of these measures expand upon and develop what has been included under immediate and early help. Measures that can be useful are listed in Box 7.3.

Box 7.3 Help measures

Intervention methods
- Communication of facts
- Systematic conversation for the individual and/or group
- Information about common reactions
  - Oral
  - Written
- Return to the scene of the event
- Classroom and small group intervention
- Parental counselling
- Counselling for other adults
- Play and drawing
- Other forms of expression

Different forms of expression can be used
- Drawing and play
- Artistic forms of expression
- Stories and metaphors
- Written forms of expression (writing assignments, essays, and fill-in-the-blank exercises, etc.)
- Participation in rituals and prayer
- Library guidance and literary texts
- Other 'gentle' methods

Communication of facts

Children need to gain knowledge of new facts that come to light about traumatic events that they have experienced or that have affected them. This can be a matter of information from rescue and healthcare personnel about factors in connection with an accident, a death or an acute illness. It can be a matter of receiving information about what is mentioned in the newspapers, knowledge about what is happening in a trial, updates on how the illness of a close family member is progressing (prognosis), etc.

The day after an accident where the father of a 6-year-old boy died, the mother let him see the photographs of the accident in the newspaper. Later the same day she brought him to the scene of the accident and explained what they saw there and what she knew about how the accident took place. Later, after more information came to light, she made sure that he received this. She also provided him with toys that made it possible for him to play the events of the accident. She spent time with him answering the many questions that he had and explained as best she could what had taken place during the accident.

Even if the child immediately receives good information, this is often forgotten with respect to new information that adults may receive in the following weeks. Even though this need not be so important in all cases, lack of information can in some cases lead to misconceptions or fantasies constituting the basis of the child's understanding.

Systematic conversations about what occurred

Children must be given the opportunity to go through what they have experienced in detail under secure and supportive conditions. This review must allow them to tell, write or play out what happened. This helps them to express the thoughts they are wrestling with and the impressions they have taken in. Through this type of help the implicit, unprocessed memories can be made explicit. It is usually easier to do this a short time after the incident rather than postponing it. At the same time, research findings indicate that this perhaps should be avoided during the initial days, because emotional activation can contribute to reinforcing the memories. Such a review also serves important memory functions, especially for young children. They need adult support to find words to express what has happened. Without such support, what has happened is not adequately integrated in the autobiographical memory. With the help of this type of review, children can acquire a more comprehensive understanding of what happened; they can express thoughts and emotions in connection with the event, gain more control over their own memories and avoid having to utilize unconscious avoidance strategies, strategies that are associated with more tension and long-term problems. Children need the help of adults to organize a sequence of events along a time axis and arrange what happened in the right order. While adults can utilize their experience in such a context, children have less life experience to draw from. Without such a structuring of the facts, mistaken perceptions of the event and its causes can more easily arise, sometimes with self-reproach as the result.

The structured review that is described in the section 'Debriefing groups for children' (Chapter 8, p.132) can also be followed in work with individual children or families. In contrast to work with groups, with individual children it is possible to move back and forth between facts, thoughts, impressions and reactions. When a child describes what has happened, one can ask, 'What did you think then?' in order to be able to identify constructive things that the child did or thought. At the same time, in subsequent conversations it can be important to make a mental plan of what the child can do if a similar situation arises in the future. There can often be positive moments within a traumatic situation that are important for long-term progress, such as a person who tried to help when they felt the most powerless.

> A teenage girl experienced that after a traumatic event she was met with a lack of understanding and care. Many people put unnecessary burdens on her shoulders. A policeman, however, understood how she was feeling, made sure that she received information and gave her support in the situation. In many ways his conduct counteracted the behaviour of the many people who ignored her.

Information about common reactions

Psycho-educational information for children about common reactions can be exceedingly important in terms of the prevention of subsequent problems. The strong reactions that can arise after a traumatic situation are unexpected, painful and can create a strong sense of fear in children and young people as to where the reactions will lead or that they are going 'crazy'. It is therefore important that the adults who have contact with the children have knowledge about common reactions in children, which is then passed on to the children themselves. The significance of counselling for adult caregivers should not be underestimated in that it is from these individuals that children receive verbal and non-verbal messages about 'the correctness' of their reactions. Such counselling should also include advice and tips as to what children can do personally to cope with the situation that has arisen. This will be discussed in further detail later on.

School-age children should be told about common reactions in order to avoid unnecessary fears or misconceptions. Children can be told in simple language what is commonly experienced, while they are also informed that it is not the case that they 'must' react in this manner. In the information for individual children or groups of children, the fact that it is natural to react to such unexpected events is emphasized, along with how one often reacts and how the reactions usually progress. It can be expedient to use simple, written information folders, especially for older children and adolescents. Such folders should not contain a list of all the problems or symptoms that can come about, but rather provide an intelligent presentation of common reactions, supplemented with what can be done to normalize the situation or cope with any symptoms they might have or later develop. In addition, it should contain information about where and how they can find more help if they should need it.

A child needs external permission, encouragement and assistance to express or acknowledge reactions they are embarrassed about or believe to be unusual. An acceptance of their reactions on the part of adults, and information about the normality of the reactions, increases children's tolerance for the negative emotions the incident may have produced. Confirmation of the normality of their reactions, and acceptance that it is usual and normal to react as they do, becomes more important as children grow older, because it becomes correspondingly more and more important not to be seen as different from others.

Information about handling traumatic reminders can have special significance. Without preparation for such 'triggers', and without adult support, children will have more difficulties managing to understand and tolerate their own reactions. They can be told of how others have experienced such reminders, who they sought support from and how they can learn to manage the pain that such memory triggers can produce.

Such reviews allow children to identify many aspects of the situation, aspects that in daily life function as reminders of what happened. It also helps them to expect, understand and handle such reminders, and it provides them with an opportunity to normalize their feelings and thoughts. When, in addition to this, they can share the experience of these reminders with parents and teachers, it facilitates their daily life within the memory landscape that they inhabit.

If children are also prepared for parents' reactions, they can to a lesser extent assume responsibility for the task of comforting, placating or protecting their parents. By gaining knowledge of the common trauma reactions of parents, the risk of a breakdown in the family's internal communication is also counteracted.

Return to the scene of the event

Traumatic events are as a rule tied to a location. The place where a traumatic event took place is associated with anxiety, often avoidance and not infrequently with an unclear perception of the location, size, view, etc.

A return to this place can be important in terms of developing a better understanding of what happened, how it happened and what one remembers about what happened. If a friend dies in a traffic accident, friends who have not seen the scene of the accident (or the car, motorcycle, etc.) will often 'demand' to see the site, both to understand and as a means of acknowledging and commemorating the situation. In such a case, they can visit the site carrying lit candles, and lay down flowers, photos, etc. Such spontaneous rituals at the scene of the event help to express feelings, make grief and pain concrete and the unreal real. The important function of rituals in such situations is described elsewhere (Dyregrov 1996).

A number of children struggle with the fear of anything that reminds them of the event, or with 'blanks', in which case they have an absence of memories about what happened. An important strategy for helping children in such a situation is in different ways to support them, in practical terms, to approach what happened, in their thoughts and/or in reality. This can be done in a number of ways. By talking in great detail about what happened, the child will often be able to fill in 'blanks', because it is easier to remember when one addresses the event in detail. Should they have misconceptions about the situation, adults can then clarify these. At the same time, this procedure enables one to understand more of the child's emotional reactions and, where relevant, any misconstrued help-fantasies the child may still have. In this work, a reconstruction of the physical context in which the event occurred – in other words, returning to the place where the incident took place, looking at photographs, newspaper clippings, etc. – will also help to build up a complete understanding of the event. Sometimes a redramatization together with the child, the creation of models or drawings of the event, and maps or sketches of the site can also serve the same purpose.

Returning to or visiting an accident site can help children to understand what actually happened. Some children do this spontaneously, without adults' knowledge.

> The father of two boys in their early teens was killed in a small-boat collision. The boys sneaked in and opened up a gap at the edge of a canvas, in order to see just how destroyed the boat that their father had been navigating had been after it collided. It was only when they first saw the degree of damage done to the boat that they understood that their father could not have survived. That the children had been to see the boat came as a surprise to the others in the family, who had thought about doing the same thing. The children's account made it easier to accept the advice that everyone should go along to visit the accident site to see where it had happened.

Exposure to an accident site or site of a traumatic event can cause discomfort, anxiety and other reactions. An adult, who can provide support, comfort or simply just be there, should accompany children. In such situations we shall remember that something that is painful can also be important, and we shall help children or young people to gain clarity about what happened by looking at the location, vehicle, etc. whether it is for the first time (when someone they know was affected) or it is a return to a place or vehicle in which they have experienced the trauma personally. While this is often relatively easy to organize just after an incident, it can be difficult to bring about a long time after the event. Such reconstructions function as a support for the memory, while also creating a context for what took place. Heir and Weisæth (2006) have referred to how different kinds of fear, such as of water or waves, and separation anxiety, were diminished when children who survived the tsunami took part in a trip back to Thailand.

Adolescents will as a rule personally verbalize a wish to return to the scene of the event, while adult caregivers must take responsibility for this when younger children are involved. It can seem brutal to bring a 5-year-old back to the bus that the child had been travelling in when a crash occurred, but often it is only after having returned to the destroyed bus or place that children will ask questions that serve to disclose any misconceptions or fears they may be carrying.

If children are to return to a site of an event, it is also important that they are accompanied by an adult whom they trust, that they are allowed to spend all the time they need there and ask any questions they might have, and that the adult companion attempts to anticipate or imagine what they are stumped by or wondering about, and to carefully ask about this or provide unsolicited information. Before such a return visit, one should explain to the children why one is doing it (e.g. as a means of support for the memory and to gain clarity about what happened), how this will be done and that they can personally control the pace of the approach. The children can receive information about the discomfort they might feel and, where relevant, training in simple breathing exercises (see Chapter 9, pp.174–175) that can alleviate tension. After the visit, spend some time talking to the children about the experience. The children shall not of course be pressured to return to such a site.

Classroom and small group intervention

Small group intervention can be a good means of reaching children when several have experienced the same or a similar trauma situation. This can apply to groups of children who have experienced incest, children who have witnessed domestic violence or children experiencing the divorce of their parents. Wagar and Rodway (1995) showed that a group of children who had witnessed violence against their mothers experienced a significant decrease in the responsibility that they felt for their parents and for the violence they observed (the responsibility was assigned to the correct person) after having taken part in a group for children who had experienced the same thing as they had. Following participation in the group they also demonstrated more suitable attitudes or reactions to the use of violence as a response to anger and for conflict resolution.

In Chapter 8 the procedure is described for handling school children in the context of an incident that has affected more than one individual person. Also in this chapter, and in Chapter 9, other factors of significance for group work with children are described in further detail.

Parental counselling

A large number of trauma situations that affect children also affect the parenting system so that parents during a period of time find that they have a reduced capacity for taking care of their children. This can lead to parents:

- being less emotionally sensitive to their children's needs
- having difficulties upholding rules and discipline and becoming more indulgent with their children
- becoming more irritable and quick-tempered
- becoming more over-protective and frightened.

In practice this means that good support for children is promoted by help for the parents so they are better able to cope with what has happened. This help can include, in addition to assistance in processing the event for the parents, information and counselling for parents about children's needs, children's common reactions and how parents can support and help their children. In addition, parents can be given guidance about when it is necessary to seek professional help for their children and simple advice on how they can help them (see Appendix).

Parents should be informed that it is a myth that children are so resilient that they need only put what has happened behind them. Children are seldom helped by not thinking at all about what has happened but need adult assistance in taking it in, little by little, so they do not become overwhelmed. This does not mean that they are to be forced to 'get it out', but rather assisted in finding ways to express and process the experience.

It is of particular importance to ensure openness and directness in the family's internal communication, so that new facts about the trauma situation are also passed on to the children and that problems do not arise in the interaction between the children and parents. Many parents struggle with a guilty conscience for how they have treated their children.

> A mother and her two children experienced a dramatic death in the mother's family. During the first two weeks everything went well but in the course of the first six months, the mother became more and more depressed, in addition to her blaming herself for what had happened. Therapy for the mother helped her to take control of her feelings of guilt, and she became less depressed. When she was able to acquire some distance from her problems, she was filled with feelings of guilt in relation to the two children: 'I have not managed to take care of them. I have been so short-tempered and angry. How painful this time must have been for them.' In particular one of the children

was heavily traumatized by the experience itself (present at the death) and later needed help from a psychologist. Help for the mother involved a recognition that she was completely wiped out, that she had done the best she could and that she could learn from this. At the same time, her self-reproach was out of proportion to the situation, so that a review of what she had in fact done for the children contributed to a more realistic assessment of the situation.

In such situations, other caregivers can be important to children. If parents can accept that for a time they do not have anything left over to give their children, they can more easily understand that other adults whom the children trust can be helpful individuals from whom the children can receive support in the period following a trauma. Parents must understand that there is a difference between not having the energy to take care of their children as well as usual, and neglecting their children.

Parents can also be encouraged to use touch, and light massage, in the period following type I traumas. Research has shown that such physical contact has an immediate effect of soothing bodily activation. Tactile stimulation in the form of a massage appears to diminish the production of the stress hormones noradrenaline and cortisol, it soothes reactions of pain and has been shown to lead to fewer post-traumatic symptoms in children who have experienced a traumatic event (Diego, Field and Hernandez-Reif 2009; Field 2006; Field, Seligman and Scafidi 1996). It bears mentioning that traumatized parents often diminish the physical contact that they have with their children. For this reason, encouraging parents to spend time on this type of contact leads to more interaction between children and parents. It is clear that this is not a measure that is encouraged if the child has been subjected to sexual abuse within the family, and other adults should neither start giving a massage if the situation can be misunderstood or if this can increase the risk of the child being abused.

Advice for other adults

There are a number of things that can be done by considerate adults in the child's immediate environment to help the child following traumatic events. These include:

- giving children and young people explicit permission to react. When children and young people are uncertain about how reactions will be received by adults, they can hold back their reactions. It can therefore be a good idea for adults to say that it is okay to react in the way they do and that they need not hold back their reactions for fear of being laughed at or criticized by the adults.

- working to ensure that the child acknowledges and accepts what has happened. This does not mean that one should overlook the need a child might have to take things in a little at a time, but that one does not become complicit in a common denial of what has occurred. By making the occurrence real, such as by saying, 'I understand very well that it is difficult to understand that it is true that your best friend has been killed, but the message we got from the police was not to be misunderstood', one avoids unnecessary optimism or denial.

- saying that you will be there to support them in the upcoming period. It is good for children to know that somebody is there if they need someone to talk to and that they can count on this support over time. Many have experienced being let down previously and can be vulnerable to another rejection.

- encouraging use of the network of friends. As adults we must remember that children as a rule seek support from their friends in critical situations rather than from adults. By encouraging them to spend time with friends, by giving them advice on how they can speak to friends about their thoughts and reactions, and by speaking to them when they experience that their friends do not understand, we can help children to maintain their social network.

- helping them search for an underlying theme – a deeper meaning. Children actively look for frames that they can use to understand what they have experienced. They must reformulate assumptions about the nature of the world, other people and themselves, and, particularly in adolescence, traumatic events can be the cause of many thoughts about the deeper aspects of existence. It is therefore important to pay attention to the thoughts behind their questions and comments, and to be willing to discuss thoughts about areas where there are not always clear answers.

- normalizing and legitimizing thoughts, feelings, wishes, behaviour and experiences. The intense and often unfamiliar reactions that children experience can be frightening because children and young people do not have a former and comparative basis at their disposal to use in helping to understand these reactions. They can easily view their own reactions as unique or as a sign of illness or deviance, with subsequent negative thoughts about themselves, their worth as a human being and their future prospects. Even when children keep such thoughts and feelings to themselves, it can be important for adults to put into words common thoughts and feelings in such a situation, so that the child understands what is happening inside them.

- helping children and young people to identify, name and differentiate between feelings. Traumatic situations involve such intense experiences for children that the feelings can be pushed away completely or be experienced as a whirlwind of strong emotions over which they have no control. While adults have developed the ability to differentiate between feelings, children need the help of adults to put into words, understand and distinguish between different feelings. Traumatic events make it difficult to regulate the intensity of reactions, which can lead to children either attempting to evade the strong feelings or feeling completely overwhelmed by them. Particularly younger children benefit from parents helping them to put into words what they are feeling and to regulate the strength of their reactions.

Play and drawing

Even though it is young children who benefit most from play and drawing in the follow-up of a trauma, such methods can also be used for older children and adolescents. As mentioned previously, many children will spontaneously utilize play as a means of expression. At the same time, play can provide signals indicating whether or not the trauma has become stuck, as is the case with compulsive, repetitive play. This means that the child is constantly re-enacting what happened through play, without this providing any reduction in tension, or the reduction is short-term. In such cases, adults must help the child to find a better 'solution' for their play, by carefully introducing ideas for another ending or by playing with them to see if the game can be developed, such as through simple suggestions.

Play and drawing allow a 'safe' working through of traumatic moments. Often the contents of play can give us a good insight into key traumatic themes. The child can express through a drawing what was most important to them about the experience, and they can directly or in symbolic form give us an idea of what is important to process.

A girl who experienced that one of her grandparents was seriously injured in an accident drew the picture shown here as Figure 7.1.

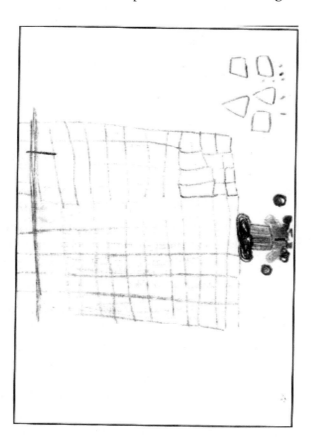

Figure 7.1 Being witness to a grandfather's death

The colour red represents the blood, which was the worst part for the child to witness, and which returned to her in the form of intrusive memories.

A number of authors have described thoroughly how play and drawing can be utilized in the assessment of a child's condition and in help measures and treatment (Einarsdottir, Dockett and Perry 2009; Nader and Pynoos 1991). When drawings are used after traumatic events, children must not only be given the opportunity to draw the trauma but also to draw pictures of coping where they can repair damages, draw a new house in addition to the fire-damaged house, etc.

> Silje was molested by an older man who threatened her life. She drew him in detail, down to the colour of his trousers and jacket. To the question of whether she would like to draw a picture in which she felt safe that he could not do anything to her, she began drawing with great intensity. She drew him locked up in prison and with bombs dropping on the prison, a fire burning there, etc.

Drawing permitted her to take revenge in her imagination, but it was also a coping strategy (she drew several such pictures later) in which she activated her imagination as a partner to help her cope with the situation.

Pynoos and Nader (1993) have shown how children's rescue or help fantasies are complex attempts to handle external and internal dangers that they experience during and after a traumatic situation. In their imagination children can change the triggering event, stop the traumatic episode or reverse fatal consequences. They can also take revenge, acquire safe distance, or prevent future traumas or loss.

> Sigurd drew in great detail his revenge fantasies after his father was beaten to death. He stabbed the criminal with a knife, burned him and cut off his hand. The drawings were grotesque but important for the boy in his processing of what had happened. He could take control over the perpetrator, he could reverse his feelings of helplessness and he could express strong feelings that were difficult to put into words. Before he drew these drawings he had plans of killing the perpetrator when he was released from prison. When asked later if he still had such thoughts, he said no. It is likely that the drawings had enabled him to process the aggressive feelings and led to improved impulse control.

Unchanging intervention fantasies can, according to Pynoos and Nader (1993), result in 'becoming fixated on the trauma' or 'identification with the aggressor' (perpetrator), or to put it simply: the event remains more unprocessed in the child's emotional life. Play and conversation can help the child to express such fantasies but are contingent upon adults understanding something about the dynamic of these, and being able to accept potentially grotesque contents.

Play also allows children to put things into perspective, create order in their thoughts and, in a symbolic and visual form, express feelings. When children act out the funeral of a preschool classmate, they can better understand death and its finality through this type of play.

Pynoos and Eth (1986) incorporate drawings in a work method for use in meetings with traumatized children (especially those who have witnessed violence). They let the child start by drawing a picture while telling a story for the drawing. The free drawing and storytelling allows children to express themselves using their imagination. Usually the violent act(s) will appear in this 'neutral' drawing or the story, and interviews can then utilize this connection.

In the next part of 'the conversation' the interviewer points out the part of the drawing or story that is connected to the trauma and gives it an interpretation. Eth and Pynoos (1994) give one example: if a drawing contains a policeman, the interviewer can say it would have been so much better if he had been there to stop the violence from taking place. Such a reference to the traumatic event can cause a strong emotional reaction in the child, which facilitates the continued account of what took place. The child can then explain and re-enact the event through play or drawing. The interviewer's task is to help the child to go through all the aspects of the violent incident, including what occurred before and afterwards. This can be done by asking the child to draw, for example, the worst moment, revenge fantasies and rescue fantasies. By way of sensitive questions, details can be clarified and the child's understanding explored.

Towards the end of 'the conversation' the themes that have emerged are reviewed along with the child's current symptoms and fears about the future. The child is given confirmation of how understandable his or her reactions are and before the meeting is over, the child receives the chance to give feedback on the experience of the meeting. The core of the traumatic incident can in this way be approached with a point of departure in the child's experience as this appears in drawings and play.

If the incident is not too far back in time (less than about three months), it is usually possible to more or less directly relate, re-enact or draw what took place, even if this involves a lot of anxiety. The medium of play is safer than conversation alone, because small breaks for 'neutral' play can be included.

It is clearly beneficial if there are toys available that enable a reconstruction of what happened (a boat if children experienced a shipwreck, cars if children were in a car accident, etc.). In the game the children can go through, explore and test out the chain of events, understand particularly difficult moments, express the wish that they had been able to do something to help, etc.

A 'playful' approach can also be used following large-scale events. A kindergarten in England was the next-door neighbour of a transformer that exploded. One man was killed, another seriously injured. The children witnessed all the drama because the injured came running out in flames and collapsed just outside the kindergarten. In the post-traumatic work a model of the kindergarten, the garden outside and the transformer station was constructed. Tiny dolls represented the children, the staff in the kindergarten and the two people who were burned. In addition to this, there were models of the fire engine, ambulance and helicopter that arrived at the scene. The children were then asked to imagine that the models were the kindergarten, transformer, etc. and to select a doll to represent themselves. They were subsequently asked to position 'themselves' where they had been when the explosion occurred (called 'the big bang'), and describe what happened. If the children did not give a description, they were asked: 'Was there a fire?' 'What happened here?', while pointing at the transformer. If the children answered, they were asked to describe details. While communicating with the children, a lion puppet was also used that wondered how they had felt during the fire. In this manner the preschool children were helped to speak about and express different thoughts and feelings about the accident. Drawings were also used.

The children's ability to acknowledge how much fear and uneasiness they felt was much more limited than their ability to describe the events (Misch *et al.* 1993). Even children as young as 2 years old managed to describe their experiences of what happened during the explosion. Those over the age of 3 could communicate more of their feelings. It was interesting that they allowed the hand puppet stronger feelings than they allowed themselves – perhaps this is an expression of the fact that their own feelings are more manageable when they are transferred to another.

Although the method described here was part of a study designed to observe how children understood what happened and how they reacted after the accident, the method represents a sensitive and direct approach to a traumatic event. Misch and others (1993) point out that the method had a therapeutic function, in allowing the children to describe the event in detail within a supportive atmosphere. When the kindergarten staff took part in the interviews, they were able to learn how they could then help the children. Several of the adults who worked in the kindergarten also needed help personally before they were able to help the children.

Children who have lived in homes characterized by abuse and maltreatment often lack the ability to take part in symbolic play or imagining, or this ability has been seriously inhibited. These children will often need time and assistance in learning to play before they will dare take part in activities that are pleasurable. Pretend play or playing 'as if' they were another is often absent in these children. This type of play is important in order to be able to understand the perspectives of others, and accordingly to be able to communicate well with them. Children with such a background therefore often need long-term therapy, both to enable them to dare to be a child again and to process the effects of the long-term trauma.

Other forms of expression

It is fully possible to utilize other forms of expression to help a child. Dance, theatre, drama, writing, painting, creative games and role-play can be used both for individual children and groups. In the work following disasters, such activities have been used to provide form and structure for various aspects of the experience, and to express feelings that are perhaps more difficult to put into words, whether in speech or in writing.

The use of stories or narratives and metaphors can be useful both to express feelings and for the creation of meaning. Together with adults, children can create stories that resemble what they have experienced but where one can also use the imagination to introduce magic helpers who can assist them, where the different characters serve to express feelings, create good thoughts, perform rituals, etc.

The use of diaries, essays and fill-in-the blanks can serve an important function in helping children, and have been used by teachers and other adults after traumatic events. In the chapter about therapy (Chapter 9) such methods will be described in further detail.

Taking part in rituals and prayer can help children to find expression for feelings, to present their thoughts to God, to remove troublesome thoughts from their shoulders and to commemorate or find closure for important events in their short lives. Aspects of this are also described in more detail in Chapter 9.

Library guidance and the use of literary texts can be used for groups and individually. Teachers frequently have a good insight into short stories, novels and poems about subjects with clear parallels to what children have experienced. Books can be read in class as part of the curriculum or children can be permitted to bring home relevant books that they can read on their own or with their parents. In kindergartens there are many books about divorce, death, accidents, etc., which are appropriate for reading out loud to groups. In addition to identification with the main characters in the text, discussion about, questions and comments on the text can help the children in their handling of trauma.

Help methods

It is not uncommon that children and particularly adolescents (boys) will not want to speak very much or at all about what has happened. This is a part of the avoidance patterns that function as protection against painful memories and anxiety. At the same time, such avoidance patterns can prove negative over a period, because the tension in the body increases and thoughts and memories pop up spontaneously and distort the emotional and cognitive life. The problems become evident first and foremost when children consciously repress thoughts and memories, and avoid discussions about what has happened, more than when this occurs spontaneously. If feelings must be actively restrained, this requires cognitive resources and energy (Richards 2004). When this occurs automatically and subconsciously, such mechanisms actually appear to be useful in terms of getting through a difficult situation (Bonanno *et al.* 1995). Should adults prematurely and with excessive force intervene to pressurize children to speak about things that they do not want to speak about, this can easily be experienced negatively by the children and the communication can become deadlocked. For this reason, the precautionary measures listed in Box 7.4 are proposed:

Box 7.4 Discussions with children and young people

- The doors must be opened carefully
  - be sensitive
  - listen to their wants — do not say, 'You poor thing'
  - do not say, 'I know how you are feeling'.
- Some will not want to speak about what has occurred
  - they can personally choose discussion partners
  - another person can perhaps help — be patient, wait for an opportunity.
  - Be sure that a lot of different people do not ask about the same thing (e.g. How are you doing?).

The desire to refrain from speaking about what has happened after a traumatic incident is a reflection of the need to take in the incident step by step — in other words, to absorb the pain in small, digestible doses. If children over time continue to push away what has happened and are suffering because of this, a more active approach must be used to prevent long-term problems. But if the children are functioning well at school and with friends, there is less of a need to push them. Traumatized children usually do not like sympathy in the form of 'you poor thing' or 'how terrible that this could happen'. Such statements can lead to their losing control over their feelings, something that is uncomfortable for both adults and children.

It is also a matter of giving the children control with regard to what is to be said about the event, such as at school or with a sports team. Include the children's input when a strategy is to be chosen. One example can be to say:

> What happened is something we will have to speak about in class but you can choose whether you want to be present or not. I would prefer it if you were there, but understand if you do not want to. Regardless, I want to say something about how you would like your classmates to approach you in the coming days in connection with what happened. Do you want

them to talk about it with you or would you prefer to be able to bring it up personally when you feel ready?

This approach demonstrates sensitivity to the needs of the children and will contribute to building up a sorely needed sense of regained control in a situation that can be chaotic and unpredictable.

The precautionary measures mentioned here can be carried out in such a way that the child knows that adults are willing to talk about what has happened, but that the child personally can play a part in deciding when. Our experience has been that even the most difficult and most intense parts of an experienced trauma can be spoken about quite directly with children.

Tell them what will happen

There is an emphasis on an active and direct approach in the work with traumatic experiences. The intention of a conversation that a helper has with a child must be communicated:[1]

> My name is Fred. I am a psychologist. I talk with children about sad and painful things. I know that you have experienced something that many children find frightening. Your XX has told me this. She/he told me that you often wake up because of nightmares about the horrible memories. I have talked with many children who have experienced awful things and who sleep poorly. In order for me to be able to understand how you are feeling, I am going to ask you about what you have experienced and I want to talk with you about the worst memories you have about what occurred. I know that you might feel that it is difficult to talk about, but we have plenty of time. You also need to know that no matter how terrible what you have to tell me might be, I am capable of hearing it (here one can lean towards the child and extend both hands with the palms facing upwards as a concrete sign of the ability to receive this information). I will ask you about the memories you have been struggling to get rid of, about things that you perhaps see as pictures or a film inside your head or things you hear that make you believe that it is all happening again.

---

1   The remaining presentation in this chapter is taken predominantly from Dyregrov and Raundalen (2009).

I know that when you tell me this you might become upset and that this can continue after we have finished speaking. But although it may feel worse when we are talking, I also know that often this gets better afterwards, especially if you can follow some of the advice I will give you.

Dare to speak about the worst parts

After giving such an introduction, which is done slowly, gently, one can move quite directly on to the painful themes, including the worst memories. Even if one makes only relatively brief introductory comments before beginning to speak about these painful topics, the pace should be slow. When children relate what they have experienced, respect is demonstrated for their story, as well as restraint, so that they can control the telling as they wish, but nonetheless with enough activity to ensure that they do not feel alone due to the helper's silence. The initiative is not to be taken from the children, although they might need help in the form of precise questions about what they have absorbed through individual sensory channels. In particular, younger children are dependent upon external reference points, such as in the form of an adult's questions, in order to sift through their memories in a good, systematic fashion.

Listen to the child. Accept and confirm what is expressed.

A nice type of attunement takes place between the adult and the child when the conversation is taking place. The child is given full attention; your face is turned towards the child, you move closer and lean back a bit, in a rhythm adapted to the intensity of what the child is relating, and you can reach out your hands or a hand toward the child as a gesture of acceptance or support. At all times you can intensify your presence by the way in which you use your eyes, voice and by simple touch (particularly during the more difficult sequences). These measures combined serve to develop the dialogue and relationship and the child feels secure that you can receive the information being related.

The confirmation of what the child tells you occurs both through this non-verbal contact and through words. Your follow-up questions will also give the child a clear understanding that you have heard and that you are able to accept it. The child can nonetheless need a more direct verbal confirmation, for example: 'I hear what you are saying and I know that you are sad now. I also feel sad.' Or: 'Now you are angry and I understand that you are angry.' If one is not sure what the child is experiencing emotionally when describing an experience, one can carefully ask for confirmation of what one believes: 'I am not quite sure, but now I believe that you are very sad.' 'I see the tears in the corner of your eye now, and that makes me think that your thoughts made you sad.' When the child expresses strong reactions, it is important to confirm the feelings. If children are sad, we say that we understand that they are sad and that they have every reason to be sad.

'Follow' the child

The helper's task is to ask questions or provide conversation-bearing elements, which make the child's task of relating what happened easier. This can be done by encouraging the child to make comments, such as by saying, 'Can you say more about this?' or 'You said you were frightened but can you describe that feeling in more detail or describe other feelings you had?' When the child gives signals indicating references to a difficult subject, you can confirm that you have understood this by saying, for example: 'Now I know that you are going to talk about very sad things. Can you tell me more about what happened when you saw that your father was dead in the car beside you?' Usually we follow up on what the child says, but it is also necessary to take the lead sometimes. On those occasions when one leads the child into painful areas, one can also show respect for the child by expressing that one knows that it is painful: 'I know that what we are going to talk about now is painful and that you can feel afraid of talking about it but you need to know that I can listen to you and that it often feels much easier after you have said it in your own words.'

Follow up on what the child says

During the conversation we will attempt to normalize the child's reactions along the way and, towards the end of the conversation, give specific advice regarding what the child can do to feel better. One example of this kind of normalization follows:

> You have told me how time almost stood still when you were
> so afraid that your father might be dead when the accident

happened. At the same time, you told me that thoughts raced through your mind and that you spent such a long time trying to decide what you should do and then you couldn't do anything because you were too afraid. You have also told me that you see images of your father all the time, even now, such a long time afterwards. I want to tell you a little bit about what takes place in the brain when we experience something as dramatic as what you have experienced. When something like that happens, we prepare ourselves to meet danger. The brain can work very fast with many thoughts at the same time. When so many thoughts arise in the course of a very short time, it seems to us as if time stops, even though it is passing just as quickly as usual. It is then easy to blame oneself for not having done enough, such as that you did not prevent the accident. But you couldn't have. When we experience something so terrible, the memories are also stored in another and stronger manner than usual and they remain inside the head and it can be difficult to push them out again. Because they are so strong, we have no control over them. But perhaps you have found something that you can do to help you keep them at a distance? I am going to give you some simple tips that you can use until the next time and then you can tell me how it has gone. If this does not help, we can talk about other things that can be done so you can gain control over the images so that they become less bothersome.

There are many ways to continue a conversation with a child. The main objective is to maintain the same pace and perspective so that the child does not lose heart and the strength to continue confronting what happened.

Take breaks

Even though older children and adolescents can tolerate relatively long periods of conversation about what they have experienced, our experience has been that speaking with children about their painful experiences frequently causes them to experience great emotional intensity. In order to spare them from feeling this intensity for excessively long periods of time, it is important to take breaks. This can involve giving them something to drink, or a biscuit or a piece of fruit to eat. The break can also be filled with conversation about neutral topics in connection with their recreational activities or with short games (cards, noughts-and-crosses, etc.), or by getting up and walking around the room or going outside for a brief stroll. The breaks should not be too long and it is important that one remembers exactly where the child was before the conversation stopped, and is clear about where and how the conversation is to recommence.

Share the child's feelings

We have illustrated how the helper receives and confirms the feelings of the child. It is important to show empathy, but it is just as important to be careful showing your own feelings. You share nonetheless the child's feelings through your facial expressions, by changes in intonation, head movements or through gestures to illustrate sadness, anger or fear. It is important that your communication of your own reactions is subdued compared with the child's own emotions. Traumatized children will quickly begin to protect you if they sense that you are having difficulties hearing what they are telling you, if the impressions they describe awaken disgust in you, etc. If this happens, they understand that you cannot bear to receive the information and they will hold back important details. Many children have stopped speaking about what they have experienced because it became too much for those who were listening.

Wait your turn

Good communication resembles a game where the ball is sent from one side of the court to the other. The ball should mostly be in the hands of the child, but in a real-life conversation there is usually play back and forth. You should be particularly attentive if the child addresses you directly with a question or comment, for example: 'I think I am going crazy.' You will hear the question and anxiety in this statement and understand that the ball is in your court. You then pick up the ball and hold it, make a few soothing comments and possibly give some advice, before you send it back.

Rhythm, respect and sharing

In this relationship building with children there is a rhythmic activity where they tell and describe their story to an active partner; a person who is supportive without dominating the conversation, at all times attentive and appreciative of the meaning, feelings and thoughts that the children relay. Through a strongly felt, supportive presence, the children are aided in relating or reconstructing what they have been a part of, but we also want to be a positive influence on their capacity to experience meaning and continuity in existence, while they are gradually able to learn how to better regulate their emotions. The interaction with children is not a mechanical activity where they tell you what happened. As a helper, you become an active witness to what they have experienced with the consequences this has for their thoughts, feelings and behaviour. Through precise questions, active confirmation, support, comfort, recognition, patience, respect and normalizing activity, the events are clarified and the children can both achieve greater control over and experience more sense and structure in what they have experienced.

Emphasizing 'positive' aspects

During critical or life-threatening events, psychological mobilization mechanisms are activated that increase our chances of survival. I have elsewhere, with colleagues, described such mechanisms in greater detail (see Dyregrov, Solomon and Bassøe 2000). For those who experience cumulative traumas, the survival mechanisms will potentially include denial, suppression of pain, attempts to hide, submission, etc. In the conversations with children we highlight, explain and illustrate for them what caused them to act, think or feel as they did. In certain situations they can be obliged to quickly make use of former experiences and lessons, and combine this with information from their surroundings. Then they can protect themselves, escape from or reduce the risk of injury.

During the conversation, confirmation and recognition will contribute to emphasizing the respect we have for what they managed during the event, for the reactions they experienced afterwards, and what they now do to get better. We will ask what they have done to feel better, what has helped them, praise and cultivate their initiative, and propose alternative strategies if they are employing unsuitable ones. When we give them small pieces of advice about what they can do to help themselves, it is in order to support their experience that they can take control, and that they have some influence over themselves and their experiences. We want to counteract the helplessness and hopelessness that the traumatic event(s) may have created, but most of all we want children who can sense that things they do personally can lead to change. In spite of the fact that we continually seek to approach the worst things that the children have experienced, the conversation shall give the children faith that they can actively take part in improving their situation and that we can help them with this. This investment in activities that give the children increased self-esteem and an experience of control must of course be followed up by measures in the children's caregiving environment, at school or kindergarten, or at home or foster home.

If children have experienced sexual or physical abuse and have had to shut out emotions and employ dissociation as a means of protection from the abuse, one must proceed more carefully. In this case a more long-term trust-building process is required and often the child must develop their emotional regulation abilities before addressing the core of the traumatic events. That does not mean that one cannot allow them to be given strategies to handle distressing memories but that they are spared having to relate the memories in detail, until such time when they have learned strategies to handle the emotions this can trigger.

In Chapter 9 concrete work methods are described that can be used in therapeutic work with traumatized children. A number of these trauma-specific methods can also be employed as self-help methods. This implies that also helpers without formal therapeutic training can use them in their contact with children.

References

Bonanno, G.A., Keltner, D., Holen, A. and Horowitz, M.J. (1995) 'When avoiding unpleasant emotions might not be such a bad thing: verbal autonomic response dissociation and midlife conjugal bereavement.' *Journal of Personality and Social Psychology* 69, 975–989.

Diego, M.A., Field, T. and Hernandez-Reif, M. (2009) 'Procedural pain heart rate responses in massaged preterm infants.' *Infant Behavior and Development 32*, 226–229.

Dyregrov, A. (1996) 'Children's participation in rituals.' *Bereavement Care 15*, 2–5.

Dyregrov, A. and Raundalen, M. (2009) *Manual for Trauma Therapy for Children Exposed to Violence*. Bergen: Center for Crisis Psychology.

Dyregrov, A., Solomon, R.M. and Bassøe, C.F. (2000) 'Mental mobilization in critical incident stress situations.' *International Journal of Emergency Mental Health 2*, 73–81.

Dyregrov, K. (2003) *The Loss of Child by Suicide, SIDS, and Accidents: Consequences, Needs and Provisions of Help*. Doctoral dissertation (dr. philos) HEMIL, Psykologisk fakultet. Universitetet i Bergen. ISBN 82-7669-099-8.

Einarsdottir, J., Dockett, S. and Perry, B. (2009) 'Making meaning: children's perspectives expressed through drawings.' *Early Child Development and Care 179*, 217–232.

Eth. S. and Pynoos, R.S. (1994) 'Children who witness the homicide of a parent.' *Psychiatry: Interpersonal and Biological Processes 57*, 287–306.

Field, T. (2006) *Massage Therapy Research*. Edinburgh: Churchill Livingstone Elsevier.

Field, T., Seligman, S. and Scafidi, F. (1996) 'Alleviating posttraumatic stress in children following hurricane Andrew.' *Journal of Applied Developmental Psychology 17*, 37–50.

Glad, K.A., Jensen, T.K., Nygaard, E., Dyb, G. and Hafstad, G.S. (2009) 'Møtet med hjelpeapparatet etter tsunamien – behov og tilfredshet.' *Tidsskrift for Norsk Psykologforening 46*, 472–475.

Heir, T. and Weisæth, L. (2006) 'Back to where it happened: self-reported symptom improvement of tsunami survivors who returned to the disaster area.' *Prehospital and Disaster Medicine 21*, 59–63.

Holmes, E.A., James, E.L., Coode-Bate, T. and Deeprose, C. (2009) 'Can playing the computer game "Tetris" reduce the build-up of flashbacks for trauma? A proposal from cognitive science.' Available from: www.plosone.org/article/info:doi/10.1371/journal. pone.0004153 (accessed 6 Feb 2010).

Misch, P., Phillips, M., Evans, P. and Berelowitz, M. (1993) 'Trauma in pre-school children: a clinical account.' Occasional paper presented at the ACCP day meeting, *ACCP 8*, (Association for Child Psychology and Psychiatry) 11–18.

Nader, K. and Pynoos, R. (1991) 'Play and Drawing as Tools for Interviewing Traumatized Children.' In C.E. Schaefer, K. Gitlin and A. Sandgrund (eds) *Play, Diagnosis and Assessment*. New York: John Wiley.

Pynoos, R.S. and Eth, S. (1986) 'Witness to violence: the child interview.' *Journal of the American Academy of Child and Adolescent Psychiatry 25*, 306–319.

Pynoos, R.S. and Nader, K. (1993) 'Issues in the Treatment of Posttraumatic Stress in Children and Adolescents.' In J.P. Wilson and B. Raphael (eds) *International Handbook of Traumatic Stress Syndromes*. New York: Plenum Press.

Reese, E. and Newcombe, R. (2007) 'Training mothers in elaborative reminiscing enhances children's autobiographical memory and narrative.' *Child Development 78*, 1153–1170.

Richards, J.M. (2004) 'The cognitive consequences of concealing feelings.' *American Psychological Society 13*, 131–134.

Stallard, P. and Law, F. (1994) 'The psychological effects of traumas on children.' *Children and Society 8*, 89–97.

Wagar, J.M. and Rodway, M.R. (1995) 'An evaluation of a group treatment approach for children who have witnessed wife abuse.' *Journal of Family Violence 10*, 295–306.

8

Groups for Children Following Trauma

Children who have experienced traumatic events can benefit from different types of group gatherings. Such groups are particularly useful when many children have experienced or been involved in the same event, but it is also possible to organize groups for children who have individually experienced events with a common theme, such as the sudden loss of a family member, having been the target of violence, bullying, etc.

The purpose of gathering in a group setting

The most important thing about such groups is of course that it gives children the opportunity to hear that others react in the same way as they do; in other words, they receive a means of normalizing their reactions. But our experience has also been that children who meet in groups can share coping and problem-solving methods, such as with respect to what they can do to facilitate falling asleep at night, or how they can handle 'difficult' teachers. Some of the children can also hear that others are having an even more difficult time than they are, and such a 'downward' comparison can help put their own situation in perspective.

Groups can also contribute to building up a new network of friends, although we should try to encourage children not to abandon their former network completely to spend time exclusively with others in the same situation as themselves. If the children are in the same class or on the same sports team, a sense of solidarity and community will of course be encouraged in this group. In crisis groups, children can also discover that they can help others, while they are also given the opportunity to express thoughts and emotions about what has occurred. When the group members have experienced the same situation, as a group they are in possession of more information and facts than individuals, and when these facts are shared in the group it will contribute to the individual's acquiring a more comprehensive understanding of the situation and thereby a better grasp of the events. In the group the children can receive encouragement towards a more optimistic view of the future, by hearing about someone who has come a bit further along in processing such an experience than they have personally.

From a professional standpoint it is clear that through groups one can reach many and at the same time identify those who might need more professional help.

Experiences from groups for traumatized children

From our experiences from work with groups after traumatic situations, the following points can be mentioned. Children appear to want to spend time together without necessarily only speaking about the trauma. This is a reflection of a lower tolerance for psychological pain, and some may have a need to allow the conversation to wander into more neutral topics along the way. The frequency of the meetings is often determined by practical circumstances and varies from every other week to once a month. How long a group should continue need not be decided in advance, but, if the group was started after an event that involved many people (e.g. a large-scale accident) it will be natural to hold regular meetings that are scheduled over time in the beginning, then less frequently, and finally a meeting shortly after the one-year anniversary, to discuss how they experienced this day and how they commemorated it. The literature that addresses therapeutic groups for children often recommends a group size of 6–8 children, and it is viewed as advantageous if the children are around the same age and have the same maturity level. We have had somewhat larger groups in the aftermath of critical events and have found that groups of 8–12 children also function well.

In addition to discussion about what happened, expressive activities are utilized, from artistic forms of expression to creating a video film about the event. It can prove of interest to divide the groups up by gender, because the gender difference in reactions over time can be quite pronounced. It is less suitable to do so immediately following a traumatic event than after some time has passed. A parallel group for the parents can also be expedient, particularly due to the intense impact that the situation can have had on them, but also because it is reassuring for parents to hear that others can have the same reactions that they are having.

Parents must of course be informed of how one works in a children's group so that they have an understanding of any reactions that may arise following the group meetings. Such information can be provided orally or in writing, while specific details of what individual children relate are of course not to be passed on without first receiving the consent of the group members.

Among the factors that must be taken into consideration with the start-up of groups for traumatized children are:

- Should the group be open or closed – in other words, should the same children meet every time, or can new members join and others leave?

- Shall one create a group where everyone is close together in age? The difference between a 7-year-old and 12-year-old can be enormous, while the difference between adolescents can be less.

- How often shall the group meet? Once a week is too much; many have chosen to meet once a month or every three weeks.

- Who will lead the group? Here I would recommend that qualified professionals lead the group, particularly because this ensures the most proper treatment of difficult topics and the possibility for referrals where necessary.

- Should there be one group leader or two? Experience shows that it is best to have two leaders.

- How should one establish a good group process? Can it be appropriate to have activities that break the ice?

The structure and flow in the group meetings is dependent upon leaders who understand what is taking place in the way of positive and potentially negative processes, so that they can encourage positive processes or prevent negative ones through their authority in the situation.

In many groups different activities are employed to stimulate mental and emotional processing of what has occurred. This can involve:

- letter writing

- poetry writing
- making up stories
- making videos
- recalling good memories
- rituals
- collective expressions
- paintings
- posters
- theatre games and role-play
- music
- movement games
- relaxation exercises.

Through the activities a more direct emotional expression than words can be utilized, or words can be given a form that differs from simply conversation. Depending upon the type of group, different topics can be addressed. The group leaders can in advance decide which topics to address, or they can together with the group decide which topics will be addressed in the next meeting. For some topics it can be suitable to invite guests into the group, such as a child or adolescent who can pass on experiences from a former group. On other occasions a police officer or a doctor can come and present information that is then discussed in the group.

Topics that can be appropriate to address in a group can be:

- learning from the experience, and reactions to it
- friends' reactions and problems with friends
- the school and teachers, and problems with understanding as time passes
- differences between the reactions of children and adults (parents)
- traumatic reminders and red-letter days
- coping with fear, pain and other problems
- difficult feelings (guilt, anger, sadness, etc.)
- good advice for coping on a daily basis.

Additional topics for bereavement groups can be:

- 'the presence' of the deceased
- grief over time
- life after death
- differences in the pace of a grieving process
- the personal belongings (clothes, possessions, etc.) that the deceased left behind
- children's versus adults' grief
- creating meaning.

In addition to the positive effects such groups have on children, they can also entail stress for both children and parents. Peled and Edleson (1992) have used groups in work with children whose mothers had been subjected to violence. They speak of how the children, as a result of the knowledge acquired in the group, criticized their mothers for their conduct. The children were able to view their parents' behaviour and parenting methods in new ways and challenged the mothers with their knowledge. Children who took part in the groups could also express pain, anger and other feelings more directly, something which could have an impact on the entire family, and which was not always easy to handle. For this reason, among others, parallel groups for parents are recommended so that parents are better equipped to understand their children's reactions. Otherwise, the authors emphasized that these groups had a clearly educational effect. The children learned a) that maltreatment is not okay and that it is not the fault of the child; b) that it was good to feel and express feelings; and c) that they could share personal experiences and recognize that they were not alone in having such experiences.

Debriefing groups for children

In a number of other contexts I have described the procedure for carrying out a session where one talks through a traumatic event with a group of children or young people (see Dyregrov 2008 and Box 8.1).

Box 8.1 Addressing a traumatic event in a group

- Share facts to increase the understanding of what happened.
- Prevent confusion and reduce misconceptions.
- Give the opportunity for emotional expression.
- Re-establish stability and security.
- Stimulate contact with friends.
- Maintain motivation for school and learning capacity.
- Increase coping abilities.

Talking through a topic in such a systematic manner, which is also called a psychological debriefing, should not take place on the same day as the event, because the shock reactions and emotional mechanisms that maintain distance protect the child from taking everything in. Talking through things too early can also consolidate emotional memories so that they are intensified rather than weakened. If one waits a few days before holding the systematic talking-through session, this does not mean that everything has 'sunk' in, but that the child has collected their thoughts more and understands a bit more about what has occurred. Children should of course be given the opportunity to meet and support one another immediately after such an event, but the more systematic review of what occurred should be put off until a few days later.

For meetings on the same day that the event occurred, allow the children to have the opportunity to sit close together, put into words what they wish, light candles or symbolically commemorate any losses they have suffered, and give them simple advice about what they can do after leaving the meeting to feel safe, etc. (see Box 8.2).

Box 8.2 Simple advice for the day the trauma occurred

- Don't stay alone all evening. Spend time with friends or adults.
- Write down thoughts and feelings.
- It is okay to sleep late or not to sleep well on the first night.
- Don't hold back your reactions, but allow someone to hold you, stroke your back, be there for you, etc.

- Know that people react very differently, but that increased fear and anxiety, and restlessness are very common reactions.
- Take part in the meeting that will be arranged later. Many feel calmer when they know they will have a chance to speak more about the event at this meeting.

When one is to carry out the systematic talking-through session, one should choose a well-lit and pleasant location (classroom, meeting room, etc). Adolescents feel comfortable if they are seated without a table in front of them, while adults often feel more at ease sitting behind a table.

Who is to attend the meeting depends on what has happened. If it is a classmate who has passed away, it is natural to gather the entire class, perhaps along with the classmate's best friends from outside the class as well. If it is a group that has survived an accident, one should think about exposure-related similarities – for example, everyone who was on the same bus in one group and witnesses who were on the next bus in another group, etc. If it is a matter of a school class, it is a good idea for the class teacher to lead the meeting, but this is contingent upon the teacher not being so affected by what happened that he/she is incapable of leading the meeting in a satisfactory manner.

If it is a matter of a serious accident, it is advantageous to use a professional who has experience of leading such meetings, a person who knows how to promote the group process to the group's best advantage. A school psychologist or other mental health professional will often have the requisite professional background for leading this type of meeting.

Small event-related groups for young children

It is clear that the older the children are, the more they will benefit from speaking about what has happened. Preschool children must to a greater extent be involved in games and activities. Wraith (1995, 2000) has used such meetings for preschool children, where they have sat in a circle on the laps of their parents and then talked about what happened. The conversations with young children should be brief, but perhaps more numerous, while school children are capable of speaking about a traumatic event over a longer period of time (1–1.5 hours). Adolescents can sit together longer than this, up to 2–2.5 hours, without it becoming too much for them. Younger children are more dependent upon someone they know leading the activities, while older children have an easier time relating to strangers whom they know are informed about their situation.

Small event-related groups for young children must take into consideration the children's:

- age and maturity level
- verbal skills
- need for making things concrete
- need for security and structure
- limited coping repertoire.

If one is to go through an event with preschool children, the parents should be present. The group can sit in a circle on the laps of their parents during the meeting. This provides a sense of security while speaking about painful things, and a shoulder to cry on if necessary. For this age group the meeting must be concrete, in language that the children can understand, and gentle encouragement should be given of the children's accounts. Drawings, hand puppets, etc. can be used simultaneously to encourage spontaneous expression. Adults may have to repeat factual information and at the same time ensure that young children have understood the events. Children in this age group can have insufficient verbal skills with respect to expressing different aspects of the event, but can be encouraged by what the other children say and the adult support they receive. There is a limit to how much information can be given to this group about common reactions, but preschool children can benefit from simple, concrete advice about what they can do if unpleasant or scary thoughts arise:

- Speak with mother or father about it.
- Allow good thoughts to come and take the unpleasant or scary thoughts away.
- Create a trap for the unpleasant or scary thoughts, etc.

Young children have a more limited coping repertoire and must therefore be given simple advice about what they can do. Sometimes the ideas come more easily if one says, 'If scary thoughts arise about what has happened, what can we do then?' Young children can sometimes come up with a whole list of ideas, if they are only given the chance to use their imagination.

Small event-related groups for school children and adolescents

This type of meeting is most suitable for children who are older, and adolescents. It follows a fixed structure that has been implemented with positive results. Experience has proven the structure to be well suited for helping children and adults in the aftermath of critical or traumatic events. The structure is presented in Box 8.3.

Box 8.3 Small event-related groups for older children and adolescents

Introduction
- Presentation
- What happens now and why
- Rules

Facts
- Review of the events – what happened
- Everyone takes part
- New facts
  - Can be presented by teachers, the police, a physician, etc.
- Make it concrete
  - Utilize drawings, maps, etc.
- Questions

Thoughts
- Immediate thoughts
- Other thoughts
- Emphasis on coping thoughts

Reactions
- Sensory input – NB! Proceed with caution
  - Vision, hearing, smell, touch, movement, taste

- Different reactions immediately and later
  - Somatic reactions, feelings, actions
- Use of different forms of expression, such as rituals

Information and advice

- Give information about common reactions
- Advice about coping
- How to help others

Conclusion

- Mobilization of solidarity and learning
- Where necessary, agree upon a new meeting date

The introduction is important because through it the leaders (it is best to have two leaders) of the meeting establish a good atmosphere, where the children feel secure enough to speak without being ridiculed. The trust between the children and the leaders is built up in the initial phase of the gathering. If the leaders explain briefly about why the group has been convened, this will serve to motivate participants. At the same time, it is useful to have some 'rules' for the meeting: 'There are some things that I want you to remember or that I want us to agree upon before we begin.' Such 'rules' provide security and establish a clear structure for the children. Things to be emphasized include that:

- nobody is to be teased or laughed at for things they say in the group or afterwards
- nobody is to hear of things that they have spoken about from others
- everyone is to be respected for his or her contribution
- everyone speaks for themselves, nobody speaks for anyone else.

During the fact phase the children speak about what happened, as they experienced it, perhaps on the basis of the following questions: 'How could you tell that something was about to happen?' 'Can you tell us where you were when it happened?' 'How did you find out about what happened?' 'Who told you?' 'What were you told?' 'Where were you at the time?'

When everyone tells their story, many details are filled in and everyone is thereby able to develop a more complete understanding and overview of the incident than they had individually. Sometimes it can be best to allow the children to tell their stories according to the order in which they became involved, such as 'Who was notified first about what had happened?' Often children have an incomplete or erroneous understanding of what has happened, which can be corrected during the meeting or by receiving information from adults. Representatives from the police, rescue service, healthcare service or others can be brought in early on in the meeting to help the children develop a correct and more comprehensive understanding of what took place.

> After an adolescent committed suicide by hanging, several in the group that had come together for a meeting believed that he had been found lying on the ground. This resulted in a number of them thinking that something criminal was behind the death. Through information from the police describing where and how he was found, these rumours were diminished and the adolescents acquired a more correct image of what had taken place.

After everyone has had the opportunity to explain their experience of what happened, the leaders ask about the type of thoughts that went through their minds in the course of the critical situation or when they learned about it. This allows them to get in touch with what they said to themselves and what they did to cope, survive or get through the incident. Many are left with feelings of helplessness or with extremely negative feelings and thoughts about what they did or did not do. By focusing on the immediate thoughts they had, it is often possible to help children or adolescents to understand that they made many correct decisions, which helped them to survive, to contain the fallout or to get through a difficult waiting period, alleviate pain, etc. They can also come to understand that when they afterwards think about what they should have done, that this was in fact not possible in the midst of the hectic situation.

By emphasizing these thoughts, the feeling of helplessness is reduced and simultaneously a greater sense of control is established in that such direct questions about thoughts serve to support a construction of a complete recollection of what took place. Often questions about thoughts lead to discussions about the most important emotional topics.

This indirect manner of approaching emotions is particularly important for boys, who tend to have a more difficult time speaking directly about their feelings.

If all the members of the group of children or adolescents have taken in powerful sensory impressions, the discussion is guided into different aspects of these. A clearly detailed review of what they saw, heard, smelled, touched or sensed in the manner of movements and physical sensations can help the children to find a verbal expression for memories that otherwise can begin to live a life of their own. Verbalization of these sense memories can moderate the frequency of intrusive, distressing memories.

If only one or a few members of a group have absorbed intense sensory impressions, one should demonstrate extreme caution in allowing them to speak in detail about these to the rest of the group. This can in the worst case traumatize others. If the group composition is such, one should be sure that the exposed children receive the opportunity to describe their impressions in detail later, either individually or with others who have absorbed corresponding impressions.

> In a bereavement group one of the adolescents present spoke of how her mother died in a car accident. Another one of the group members understood that she knew something about this accident and started to speak about how the car had been brought to her father's garage afterwards and that there had been a lot of blood. The group leader had to quickly intervene before she could relate further details. Although it was not possible to know ahead of time that this young person would start to speak about this, it was extremely important that the group leader quickly stepped in and stopped the discussion and said, 'I don't want you to tell us about this here because Lise was not prepared for you wanting to say this. If she wants to know more about what you have to say she can ask you about it later.'

The example illustrates that a good group leader is required during such discussions and that it is important that the leaders know how to handle difficult subjects (see Dyregrov 1997, 1999, 2002 for further descriptions of how to handle debriefing groups).

Conversations about thoughts and strong impressions naturally lead into discussions of different types of reactions, whether of a physical or emotional nature. The children will usually make the most important topic apparent when they describe facts and thoughts. In some meetings children and young people can exhibit strong feelings during the course of the discussion; in other cases the discussion takes place without the expression of any intense emotions. Drawing, fill-in-the-blank exercises (e.g. 'the worst thing about what happened for me was…') or a ritual commemoration (e.g. lighting candles) can be utilized as means of expression during this part of the discussion. It is important that one does not explore in depth the feelings that are spoken about. This can be done in one-on-one sessions if necessary. The most important thing about the group discussion is that participants are able to hear that others react as they do, with the normalizing effect on their reactions that this entails.

It is particularly in the thought and reaction part of the discussion that the children have the opportunity to hear other children describe thoughts, feelings, or actions corresponding to those they have personally experienced or carried out, and which thereby confirms that there is nothing unusual about them. When someone mentions a reaction that one knows to be common, this normalization is encouraged by the leader saying, 'Has anyone else experienced the same thing?' If more unusual reactions are mentioned, the leader of the discussion must either request other comments 'Other reactions?', or comment on the basis of own experience: 'I have heard about what you are telling us from…'

Sometimes the group leader must personally take the initiative to address sensitive subjects that are important but which the children do not address themselves, such as:

> I am thinking that because Morten has suffered such extensive injuries that he will never be the same again, that he most probably will be bedridden for the rest of his life, that there are a number of you who have perhaps thought that it would have been better if he had died. Has anyone had such thoughts?

After the children have had the chance to speak about different thoughts and reactions, it is the leader's turn to present information that further confirms the normality of what they are communicating in the way of experiences and reactions, and also to give preparatory information about reactions that may arise in future. Then advice is given that can be helpful for them. In this part of the meeting, any misunderstandings or expectations about reactions are clarified. The following suggestions may be useful:

- Speak with friends and parents about what has happened.
- Put your experiences into words (facts, thoughts and feelings) in another way, such as in a diary, letter, poem, on a computer, or by speaking into a tape recorder.
- Seek out more information about what happened.
- Visit the site of the event accompanied by others.
- Resume ordinary routines as soon as possible.
- Take part in activities that alleviate tension: sports, music, or recreational activities.
- Accept help if you feel that things are not going well.

There are limits to how much one can say. It can therefore be useful to give young people simple written information about reactions and coping. This should not be a long list of symptoms, as this may well have the effect of producing a self-fulfilling prophecy. Briefly explain the most common reactions, but also let it be known that it is fine not to have any reactions at all. Even younger school children can take such information home to their parents. Following situations during which children have absorbed powerful impressions, they should be given instructions for specific methods they can use to alleviate the reliving of these, if the impressions become disturbing and do not subside as a matter of course (see Chapter 9 for descriptions of such methods).

Before the discussion is concluded, children and adolescents should be encouraged to contact one of the leaders if they have questions or want to talk more about something. An agreement can be made to meet again to speak together after a few days have passed, or later, depending upon what has occurred. After the meeting the leaders, of course, should speak individually with pupils who are clearly in need of help.

Upon ending the meeting, the children can also agree on a group activity, such as a gesture for the family most heavily affected, in the form of a letter, group drawing, or something similar.

Stallard and Law (1993) showed how such a meeting effectively reduced intrusive memories, even when the meeting was organized several months after a serious traffic accident that affected a group of young people. When Paul Stallard et al. (2006) applied the debriefing format in individual conversations with children following traumatic events, they found that both the control group and those who were given shorter debriefings showed a large reduction in reactions. The authors speculate about whether even the act of simply filling out a questionnaire on what happened functioned as a debriefing.

There are a number of other factors with respect to the composition of the group, training of group leaders, follow-up afterwards, etc., which for reasons of space will not be discussed here. If the reader is interested, more information is available in Dyregrov (2002).

References

Dyregrov, A. (1997) 'The process in critical incident stress debriefings.' *Journal of Traumatic Stress 10*, 589–605.

Dyregrov, A. (1999) 'Helpful and hurtful aspects of psychological debriefing groups.' *International Journal of Emergency Mental Health 3*, 175–181.

Dyregrov, A. (2002) *Psychological Debriefing. A Leader's Guide for Small Group Crisis Intervention*. Ellicott City, Md: Chevron Publishing Corporation.

Dyregrov, A. (2008) *Grief in Children. A Handbook for Adults*. 2nd edition. London: Jessica Kingsley Publishers.

Peled, E. and Edleson, J.L. (1992) 'Multiple perspectives on groupwork with children of battered women.' *Violence and Victims 7*, 327–346.

Stallard, P. and Law, F. (1993) 'Screening psychological debriefing of adolescent survivors of life-threatening events.' *British Journal of Psychiatry 163*, 660–665.

Stallard, P., Velleman, R., Salter, E., Howse, I., Yule, W. and Taylor, G. (2006) 'A randomised controlled trial to determine the effectiveness of an early psychological intervention with children involved in road traffic accidents.' *Journal of Child Psychology and Psychiatry 47*, 127–134.

Wraith, R. (1995) Debriefing for children: are the techniques and processes the same as critical incident stress debriefing for adults. Paper presented to Third World Congress on Stress, Trauma and Coping at the the Emergency Services Professions. Baltimore, April.

Wraith, R. (2000) 'Children and debriefing: theory, interventions and outcomes.' In B. Raphael. and J.P. Wilson (eds) *Psychological Debriefing. Theory, Practice and Evidence* (pp.195–212) 'Cambridge: Cambridge University Press.

9

Post-Traumatic Therapy

What works?

As stated below, first and foremost cognitive behaviour therapy (CBT) has a well-documented effect in the area of trauma. This does not mean that other child therapy approaches, such as play therapy, various forms of art therapy approaches or psychodynamic therapy do not work. These methods have not as yet, however, been empirically documented as suitable forms of treatment in work with child trauma. In the recommendations given following a review of treatment studies, CBT is primarily recommended (National Institute for Health and Clinical Excellence (NICE) 2005; Task Force on Community Preventive Services 2008).

Cognitive behaviour therapy (CBT)

An empirical basis for the effects of CBT in helping traumatized children has been established for both individual and group therapy (Silverman *et al.* 2008; Taylor and Chemtob 2004; Wethington *et al.* 2008). CBT, however, involves many different types of approaches and the most effective elements have not yet been determined. While many so-called randomized controlled studies have been carried out, the effectiveness of the treatment in everyday clinical practice has proven more moderate (Ollendick and Davis 2004). Although involvement of the parents in therapy is emphasized, this has not been shown to be of major significance to the child's trauma symptoms (Stallard 2006).

It is primarily in the area of sexual abuse that most of the controlled studies have been carried out and here CBT has shown good results (Cohen *et al.* 2004; Deblinger, Lippman and Steer 1996; Deblinger, Steer and Lippman 1999; King *et al.* 2000). For example, Cohen *et al.* (2007) demonstrated that so-called trauma-focused CBT reduced PTSD, depression and the total number of behavioural problems, compared with a child-centred treatment for sexually abused children. The CBT treatment included training in expressive techniques, understanding of the relation between thoughts, feelings and behaviour, graded exposure, cognitive processing of events, joint sessions between children and parents, psychoeducation on the subject of sexual abuse and training of parents in their handling of children. The child-centred treatment involved a greater emphasis on the therapeutic relationship, active listening, reflection, empathy and supportive conversation about feelings, and the building of confidence in children's and parents' coping mechanisms. In addition, psychoeducational information was provided about sexual abuse. Twice as many children in the age group 8–14 years who had received the child-centred treatment still satisfied the PTSD criteria subsequent to treatment, compared with those who received trauma-focused CBT. The children in the CBT group also showed a reduction in shame and negative self-attributions. The parents in the CBT group reported less depression, more support of the children and better parenting skills than did the control group. The methods described here are to a significant extent taken from the area of CBT.

Groups for children with PTSD or PTSD symptoms

Goenjian *et al.* (1997, 2005) have shown good results from trauma- and grief-focused treatment of children in early adolescence after an earthquake in Armenia. They combined classroom intervention in a group (four meetings) with two individual consultations. They put an emphasis on five areas in this follow-up:

1. reconstruction and processing of the traumatic event
2. handling of traumatic reminders
3. stress experienced after the catastrophe and other negative events
4. grief and the interaction between grief and trauma
5. developmental progression.

Discussions, drawings, different activities and training in relaxation and problem solving were included in this intervention. On an individual basis, they worked with the processing of particularly traumatizing moments. For the intervention group, the post-traumatic symptoms were reduced and depressive symptoms did not become worse, while both post-traumatic problems and depression grew worse in the control group. The effects of the treatment were maintained over the course of several years (Goenjian *et al.* 2005).

In the subsequent development of this group protocol, Layne *et al.* (2001) have shown good results among children who have experienced war or extreme violence in inner cities in the USA. However, here as many as 20 group meetings were held, where the children met in smaller groups (5–7 participants). Participation resulted in the improvement of post-traumatic symptoms, complex grief reactions and school grades, respectively, while depression showed little change.

After earthquakes in Turkey, Greece, Iran, China and Pakistan, a group protocol (Smith, Dyregrov and Yule 1998, 1999) developed through a collaboration between the Center for Crisis Psychology in Bergen and the Institute of Psychiatry in London has been used with good results. Here many of the methods that will be described later on in further detail are included and there is an emphasis on teaching children and young people methods they can use to alleviate post-traumatic symptoms. They meet five times for 1½–2 hours and parents or guardians meet at the beginning and conclusion. There is one manual for children who have experienced war, another for those who have experienced disasters. Studies indicate that use of the manual results in reduction of post-traumatic symptoms (Giannopoulou, Dikaiakon and Yule 2006; Shooshtary, Panaghi and Moghadam 2008; for more documentation, see www.childrenandwar. org). Other CBT group programmes have proven to be correspondingly beneficial (Chemtob, Nakashima and Hamada 2002; Kataoka *et al.* 2003; Stein *et al.* 2003). Most of the programmes focus on the children's concrete experiences, and the children are exposed through the telling of their stories either orally or in writing, in addition to their being taught concrete techniques that help them to handle the consequences of the trauma.

Other treatment methods for PTSD

Eye Movement Desensitization and Reprocessing (EMDR) has been shown to be an extremely powerful technique in the treatment of adults with post-traumatic problems and there are increasingly more research findings confirming that this is also the case for children (Ahmad, Larsson and Sundelin-Wahlsten 2007; Fernandez, Gallinari and Lorenzetti 2003). The basis of the method is that the child recalls the traumatic image (or other aspects) of what they have experienced while simultaneously following the hand of the therapist with their eyes, as the hand is moved rhythmically back and forth before the eyes of the child. Another option is alternating tactile or auditory stimulus, by tapping in turns on the right and left hand, or by presenting auditory stimulation alternatively to the right and left ear.

The method seems very simple when it is described. However, it should only be used by an experienced therapist who has established the secure therapeutic relationship that is necessary for good treatment of traumatized children. Because the effect occurs so quickly and the method sometimes causes strong reactions, it is important that it is carried out by professionals who are well trained in application of the method. The reason why the method works as well as it does is not known, but research indicates that it triggers an immediate relaxation response (Aubert-Khalfa, Roques and Blin 2008; Elofsson *et al.* 2008) in addition to a simultaneous desensitization and cognitive restructuring of memories. It is also believed that the eye movements (and the other bilateral stimulus) promote the transfer of information between the two sides of the brain and possibly between deeper areas of the brain and neocortex. Through alternating tactile hand stimulation, the method has been used with good results even among young children (clinical accounts). We have also used the method in the treatment of disturbing fantasies in connection with traumatic situations.

> Roy (12 years old) had episodes where he imagined that his dead father was suddenly in the room. He would see his father in front of him and was afraid of what his father would do to him. Through the use of EMDR spontaneous changes occurred. He speaks with his father during the fantasy. He is able to express things that he wishes he had said to his father before his death. While the eye movements are being carried out, Roy sees his father turn around and leave the room. He understands that his father does not wish to harm him. The boy experiences an immediate alleviation of tension

and reports no disturbing fantasies over the course of the following months.

Chemtob, Nakashima and Carlson (2002) used the method on 32 children with PTSD, after other methods of treatment had been tried without results. They documented a clear reduction in post-traumatic scores, but less of an impact on depression and anxiety. Subsequently, Ribchester, Yule and Duncan (2004) treated 11 children who developed PTSD after traffic accidents. One withdrew from treatment, but the ten others no longer qualified for the diagnosis after an average of 2.4 EMDR treatment sessions. De Roos *et al.* (2004) report a randomized controlled trial (RCT) study of 52 children after an explosion catastrophe in the Netherlands in 2000. EMDR fared well compared to CBT. Both treatment methods resulted in a significant reduction in stress symptoms, with EMDR slightly more effective with fewer sessions. Ahmad *et al.* (2007) have in a small RCT study reported that children treated by EMDR showed a clear improvement in post-traumatic reactions compared with a waiting list control group, particularly with regard to intrusive memory material. The children had experienced different types of trauma, the most common involving maltreatment, sexual abuse and traffic accidents. Group methods based on EMDR are also used. Here bilateral stimulation is used where the child does a so-called 'butterfly-hug', where they cross their arms in front of them and alternatively pat themselves on the left and right shoulder while focusing on drawings they have made of their traumatic experiences. The results of the method are extremely promising, but the studies have been methodologically weak (Adúriz, Bluthgen and Knopfler 2009). There are several good books describing the use of EMDR with children (Greenwald 1999; Tinker and Wilson 1999).

Tiffany Field *et al.* (Diego *et al.* 2002; Field, Seligman and Scafidi 1996a; Field *et al.* 1996b) have in several studies shown that massage can reduce post-traumatic symptoms and other problems in children. Such methods of physical therapy comprise an important supplement to more cognitive-based methods.

Different types of narrative therapy have also been utilized for traumatized children. These methods have their roots in work done in South America, where individuals who have experienced political violence tell their story, which is then written down by the therapist. Combined with methods taken from CBT and James Pennebaker's work (1997, 2004) where clients write in detail about what they have experienced, the idea is that the method can help with the integration of fragmented memories. Neuner *et al.* (2008) have shown that the use of so-called narrative exposure therapy (NET) with traumatized children lead to good results.

Commencement of therapy

This is not a book for psychotherapists on how they are to go about helping children following traumas. But both with an eye towards creating 'treatment optimism', and towards giving parents and other adults a certain insight on different therapeutic work methods, it is appropriate here to describe some of the methods that can be used to help children who have developed PTSD. At the same time, some of the methods described here can potentially be used as self-help methods that can be explained to children by adults. A lot of what follows has therefore a clear relevance to all helpers, from parents, teachers, and preschool teachers to healthcare personnel.

Before treatment is started, the child is evaluated through interviews with the parents, alone and/or accompanied by the child. As well, a consultation can be held with older children without the presence of their parents. Through conversations, sometimes the use of a questionnaire (older children) and tests, the child's history is mapped out (developmental history) along with any former crises, loss, or traumatic events. Through the accounts of both the parents and the child, a clear image of the traumatic event(s) the child has experienced is created. On the basis of this a treatment plan is developed.

At an early stage in the meeting a conversation is held with the child about why they have come to see the therapist. Sometimes it is surprising how little children have been prepared by their parents or the kinds of perceptions they have about what is going to take place (see Chapter 7). The therapist explains what is going to occur, his or her role in this, and what the child's contribution will be. It is important that the child is prepared for the fact that the consultations will contain elements of fun and play but that it can also be hard to approach the painful things that have happened.

All therapy depends upon the development of a good relationship between the therapist and the child and family. Through respect for the child, directness, and warm, open communication and empathy as an important part of the frame for the interaction, a good foundation is created for the therapeutic contact. For children who have experienced repetitive traumas, the building up of a relationship can take much longer than otherwise because they may have problems trusting others. In this case a clear, strong signalling of warmth and compassion in the start phase can be frightening, because an assailant may have used such strategies in connection with abuse, or essentially because the child is unaccustomed to encountering such warmth. Regardless of the type of trauma, it is important to give signals of hope and the belief that the child is going to feel better. When the therapeutic contact has been established, one can use different types of post-traumatic methods to help the child.

Relationship building

Interaction during the first meeting is essential to the subsequent therapeutic contact. In building a relationship with children, and particularly adolescents, the establishment of this type of contact is more important and more vulnerable than is the case in other life phases. In this phase of their development, their need to demonstrate independence and autonomy can make them extremely critical of adults who either attempt to be one of them or who seek to involve themselves in areas that they personally wish to master.

In meeting with children who have experienced trauma, our point of departure is that they are to experience receiving something helpful as early as the first consultation. Traumatized children often struggle with specific problems, such as sleep disturbances and intrusive memory images, or other things that they experience as extremely upsetting. If, towards the end of the first consultation, the therapist gives the child one simple, concrete piece of advice (self-help methods that will be described later) that can be applied during the time period before the next session, as an initial attempt to alleviate these problems, it will strengthen the relationship. One way of doing this is to ask what is disturbing the child the most now, and then to give a concrete piece of advice in relation to this. Even if this does not result in a dramatic improvement in the child's situation, it signals the therapist's willingness and commitment to meeting the child where he or she is struggling, something that can build trust and strengthen the relationship. If necessary, one can use trauma therapy methods to help the child acquire further control over the problem, but the trust has at this point already been reinforced and the relationship strengthened through the help that the child experiences having received, or the level of commitment they recognize in the therapist with respect to the help given.

In this work the therapist is an active, advisory collaborator. The aim is to awaken hope by communicating that the child's distress can be alleviated. If the self-help methods can have a positive result, both coping abilities and self-image will be reinforced, while the relationship building is strengthened and the risk of withdrawal from the therapy is counteracted. In families where the child and/or one of the parents are exposed to violence, it is almost a given that one of the parents also has been traumatized and, accordingly, parenting capacity diminished. This means that the parent personally has a need for therapeutic support and will benefit from information about children's traumatic reactions and what can be done to provide support.

Some suggestions about establishing good contact with young people are given in Box 9.1.

Box 9.1 Simple advice for establishing good contact

- Be active in contact with the child, and ask questions, preferably open questions without having any expectation of receiving lengthy answers.

- Don't be too 'eager to please' or concerned about speaking in the child or young person's jargon – they can dislike such attempts to be a part of their culture. Try nonetheless to be up to date about current trends in the cultures of children and adolescents.

- Be flexible about the timeframe; shorter 'conversations' can function particularly well for some boys, though in 'times of crisis' there can be a need for a longer consultation than usual.

- Choose informal locations as a framework for the consultation if necessary, such as a ride in the car or a walk.

- It can be a good idea to sit side by side or at a 90-degree angle so that eye contact is less intense.

- Reactions and problems can be normalized through information. Keep in mind that children have limited life experience.

- Avoid long pauses and awkward periods of silence.

- Meet the child or young person halfway by asking what the most important thing to receive help with is.

- Repeat on a regular basis, particularly in the beginning, why it is important to confront difficult things that can be experienced as painful.

- Create clear expectations that it is possible to do something about the things that are distressing now.

Can we proceed too quickly?

In the professional literature there has been discussion about how right it is to initiate conversations about children's traumatic experiences, particularly if this occurs in a setting where there are few opportunities to follow up (Hundeide 1995). Although in a consultation with traumatized children it is very important to develop a secure therapeutic relationship, our experience from the area of trauma is that we can relatively quickly approach what the child has experienced. In fact, we find that many children experience it as a new betrayal if they meet a helper who, instead of speaking with them about the worst things they have experienced, starts speaking about many other things that are, for them, insignificant. In work with research studies (most frequently in the form of qualitative interviews) in which we approach traumatic experiences relatively quickly, we have on several occasions, such as with refugees (both children and adults) investigated their experiences of this. The response has been extremely positive. Such consultations or interviews are in fact experienced as having a positive effect (Dyregrov 2004; Dyregrov, Dyregrov and Raundalen 2000), and this finding is confirmed in other research (Reich and Kaplan 1994). Therapeutic contact provides the parameters for creating a secure atmosphere, in particular because it is possible to give confirmation and advice in a wholly different manner from that possible in the context of a research interview. Cohen and Mannarino (1996a) have recommended such a direct approach also where children have experienced long-term violence (sexual abuse) in the family:

> The present study lends support to the view that, in young children who have already reported sexual abuse and have had

some form of independent validation of that report, therapy that directly addresses sexual abuse-related issues is more effective in reducing symptomatology than therapy in which the child is not required to (and frequently does not) directly discuss the abusive experience (p.49).

Post-traumatic therapy – different methods

Different work methods will now be presented. Several of these can be used as self-help techniques, but because children are less able to learn such methods by reading, and will need adult assistance in understanding the instructions, contact with a therapist is often an advantage. This also ensures an assessment of the scope and nature of the problems, and that complicated and complex problems receive the requisite follow-up. The methods are predominantly organized according to the reactions that are typical for PTSD. Thus they are grouped by methods that a) aim to reduce the intrusive memories and thoughts; b) seek to redress avoidance reactions; and c) reduce physiological arousal. Further, interventions to assist children in alleviating persistent self-reproach reactions and feelings of guilt, and methods aimed at cognitive restructuring, are included.

Therapy for traumatic memories and thoughts

Just a few years ago there were still few possibilities for helping children and adults in handling traumatic memory material. This can now be achieved through several different approaches. The nature of intrusive memories is typically such that the child has little control over them when they arise. When the imagination is implemented as a means of taking control over these memories, the child experiences more control so that they can handle the memories more actively. The imagery techniques can be used as self-help techniques, but, as mentioned earlier, adult assistance is frequently required for explanation and understanding of instructions. If the self-help methods do not provide the desired change, the methods can be utilized more effectively in an interaction between the therapist and the child, supplemented with trauma-specific methods such as CBT and EMDR.

Imagery methods

Imagery methods are useful for helping the child gain control over negative memories. They are extremely suitable for work with children, because children can use their active and vivid imaginations. Before this work is begun, the therapist attempts to establish, or activate, positive imagery. Such positive imagery is also used in connection with exposure techniques, whether these are used *in vitro* (in the imagination) or *in vivo* (in real life).

A method that is commonly used before approaching the painful memories has been given the name 'safe place', which implies that one creates a perception of a safe place. This is a method that is used a great deal within EMDR and it is based on a relaxation exercise described by Miller (1994). The child is asked to visualize, describe or draw a particularly 'good' place, a place characterized by wellbeing and security – a place it feels good to visit using imagination. Young children can, for example, visualize mother or father sitting beside their bed and reading, singing or talking and that they tuck them snugly in at night before they go to sleep. This positive image can later be activated to help the child alleviate the anxiety and tension awakened by the negative memories. When the child has created such a safe situation or place, one can then observe whether the child appears to be comfortable while they are thinking about it. Then proceed with further guidance:

> I now want you to use your imagination and really try to go to this place with your entire self. Whether you want to keep your eyes open or closed is up to you, but many feel it is easier to achieve this with their eyes closed. Summon up an image of the place and imagine that you are there with your entire self. Take a look around you and pay attention to what you see. Look at details and different colours and shapes around you. Let your eyes rest on pleasant things you see around you. What do you see if you look a bit further away? Allow what you see to help you to feel comfortable and relaxed. Remember that this is your special place, which you can return to in your imagination at any time. See if you can retrieve some familiar, good smells that you associate with this place. Notice how you take in the smells through your nostrils and that at the same time you can hear the sounds that you associate with this place. Good, familiar sounds that make you feel even more relaxed and safe. Pay attention to how it feels to sit, stand or lie down there, how your body is in contact with the place. If it is a place where you don't lie down, walk around a bit

and see how good it feels. Notice things around you, see how they look and spend a little time touching them. Perhaps you are somewhere where you can feel the wind playing around your face, or the sun warming you, perhaps there are birds flying above you or the scent of flowers you like or the smell of good food or the voice of someone you like, that makes you feel safe? In your safe place you can see, hear, touch, smell and feel exactly what you want and that makes you feel calm and secure. If you want you can bring somebody with you there who makes you feel even safer. You can go to this place whenever you want. Just by thinking about it you can feel safer and more secure.

Ask children where they went in their imagination and how it was. Give tips for how they can practise this at home, and let them know that such good fantasies can change how they are feeling. Explain to them how they can gain control over their thoughts and thereby control, in part, how the body feels as well, and that if they feel afraid or uncomfortable using the imagination this way can help them to feel better.

In the visual area we have used 'screen techniques'. Before we begin this work it is necessary to map out the elements of the visual memories that are central and the most distressing for the child, so that this aspect is made a priority in the change work:

Imagine that you are looking at a TV screen, a film screen or computer screen. Retrieve the disturbing image and put it on the screen in front of you. It may take a little time to bring it up and get it in place on the screen. Notice whether it is in colour or black and white. You can then change the colours, make it greyer or let it be just black and white. Then you can try to move so that you can see the image from another angle. If that is difficult, try several times. Maybe you can look at it from above or from the side? Then you can try something else. Imagine that you are sitting with a remote control in your hand. When you have retrieved the image, press the off-button and turn the image off. If it appears again, you push the off-button once more. How did it go? Retrieve the image again and do the same thing a few times, turn the image off and on. Usually people need to practise this several times before they succeed. Spend a little time each day in the coming days on juggling the images. It will give you control over the images instead of their controlling you. It is best that you do this well before going to bed at night, preferably in the afternoon.

Look at the intrusive image on the screen again. You may have seen a programme on TV where the upper right-hand part of the screen contains another image than what is on the main screen, such as a goal in another football match? Now you are going to put a good image up in the corner of the screen, so that it overlaps a little on the disturbing image. When you have managed that, let the two images switch places, quickly, so that the good image occupies most of the screen and the disturbing image is up in the right-hand corner. Then move the disturbing image down in the right-hand corner, then over into the left-hand bottom corner and then to the upper left-hand corner. Then remove the disturbing image completely from the screen. If you are used to working on a computer, you can imagine that you close the programme containing the disturbing image and then put it in the trashcan.

If the client does not see an individual image but a film or series of images, another method can be used:

Imagine that you have a DVD player connected to the TV. Imagine that you put in a DVD. Right before you start the movie on the TV, you push the recording button and then start recording. You then record the entire film. When the film is finished imagine that you take out the DVD and put it in a drawer with a lock. After having locked the drawer you put the key in a place where you know you can find it if you need to watch something on the film later. Sometimes parts of 'the film' are more difficult to record than others. You can then stop the film, freeze it, exactly at this part, and use the procedures described earlier. You can also play the film backward and forward past this point many times and in this manner take more control over this part.

The child can take out the DVD and replace it with another, delete it, fast forward it, etc. There are many possible variations, and many children take part in this work enthusiastically and experience spontaneously that they can gain more, sometimes even full control over the disturbing memories in a very short period of time. In the work with visual memories, they can also try to change the brightness, distance, sharpness, size, depth, contrast, movement and speed. If the child manages this, the exercise can be repeated and possibly supplemented with other control techniques. The method can be varied by saying, for example:

> Can you see what happened in front of you? How far away can you see it? Good. Can you try to move the image a bit further away from you and while you move it you make the image become smaller and smaller. Good. Can you imagine that you move it so far away that it completely disappears?

Children can change the contents. They can be asked to imagine that they see the image in the therapist's hand. The hand can be held in front of the children's face at the same distance that they 'see' the image. The hand is then gradually moved further away from the children, then quickly behind the therapist's back while saying, 'Now it is gone'. The children can be asked to move the image further and further away until it disappears into the wall or out the window. They can be asked to turn it over and change it. A frame can be put around the image and the children asked to imagine hanging it up on the wall.

Another method that can help in gaining control of disturbing visual memories is to imagine a figure, such as a square or a circle that the children are then asked to trace with their eyes. They can trace the outline of the figure with their eyes, have the line change colours and follow the line around. This image is activated every time a 'disturbing' image arises, so that it counteracts or replaces unwanted visual impressions.

With regard to auditory memories, the dimensions of the impression that the children find disturbing must first be outlined. Is it the intensity, strength, voice quality, dialect, or other elements? After this has been done, the children can imagine that they hear the auditory memory on a radio, CD, MP3 player, iPod, TV without picture – there are many possibilities. They can be instructed to turn down the volume or increase the speed. They can have the voice sound like Donald Duck or change the voice in other ways; they can play the track backwards, change the language; they can hear other words or they can simply turn off the sound. They can also imagine that the sound is burned onto a CD. The CD can be stopped, taken out and even destroyed. Here is an example of how this can be done:

You told me that you always hear... Now I want you to learn a method that will enable you to take control of this memory. Do you know what a mixing board is? Maybe you have seen pictures from a sound studio on TV? Or you have seen the mixing board that is under the speaker icon on your PC screen.

You can imagine that inside your head the sounds you hear can be reorganized on a mixing board where everything you hear or see that you retrieve from your memory can be edited – do you know what that word means? It perhaps sounds a bit strange, but you can in fact edit your memories using the mixing board in your brain. Now I want you to try this. One of the buttons on the mixing board for the loudspeaker on the computer is called 'Mute all'. When you select this option, there will be no sound whatsoever. Try and see if you can do this on the mixing board in your brain when you have brought up your auditory memory. If you can't manage to do this, then you can do what they do in a music studio. They put in new tracks, so that the old tracks are changed. If you hear a scream, you can add loud music with a heavy bass so that the scream is drowned out, or you can make a change that works better for you. There are an incredible amount of possibilities for using this internal mixing board however you like.

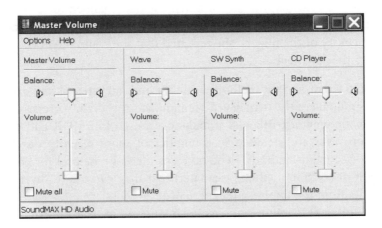

Figure 9.1 Example of a computer mixing board

Taste and smell impressions return less frequently unless there is an external stimulus that triggers them, so there are fewer cases when children need help in this area. For taste impressions one can use a counter taste – for example, have the children eat a piece of hard candy or something else to counteract the taste they repeatedly experience as unpleasant. Allow them to use their imagination to evoke a good taste, which you then, as the therapist, help them to further develop, such as their favourite dish. Ask them to describe how it tastes and ask questions such as: 'Is it salty or sour?' 'Where in your mouth can you taste it best?' 'Describe for me how it feels.' 'How does the food smell?' The good experiences can be linked to an area in the body (see the later explanation of counter-conditioning). In the following example a so-called double attention task was used:

> A girl who had been subjected to violence had had the fingers of the assailant in her mouth. They tasted awful, particularly because he had a skin disease. She was asked to let her brain find another taste that she could 'put over' the old one. She should just wait and see what her brain would come up with, and meanwhile she was given rhythmic tactile stimulation through hand tapping alternating between her right and left palms. She held out her hands with the palms facing upward while she was stimulated in approximately 1-second intervals by brief taps on her palms. A short time after her brain was assigned its task, the girl said that she had changed the nasty fingers to sugar cubes. When she was asked to recall the memory of the fingers, she repeated that she could only bring up the sugar cubes.

A double attention task method, utilizing both an internal and external focus simultaneously is believed to stimulate the brain's processing of a traumatic memory. Bilateral stimulation is used in EMDR and double attention tasks are included in a number of more recently developed trauma treatment methods. In some cases it can be helpful for children to learn distraction methods (see later) that they can use to divert their thoughts from the unpleasant experience.

For olfactory impressions counter-odours in the nostrils are a possibility. This means that the children apply a good aroma to the skin at the opening of the nostril to counteract the unpleasant odour. They can also use the imagination to contain the intrusive aroma. They can imagine that they lower a container over it, use a vacuum cleaner to suck up all the unpleasantness or have a strong wind blow it away. They can also imagine that they light a fire in their imagination and allow the heat and smoke to dispel the unpleasant odour. Allowing the odour to flow into a balloon that then becomes smaller and smaller is another option for handling odours. A more positive version is to summon up a good aroma and 'put it on top of' the unpleasant one. Here the therapist can help the child to develop this fantasy:

> Can you think of a smell that you think is especially good (give examples)? Can you smell it? Notice how good it is and how it can fill your entire nose. Let this smell replace the unpleasant one. Think of the good smell as a strong aroma that wins the battle with the unpleasant odour. Can you imagine it as a knight or a spirit with great powers? Use your imagination to give this odour strong power and become the dominant one.

The girl who was bothered by memories of the taste of her assailant's fingers in the example mentioned earlier was also disturbed by olfactory impressions. This was the experience of a particular animal smell, because the hands of the assailant smelled so strongly of this. She was therefore asked to retrieve the aroma and see how her brain could change it, while the two palms of her hands were alternately tapped. She changed the smell to a good perfume scent that she could use as a counter-aroma.

Usually both taste and olfactory impressions will create fewer intrusive memories than visual and auditory impressions, but on the few occasions where this is a problem they can be experienced as extremely upsetting for the children afflicted by them, so that we must be imaginative in collaboration with a child to find effective methods for stopping them.

Children who struggle with intrusive, recurring memories have frequently reported that the worst thing about these memories is that they are completely beyond their control. When we are to explain why such an astounding improvement takes place through the application of such 'simple' methods, we think that part of the answer lies exactly here: children experience that it helps to do something, that there are methods that can help them to gain some control over horrible elements, and this gives them the strength and self-confidence to continue the necessary confrontation with traumatic memories. When one works with the respective sensory channels, this is called working with submodalities, a method developed by the neurolinguist Richard Bandler (see Stanton 1993a, b).

Stanton (1993a) also demonstrates how bodily memories can be altered in a similar manner. A 17-year-old, who was experiencing extremely unpleasant physical sensations in his abdomen, described the experience as black, heavy, cold, circular and quite large. He managed to move this uncomfortable sensation out of his body and change the colour to a comfortable green colour, to warm it up in front of the radiator, to squeeze it into a cylinder and throw it out the window. Through the use of willpower these submodalities (parts of a bodily experience) can be changed so that children and adolescents can gain control over and master discomfort or behaviour.

Bodily memories can become invasive in nature and are usually triggered by stimuli associated with what happened. It can be something that moves towards the child in the same manner as in the traumatic situation, someone who touches them in a similar way or something they see on the telly, which directly triggers the memory. Through physical therapy, sports activities, massage and simple body-oriented methods (see Rothschild 2000), etc., they can gradually learn that physical contact and activity can be associated with something other than discomfort.

Counter-conditioning

Paunovic (2003) has developed a method for counter-conditioning that can be adapted for use with children. It is not only useful for intrusive memories, but also to reduce unnecessary anxiety. In this method one works with children in the following manner: let them speak about all the situations where they experience joy and wellbeing and which they remember as being associated with good feelings. When they have brought out these memories or situations, and recognize how good it feels to think about them, one touches or presses what is called an anchoring or conditioning point, such as in the middle of a child's middle finger. By repeatedly connecting good experiences to this point in the therapy session and then practising the same thing at home, an automatic connection can be created that children can use when an unpleasant memory emerges or they feel anxiety for no apparent reason. The procedure for counter-conditioning for adults is described in relative detail by Paunovic (2003), but is given a simpler form here adapted to children. Children who have been subjected to or witnesses of domestic violence for long periods of time can have difficulties finding pleasurable and joyful situations that can be used, and the therapist can be obliged to create situations together with a child.

Coping images or helping images can also be used by children in the 'battle' against painful memories. Children can envisage themselves carrying a weapon (e.g. a laser gun), which they can bring along in the fantasy when they are going to approach the negative memories in their mind. They can also be encouraged in the fantasy or in a drawing to stop the perpetrator, take revenge on him, transform the event or reverse it.

Sometimes the imagination more than actual memories is the source of distress for children. Different imagery activities can nonetheless be helpful.

> A girl, who was first helped to take control over strong memories from the time she found a family member who was seriously injured, had fantasies about a ghost being under her bed. Every night she was afraid that it was going to reach out a hand and pull her into another world. Together with the psychologist she constructed a 'ghost trap'. It was a large box with a lid that could be locked. Ghosts are attracted by excitement and after a little discussion she wanted to have a TV showing horror films on the bottom of the box. That's what we did. An imaginary ghost trap destroyed the fantasies.

Distraction methods

When fixed negative thought patterns have become recurring, it is important to help children to express those aspects of the incident which distress them the most. Some thoughts and memories nonetheless continue to return. The use of distraction methods can then be expedient. Here we have many possibilities. Distraction methods can entail working with hobbies, reading, watching the telly, listening to music on an MP3 player, going for a run, listening to something funny, listening to a relaxation tape – in other words, doing something that takes one's mind off painful or sad things. In studies of adults (Thayer, Newman and McClain 1994) it has been shown that there is almost a complete overlap between the methods people use to get out of a bad mood and the methods used to reduce tension and mobilize energy. Time spent with others, use of different cognitive strategies, listening to music and exercise all have such an effect. There is reason to believe that an exaggerated use of such methods leads to traumatic material not being processed. There is a difference between distraction and repression, in terms of both form and effect. Intense, positive experiences can have a more long-term distracting effect. If people have experienced something positive that they can 'live on for a long time', they have acquired a means by which to 'drown' painful thoughts for a while.

A well-known technique that children can learn to use is to wear a rubber band around the wrist (not too tight!) and each time the unpleasant thought or memory returns, the child stretches the rubber band and releases it so that it stings a bit and then the child thinks about something else. Paul Stallard has in his excellent book entitled *Think Good – Feel Good* (2002) given examples of other distraction methods such as:

- counting backwards from 123 by nine
- spelling the names of everyone in the family backwards
- naming all the players in one's favourite team.

Stallard's book is highly recommended. He has given it the subtitle *A Cognitive Behaviour Therapy Workbook for Children and Young People*, and it contains a number of good methods and practical illustrations that can easily be adapted to different trauma situations.

Different distraction methods are also used while actively thinking about the event for limited time periods. When the brain has satisfied the need to focus on what has happened, one can otherwise on that day distract oneself from the intrusive material. Here music, recreational activities, videos, etc. can be useful.

Thought control methods

Thought stopping (Cautela and Wisocki 1977) is used when it is a matter of thoughts rather than images and memories that keep returning. With this method, while children are with the therapist, they retrieve the unwanted thought and the therapist cries out 'stop' when this happens. This is repeated a number of times at the therapist's office and every time 'stop' is called out, the children are to think of a concrete, positive situation (an alternative thought). This can be a safe place or a place that fills them with a sense of wellbeing. The children are subsequently given a homework assignment to call out 'stop' loudly in their mind each time the unwanted thought arises, and then to refocus their thoughts on the safe situation. This is a method requiring a certain amount of emotional maturity and, not least, a certain amount of willpower. It is therefore a method that is best suited to those who have reached adolescence. The method is also useful for children who have developed compulsive behaviour following a traumatic event.

> Truls lost his brother in an accident. Afterwards he developed a number of compulsive thoughts and actions. He had to make sure that the door was locked, the stove turned off, etc. He reported how he had to check, again and again, that the door was locked before he went to school. If an accident such as the one that took his brother's life could happen, then anything could happen. His compulsive actions had to be viewed as a means of regaining security in a suddenly unpredictable world. By doing specific things, Truls avoided having new frightening things happen. In follow-up consultations he was given training in stopping thoughts. First he was asked to retrieve the unwanted thought and, while he held onto the thought, the psychologist shouted, 'Stop'. This was repeated several times. Immediately after the shout command, Truls was to tell himself: 'You have locked the door' (instruction) before he then thought of a specific pleasant situation, which he had personally chosen. He then practised calling out 'stop' himself, before he was asked to apply the procedure at home. He was to think the thought and shout the word 'stop' in his mind. He subsequently transferred this to the actual situation. In the course of a week, the problem was 'insignificant', as he personally described it. Parallel to this, the discussion continued on other aspects of his grief and estrangement after losing his brother.

If one exclusively uses thought stopping, experience shows that this can increase the frequency of intrusive thoughts. The method is therefore combined with an active confrontation with the traumatic event in consultations or by setting aside time to think about what happened.

Self-instruction or strong thoughts

Self-instruction or strong thoughts can be used to acquire control over unwanted thoughts and ideas.

Paul experienced his father's life being threatened by a man who had previously been convicted of murder. It took a long time for his parents to understand how much this incident had frightened Paul. When they then contacted a psychologist, Paul was 13 years old and very scared to be home alone, even when he came home from school and it was still light out. He told the psychologist about fantasies where he saw the murderer in the house, heard him in the attic, etc. Even when the fantasies were brought under control with EMDR, he was still extremely afraid at home. Together with the psychologist he wrote a list of statements (self-instructions) on a computer. These were strong thoughts he could tell himself when he was alone at home. They included: 'I was supposed to say certain things to myself. What were they again?

- The sounds I hear are ordinary sounds in the house.
- Nothing is going to happen even though I am alone.
- Nobody breaks in if they hear people rummaging about.
- I know what I can do to control my thoughts.'

In the therapy session, Paul and the psychologist listened to all the 'normal' sounds in a quiet room and Paul was given 'homework' to do the same thing at home, so that he could learn that there are always sounds in a house, sounds that do not mean that someone is in the process of breaking in.

Paul received help from his parents to gradually increase the time periods when he was alone in the house, so that he experienced having control, and he successfully used the strong, calming thoughts that he had personally played a part in developing. His fear diminished, even though he continued to dislike being home alone after dark. The reward he received through his parents' and the psychologist's praise and feedback was also significant to the strengthening of his self-esteem.

In the work with self-instructions, the following are important:

1. Children and adolescents actively participate in developing the instructions – in other words, in finding words they think are 'cool', and that they use their own language.

2. The words are written down, so that both the therapist and the children have their own versions. After children have practised using

the instructions while thinking about the uncomfortable situation in the therapy session, these are adjusted. A playful approach, using a lot of humour, increases motivation.

3. The children learn to congratulate themselves on successful use of self-instructions and the parents must be instructed in how to give praise. Also the children are given proper encouragement by the therapist when in the next session they 'report' what has happened.

An 8-year-old girl who had experienced a fire received instructions in how she could use strong thoughts to manage to stay alone in her room even though she had developed separation anxiety. She was also taught methods for alleviating distressing memories. After the first therapy session she was out in the waiting room when she looked at the therapist and said, 'You don't know what I am thinking about?' The therapist replies, 'No, but I can guess. Is it strong thoughts?' 'Yes,' she replied, 'I am thinking, I can manage to do this.' The girl was clearly highly motivated and ready to start practising.

Children can also keep a 'log' of what happens when the thoughts arrive, what they said to themselves, how it worked, etc. They can bring the log to the session and then it can be used as a point of departure for the consultation and the adjustment of what they should say, the form of the self-instruction, etc.

Through such self-instructions children can alleviate anxiety and tension, counteract fantasies and avoid having irrational thoughts ('It was my fault', 'I should have...') get the upper hand.

Set aside a specific time for anxious thoughts or rumination

Constant rumination and anxiety about what could happen, such as with a loved one, can be redressed by talking about the deeper significance and emotion behind the anxiety, but it has also been shown that setting aside a specific time (15–30 minutes a day) for such 'anxiety' in fact reduces anxiety. Children over the age of ten are old enough to learn such a method whereby they 'catch' their anxiety and postpone it to a limited time period later in the day (see Borkovec, Roemer and Kinyon 1995). Another version of this method that has been extremely useful for both children and adults is to teach them to set aside a fixed time to approach worrying or ruminative thoughts. This method has been developed by Wells and Sembi (2004) and is called the 'postponed worry exercise'. Here is a variation that I use for children:

> Now I have understood from what you have told me that you actually spend a lot of time worrying (or ruminating) every day. You are afraid all the time that something is going to happen to mother or father, you think about it a lot and it is difficult to stop these thoughts. Now I would like you to learn a method for postponing your worries. This is a method that you need to practise a great deal if it is going to be effective, so don't give up if it does not work right away. Here is what I want you to do: the next time you notice that you are worrying, just register the fact that the worrying thought has come. Then tell yourself that you are not going to worry now, but will think about this later. Then you just let the thought gradually disappear on its own. You therefore notice that the thought comes but try not to pay any attention to it. Then I want you to set aside 15 minutes, or more if you need more, late in the afternoon or in the early evening – at the latest, two hours before bedtime – during which you think about what is worrying you. Here you can worry as much as you want, but you don't have to worry if you don't want to.
>
> In 'the worry period' I would like you to think about the worrying thoughts and ask yourself how true you think it is that what you are worrying about will actually happen. You can write down the worrying thought and find five reasons why what you are worrying about will happen and five reasons why it won't happen. Perhaps you can think about what you would have said if a friend of yours told you that he or she was worried about the same thing as you are. Perhaps you will be a bit surprised about how quickly you will manage to move the worrying thought to the worrying period and I bet that you will be even more surprised about how difficult it can be to worry on command, so that on the whole you will worry a great deal less.

Therapy for avoidance reactions

Avoidance reactions are redressed through exposure techniques that allow people who have experienced a trauma to be exposed to the very situation, if possible, that they fear, in large or smaller doses so that the fear is gradually diminished. This method can be quite overwhelming for the person involved and should be used with great care in relation to children.

Yule and Gold (1993) describe the therapy of a 14-year-old boy who experienced seeing his mother trampled to death during the catastrophe in 1989 at Hillsborough football stadium where more than 90 football fans died. He became irritable at school and got mixed up in a lot of trouble. He also became extremely agitated when he heard words that included '...borough', whether it was mentioned on the news or in another way. The psychologist who treated him made a tape containing a hundred such words. The boy learned a relaxation technique and while he was relaxed he listened to the tape many times over. After a few sessions with the therapist the words lost their power; they no longer made him anxious and he could resume a relatively normal life.

Exposure is used in several CBT approaches by having children explain in detail the thoughts and feelings that were produced by what happened. This can sometimes be recorded on a tape or DVD or written down so it can be read back to the one receiving help. The children then listen to this tape or DVD several times every day until the next session. Such methods have been shown to diminish disturbing memories. Much of the work in this area consists of helping the children to handle the many reminders that surround them. Because these reminders often trigger uncomfortable feelings of fear and pain, the children need advice and helpful hints on how they can handle or confront them. Sometimes the children are not aware of what it is that triggers their reactions. They therefore avoid everything that reminds them of the incident they have experienced. By figuring out or identifying these reminders, the children can be helped towards learning a more selective type of training to confront and take in what 'hurts' in small doses.

Avoidance reactions can be understood from a phobic conditioning perspective. Each time children avoid uncomfortable situations, conversations, actions or people that can be the cause of psychological pain, discomfort or grief, they find that the discomfort is diminished – in other words, a negative reinforcement of the avoidance reactions occurs. The use of exposure, both *in vitro* and *in vivo*, can in controlled forms counteract what can otherwise develop into life-limiting avoidance behaviour. Usually the process of confronting the painful material is carried out using relaxation techniques simultaneously, such as through the use of a safe place that children can retreat to using their imagination (see earlier). Thinking about this situation can quickly reduce discomfort.

Exposure with guidance and support appears to be effective for both intrusive thoughts and avoidance behaviour. We have also used a combination of exposure through imagination with coping images to help children. They are asked to envisage what happened by recalling images, thoughts and feelings from the situation. Subsequently they are taught how to allow their imagination to replace what happened with a new scenario where they can reverse what happened. Here they can rescue themselves or others, scare away the things they fear, or magically escape what took place. They can call in all the help they want from the police, parents, magic helpers and others, and hereby see themselves mastering the situation. We create a playful atmosphere through use of the imagination, so that the children are able to believe that this is something they can manage.

As already mentioned, it is common that children wish to avoid conversations, situations and people that remind them of what happened. In the therapeutic work, they must often receive help in managing exposure to such aspects in small doses, so that they gradually dare to confront the situation and process both thoughts and feelings in connection with this. Here the work will involve teaching the children to handle the traumatic reminders. If they have developed phobias, such as about getting into a car again after a car accident, one must apply systematic training methods for them to be able to overcome the phobia. After having first learned a relaxation technique, they will then gradually approach what they are afraid of in their imagination and subsequently continue practising this in relation to the real-life situation. They can be asked to imagine seeing a car, open the door of the car to get in, sitting in the car, etc. When they feel anxious, the relaxation method that they have learned is used to help them approach the situation in their mind again once the anxiety has been reduced, until they no longer feel any anxiety. In the same systematic and gradual way they can approach the actual situation with complete control over the exposure process.

If children show avoidance reactions, have delayed reactions or inhibit their reactions, they can often be afraid of what will happen if they should release control. The fear of losing control is counteracted by:

- taking one thing at a time
- taking one's time
- informing the child that, even if they approach unpleasant feelings or pain, it is seldom the case that these reactions will come all at once or run out of control
- assurances that one will be there to give support and assistance.

Confrontation can also be achieved through exposure to concrete memories such as:

- newspaper clippings, photos, albums, video films, TV programmes
- things with a particular emotional significance
- places with a connection to the event.

> A girl who experienced that one of her parents survived a shipwreck became frightened of all ferries and express boats afterwards. She needed a training programme in which she first practised taking very short ferry trips before she could move on to longer trips.

Therapeutic rituals can also loosen up and help children to express feelings, and thus be a useful means of approaching things that they fear. Through rituals children can directly express feelings they otherwise have difficulties finding words for. Many speak of how, in an indescribable manner, they notice changes after they have lit candles, laid down flowers or something similar at an accident site, a grave, or another location that they associate with their traumatic situation.

Writing

As a result of James Pennebaker's pioneer work, different methods for writing about trauma have been thoroughly investigated and have proven to have a strikingly positive effect on our health (Pennebaker 1997, 2004). By writing down their innermost thoughts and feelings (i.e. putting these into words and putting the words down on paper) the physical and emotional health of people who have experienced traumas improves. In fact, writing after traumas can strengthen the immune system (Pennebaker, Kiecolt-Glaser and Glaser 1988) and accelerate the healing of wounds (Weinman *et al.* 2008). Inhibiting or holding back thoughts, feelings or behaviour is physiologically stressful and creates tension, and can over time result in or compound different health afflictions (Pennebaker 1997, 2004). When traumatic or intensely stressful events are put into words, whether one simply keeps a diary, writes a letter to one's therapist or to others, or expresses what happened orally, this has been shown to have a positive effect.

Unfortunately not much research has been done on the effect of writing for children, but there is no reason to expect that the same results are not valid for adolescents at any rate. Children gradually learn to understand causal relations and time sequences, and it is therefore feasible that children close to puberty will benefit greatly from the expressive writing methods developed for adults. Younger children are still learning how to regulate their emotions. It is therefore less likely that they will turn to writing methods in the same way as adults. In fact, Fivush *et al.* (2007) found that the more 9–13-year-old children wrote about problems and explanations and the negative assessments of others, the lower was their sense of wellbeing. The more children wrote about coping, the lower the level of somatic afflictions. Even though this study did not address writing after traumas, it tells us that we should tread carefully in relation to writing as a method for young children. Children do not appear to be able to create meaningful explanations on their own and, as Fivush *et al.* (2007) have written, the mere act of retelling the story brings it up again and can leave them with a strong sense of fear without an explanatory framework to diminish discomfort. For such writing to be useful for children, it must in all likelihood be done in close interaction with adults who can help them to organize the event along a timeline, put it into a context, and simultaneously explain more about the causal factors. The same holds true for adolescents as for adults: in order for the method to have a therapeutic effect they must describe, in addition to the facts, their own innermost thoughts and feelings.

The therapeutic effect of writing is presumed to stem from the fact that through writing one finds expression for repressed thoughts and feelings. Such repression is considered a main source of the unnecessary, long-term reactions following loss and traumas, and that by writing one structures the inner chaos and creates connections between the past, present and future. At the same time, by writing one takes 'control' of the memory, instead of being controlled by the memory. The writer can also retrieve the memory in small doses according to personal need. By presenting the incident in the form of a story, it can be more easily assimilated in the structures or assumptions the children or adolescents have about the world, themselves and others (or the new assumptions that have developed), and more easily situated in the long-term memory. At the same time, it is clear that one must be willing to approach negative things. Although in the short term it is painful to approach negative things, both psychologically and physically, this is nonetheless associated with a good impact on the physical and psychological health. Together with some of the foremost researchers in the field of writing, we have developed a writing manual for young people who have experienced war and disasters (Yule *et al.* 2005). The hope is that this writing process can contribute to reducing post-traumatic symptoms (see www. childrenandwar.org).

In therapeutic work children can work with creating a 'book' about the event where, in addition to describing the facts of the incident, and the thoughts and feelings they have in connection with it, they can also paste in newspaper clippings, pictures, sketches, maps, etc. that contribute to connecting their thoughts and introducing a wholeness to the event. Here children's drawings, letters to the deceased, perhaps letters they have personally received, obituaries from a funeral, etc. can also be included. Such a 'book' is useful for them to have later on, if they want to remember the way they were thinking when it happened or if they should need factual information that they have saved there. The book serves as documentation of an event that can have significance for a long time, in fact throughout their entire life if they have lost a close family member.

A special way of using writing – namely, writing letters to the deceased – is an exercise we have used in group work with children who have lost a parent or sibling. It has clearly provided an outlet for the expression of unresolved guilt and estrangement, while group members can simultaneously share this with other children who had experienced the same thing. Putting thoughts down on paper can in fact also be meaningful for children who are so young that they cannot yet write. With a point of departure in what in preschool education theory is called 'creative text writing', we have had 6–7-year-olds dictate their thoughts and feelings to us while we wrote them down. They will often go back to their own text and want to hear it read out loud, and we assume that this method helps them to build bridges between thoughts and feelings, in spite of their age.

The use of a diary can provide control over recurring thoughts and frightening feelings. Girls have a greater tendency to keep diaries than do boys, while boys often seem to find it easier to write on a computer or to tell stories orally. Our experience indicates that girls use language as a therapeutic tool more easily. It is not only that they have a larger vocabulary but they also use more words that describe feelings than boys do. The words of boys are more action-oriented, and often they tell a story. When boys write on a computer, about a friend or family member who has passed away, they will often write about situations and events they have experienced with the deceased, while girls to a greater extent describe their thoughts and feelings.

More practically oriented methods, such as the use of diagrams, fill-in-the-blank and other similar activities, appeal to boys more than descriptions of emotional states (see Chapter 4, pp.71–72). The clear gender differences would indicate the importance of a more systematic investigation of gender-adapted means of expression being carried out.

A highly suitable method, both in terms of identifying critical life events that one otherwise would not have known about and for use when entire school classes are affected, is the so-called 'log' method. This method is developed within the educational concept of 'process-oriented writing'. The idea behind this educational practice is that being able to express feelings and communicate about personal experiences and relationships is an important skill. The practical tool in this context is the logbook. This is a journal that belongs to an individual pupil, is used for group assignments, but which also offers the pupil the opportunity to write directly to the teacher and receive a response. This opens up the possibility for a 'written correspondence' about sensitive and difficult themes, such as loss, grief, divorce and other traumatic events.

Confiding in a higher power through prayer and rituals

Traumas, loss and grief tend to prompt religious or existential thoughts and feelings, regardless of the beliefs and practice of the family. It is also a well-known, clinical observation that fatal illness and accidents can 'add depth' to the existence of the person affected, and religious orientation a means of finding a language for such thoughts. We have observed that to a pronounced extent this applies to children, almost irrespective of the extent of the parents' religious commitment. From studies done on adults and experiences with children, it is clear that to pray or speak with God is a special way of channelling one's innermost thoughts and feelings. It will always be up to the individual family to personally create the frameworks for religious practice in connection with loss, grief and traumas, but, from the perspective of therapeutic motivation, it is well worth becoming informed of these opportunities for 'self-help'. Children can confide all their anxiety and painful memories to God (or Allah) in a detailed and descriptive fashion. Some children draw what has happened to them and put it beside their bed so that God can see what really happened to them and subsequently better understand their prayers. Confiding feelings and thoughts through prayer can also be done in groups by praying 'out loud'. It has been shown how helpless parents in war-stricken areas can more easily accept and hear their children's desperation when this is directed towards 'The Almighty'. Parents must understand that this can be painful and that children can begin to cry. In war situations we have experiences indicating that this reduces nightmares, releases tension, and helps children to handle difficult situations. El-Helou and Johnson (1994) have shown that the majority of Palestinian teenagers used religious rituals to manage their fear (they prayed to Allah and read the Koran) in connection with the *intifada* (uprising) at the end of the 1980s and the beginning of the 1990s.

Therapy for physiological hyperarousal

The reaction of increased arousal appears to diminish when the occurrence of the traumatic memories and avoidance reactions is reduced. Simultaneously, one can attempt to directly reduce hyperarousal by using relaxation techniques, listening to music, imagining comfortable situations from earlier in life or by creating tranquil images through use of the imagination. Physical activity, singing, dance and play also have the same effect, as does the opportunity to express oneself through drawing, painting, etc.

Relaxation methods

Physiological arousal is in part connected with the intrusive memories, so work on gaining control of the memories often has a positive impact. A combination of teaching a child relaxation methods and self-instruction to limit anxiety-producing thoughts often has a good effect. Most relaxation methods involve first tightening or tensing a muscle, maintaining the tension and then releasing it and noticing the difference. While a child over the age of eight can do this with many individual muscles, younger children must work with larger muscle groups. In addition, young children need more encouragement and guidance. Progressive muscle relaxation is described in Smith *et al.* (1999). Relaxing images can also be used, such as having children imagine that they are lying on the beach or sitting in front of a fireplace. Children as young as 7–8 years of age are capable of producing and manipulating such images. The safe place method described previously is another such method.

When children are to learn relaxation or imagery methods, it is a good idea to first test their ability to concentrate and follow instructions. A simple means of doing this is by asking them to sit still, and then observe their ability to maintain eye contact and to imitate – 'Can you do what I am doing?' (Raise your hand over your head, knock lightly on the table, knock lightly on your chest) – and their ability to follow simple instructions ('stand up', 'sit down', 'come here', etc.).

Breathing methods

Breathing methods can also be used. With the deep breathing method, also called rectangular breathing, children are asked to breath in deeply (through the nose if they can manage this), hold their breath and then slowly exhale through their mouth. While they are exhaling they are to try and relax the entire body, from head to toe. While exhaling they can also say 'relax'. They can be given an assignment to practise this at home, preferably with the aid of the instructions on a tape or CD that they can take home with them. Here are the instructions:

> Now I would like you to learn a special method for breathing that will help you to calm down quickly if you start to feel nervous or afraid. You can also use the method for calming down if you get so angry that you want to hit someone or say something that you will regret later. First I will show you what you do before you try it for yourself. I want you to breathe in deeply through your nose with your mouth closed, like this (this is then demonstrated by inhaling powerfully through the nose so that the child can hear it). You can count calmly to five while you inhale. Then you hold your breath for a few seconds, while you count slowly to five again, and then you breath out, calmly, through your mouth, like this (here again, show the child how to do this). Then you wait a few seconds without breathing in, you can count to five again if you like and then do everything all over again (demonstrate everything one more time). Note that I inhale deep down into

my stomach. You should breathe like this four or five times and you will then notice that you become calmer. Now it's your turn. Ready? Sometimes it is easier to do this if you close your eyes, but if you don't want to it's okay.

One then guides children through the method, making sure that they inhale deeply through the nose, hold their breath for a few seconds before exhaling and then wait a few seconds before breathing in again. Explain to them that, just like with sports, it is necessary to practise such methods a few times before one gets good at it, and that if one trains it is possible to learn to take control of one's body in this way. To start with it can be difficult to keep one's thoughts concentrated on one's breathing but it is a matter of practice. If other thoughts arise, just concentrate on the breathing again.

The reduction of tension takes place through calm, deep and regular diaphragmatic respiration. There is a great deal of evidence indicating that focusing on breathing also diminishes negative self-instruction by keeping the attention focused elsewhere.

Help for insomnia and nightmares

Insomnia is found among the symptoms of hyperarousal and is among the most common post-traumatic problems. It occurs most frequently in the initial days and weeks after an event, often as a consequence of disturbing memories and thoughts that surface after the child has gone to bed. Before choosing a remedy, one must first determine whether the child is having problems falling asleep or is waking up after having first fallen asleep. If it is a matter of problems with falling asleep, the child can learn relaxation techniques, fixed bedtimes must be adhered to and the parents or other caregivers can read or sing to the child, etc. Music has proven useful for many problems of this nature.

> An adolescent who lost his father had problems falling asleep because his body was so agitated. It was recommended that he listen to music. In the next session he spoke of how this first helped him when he turned the volume down so far that he had to strain to hear the lyrics.

For nightmares, editing the nightmares while awake and the subsequent rehearsal of the new version has been proven helpful for adults. So-called 'imagery rescripting', which involves creating a new, more neutral dream by changing elements from the nightmare, which are then rehearsed while awake, contributes to a reduction in the frequency of nightmares (Krakow and Zadra 2006). There are a number of different ways to proceed in creating changes in a nightmare. Here I have built upon a method that has been shown to reduce the frequency of nightmares for adults (Kellner *et al* 1992; Krakow *et al.* 1993). Originally clients were asked to describe in detail what happened during the nightmare, then to write this down with the same amount of detail. In 2006, Krakow and Zadra launched a simpler, but reportedly just as effective, version. Here the adult version called Imagery Rehearsal Technique has been simplified and adapted for children. First, the child receives a general explanation about sleep and nightmares:

> Many children have nightmares and wake up because of awful dreams, sometimes drenched in sweat and frightened. Although what happened in the nightmare never happens in real life, you can be very frightened and reluctant to fall asleep and experience it again. If you go to bed late so you can avoid having a nightmare, you will not get enough sleep and then you will be tired in the daytime and can become easily irritated and angry. It is therefore important to practise a method that will help you to have fewer nightmares. The method you will learn is one you will have to practise in order for it to work and it may not work right away.
>
> Now I am going to explain to you what to do. Do you know what a film director is? No? A film director is the boss when films are made. Now you are going to be a film director and make a film that instead of being shown in the cinema can appear in your head at night-time. First you are going to create and then show this film many times in your mind while you are awake, so that it is this film that comes at night. You can perhaps practise at making a good dream – close your eyes and imagine something nice happening to you. Maybe you are at the movies and watching a good film; you sit in the cinema and look at the screen and there you can show, for example, a cartoon. Make it a little bit funny. Practise it a few times and imagine that you are a director who can decide what is going to be on the screen. If you don't succeed in

making your own film, you can watch a little from a film you have seen at the cinema, on TV or a DVD.

Now you are ready for a larger director's task — now you are going to change a nightmare. If you have had several bad dreams, you can practise on one that is not so scary first, before you take on the worst one. You are going to create a new dream and this new dream is going to have a lot of the same elements as the one that was a bad dream – for instance, it might start in the same way. But even though it has the same elements, you are going to change it exactly the way you want, maybe make up a new ending, include somebody who makes you feel safe, a magic helper like Superman, or in another way change the dream or nightmare up in your head. When you have done this, you are going to practise this new version, so that it is 'coded' in your mind. In this way, this new version will be chosen at night.

Once you have practised this bad dream a little bit, you will be ready to take on the worst nightmare. Here you are going to do exactly the same thing. Take it into the editing room and then you start the nightmare in any way you want. Perhaps you will want to put in a happy ending, change something in the middle, or include somebody you love and feel safe with. When you have this new version ready, I want you to write it down in detail, so you will remember it. Then you will start to practise the new version. It is best if you do this a little early in the evening. You imagine the new dream and go through it again and again, until you know it by heart, backwards and forwards. Right before you fall asleep you are going to say to yourself: 'The parts of my brain that control my dreams are now going to make sure that the 'new' dream is played at the cinema.' In this way you are instructing your brain. This is exactly what athletes do before they are going to jump high or far on a ski jump, or make an important penalty kick.

In addition to the editing work the child can do something about nightmares through a symbolic action, such as by crumpling up the piece of paper with the nightmare written on it, tearing it up, or burning it. Some children will probably know what a 'dream catcher' is. If they do not know, it can be explained to them, either by finding a picture on the internet or by acquiring one to have in their bedroom. Native Americans hang a dream catcher over their bed because it allows the good dreams to slip through and catches the bad dreams before they can reach the person sleeping. Such dream catchers can be a supplementary motivational factor for the child.

A final method that should be mentioned here is that called 'lucid dreaming' (Spoormaker, Schredl and van den Bout 2006). It has been shown that it is possible to instruct the brain so that it gives and takes messages while one is sleeping. The mental instruction that children should give themselves before sleeping is that, if the nightmare should come back, they will be able to hear themselves saying that it is only a dream. They can also retrieve the nightmare while they are awake while they say to themselves that it is only a bad dream. They can also change the dream as described earlier.

From our own practice with large groups of children in regions at war, we have received feedback from clergymen and imams that reciting evening prayers or verses from the Koran have helped children to calm down and fall asleep more quickly after awakening and nightmares. When the child has woken up screaming after a trauma-related nightmare, imagery methods have helped them to fall asleep more quickly. For example, they could imagine that they packed their dreams up and put them on the back of a horse, which then ran away, or a bird picked up the dream in its beak.

Physical contact

Parents who experience traumatic events often become so preoccupied with the event and their own thoughts and reactions that for a period they demonstrate a reduced parenting capacity, both with regard to paying attention to their children and physical contact. It has been proven that children experience a clear reduction in physical contact from their parents when a family member is involved in a traumatic event (Field *et al.* 1996a). We know as well that physical contact, touch (stroking or holding), can have an extremely calming effect after a traumatic situation. It reduces tension and appears to have an important physiological healing effect. Field and co-workers (1996b) followed up on these findings and carried out an experiment after hurricane Andrew in the USA. Sixty children received massage therapy (massage students gave the massages) for half an hour daily for eight days. Compared with a control group that received a corresponding amount of attention, the children who received the massage were less anxious, less depressed and more relaxed in the period afterwards. The massage group also showed clearly fewer PTSD symptoms than the control group. Since there are taboos connected with touch due to the increased intimacy involved, physical contact used in therapy should be planned and carefully explained. The mother or father should also be present.

One can also, as Field *et al.* (1996a) propose, have teachers instruct pupils to give one another massages. In addition, parents can be encouraged to have more physical contact with their traumatized children, such as by stroking, patting and holding them, to take advantage of the beneficial healing effect that such physical contact produces.

Children who have experienced sexual abuse or physical maltreatment, or who have suffered serious illness or extensive physical injuries after accidents, can benefit greatly from different methods that create positive experiences related to the body. Some will need to relearn and practise the ability to acknowledge and experience positive physical experiences, and dare to have contact again with their own body. This can be brought about through physical activity and exercise such as swimming, team sports, ballet or other kinds of movement. Different types of breathing exercises are suitable for learning gradually to take in bodily experiences, in combination with a focus on the different sensory channels (e.g. 'Notice what your body is in contact with, the chair you are sitting on, the armrest your hands are resting on, the floor that your foot soles are in contact with. Tell me what you feel. How does it feel to touch the chair?'). Traumatized children may also need to be taught about the body, such as about why the heart beats faster and harder in certain situations, why the mouth gets dry, how pain impulses are sent to the brain, etc. Misconceptions can be cleared up and things they are anxious about can become less threatening by way of concrete information about how the body functions.

Pharmacological treatment

Very few studies have been carried out on the use of psychopharmacology for traumatized children. Cohen *et al.* (2007) performed a randomized controlled study of Sertraline (Zoloft, selective serotonin reuptake inhibitor [SSRI]) used in addition to CBT, compared with CBT alone, and found minimal support for added benefits from this. In certain situations pharmacological treatment can, however, be required, but only if it is not possible to influence the post-traumatic problems in any other way. Pharmacological treatment can be required if children are simultaneously struggling with other problems such as depression or phobias. Also, if a child is only able to take part in a therapeutic interaction to a limited extent and the problems are disabling for the child, such treatment can be used. Whether it is expedient or justifiable to use pharmacological treatment for post-traumatic problems in children, however, is far more controversial than is the case with adults. Without better studies documenting good effects and the absence of serious side effects, it is recommended to exercise extreme caution in prescribing medication, particularly because there are good psychological methods that reduce post-traumatic symptoms.

Cognitive restructuring

Ehlers, Mayou and Bryant (2003) have shown that children's negative assessment of their own reactions and maladaptive thought strategies, such as rumination, thought suppression and confusing thoughts about what happened, are of great significance to trauma reactions over time. Cognitive methods are used to change the way children think about what happened or their own reactions. Often children have become locked into certain thought patterns that have not been corrected after the traumatic event, such as the idea that there is a good chance of the same type of thing happening again. By helping children to view what happened — or what they thought or did when it happened — in another way, we can build up a constructive interpretation or reorganization of the thoughts. This helps children to construct a new meaning or a new story about what they experienced, a story where they need not be as helpless as they perhaps believe that they were.

It is possible to allow children to tell their story several times, while they have their eyes closed (if that is okay with them) and re-experience what took place. Here they are asked to recount what took place as if it were happening now and in the first person. The therapist can help the story along by asking questions such as 'What happened then?' 'What do you see now?' 'What are you thinking?'. At 'hot spots' in the story

– in other words, the most difficult parts – one can also ask children to freeze the image or situation, or stop it as if it were a video, and then have them describe what they see, hear, think and feel, etc. By 'halting' the story in this way, one can develop it in its entirety, while at the same time desensitization occurs. An assessment of how strong the discomfort is along the way offers the possibility to follow the development. By using a scale from 0 to 10, where 10 means maximum distress (or fear) and 0 means no distress (or fear), it is possible to follow the fluctuations in discomfort or feelings. This is called establishing a SUD-level (SUD = Subjective Unit of Distress or Disturbance).

When the situation is reviewed, with an emphasis on 'hot spots', it is important to identify the fearful thoughts that have become imprinted with great intensity, and where there has been little updating of the experience the children had in the situation – for example, if they were sure that mother was going to die and then this did not happen, but they continue to live as if this could happen at any moment. Even though this was the threat appraisal at the time, what they feared would happen did not, and they need to take in the corrected experience. One can then ask about what they know now that they could not have known when it happened, or they can be asked how mother survived.

Table 9.1 refers to a girl who witnessed her mother being physically abused by a live-in partner. It shows her assessment of the situation with subsequent thoughts and feelings. The first four columns represent how she thought and felt about this before the review of this 'hot spot', while the two last columns represent the change in the 'cognitive schema' after she has absorbed the new information. Intake of new information took place through a review of the story during which she was asked challenging questions, and to subsequently relive what had happened, while she was simultaneously asked to take in new information.

Table 9.1 Changing views of a traumatic event

Situation	Witness mummy being dragged out of the room by her hair.
Thoughts when it happened	He is going to kill mummy.
Feeling	Terrified.
Persistent thought, preparedness and emotion	It is going to happen again. Expecting the worst. Continues to feel afraid.
New information	It happened only on this one occasion. Mummy has moved out.
Feeling	Relief.

In this girl's head the thought that it will certainly happen again had become imprinted and prevailed. Even though she felt that the situation continued to be more dangerous than previously, in reality it was not. By having children tell the story of what happened as if it were happening in the present, while at the same time they relate out loud what happened and what they think is going to happen, it is possible to acquire insight into decisions and thoughts that have become stuck. Questions such as 'What do you know now?' 'How did you survive?' 'What did you do to master the situation?' expand the perspective and can bring in new information as with the girl in the example, who now knows that she is safe. By yet again reviewing what happened, during which the children state out loud what they thought (hot cognitions) followed by them then including the new information in the traumatic memory, a cognitive restructuring can be achieved. A condition here is that the traumatic memory must be 'online' in order for the corrective information and interpretation to be integrated. This procedure follows that described by Smith *et al.* (2007). The method described here is very suitable, too, for use in combination with writing assignments; it also stimulates perspective and reflection.

Help for 'existential' problems and feelings of guilt

While the three groups of symptoms subsumed under post-traumatic stress syndrome can be influenced through direct methods, therapeutic sessions with traumatized children can also involve helping them to build up a new sense of security in their existence. They need to establish a new sense of faith that their world from here on in can be stable and safe, that they can influence their own life situation and that other people do not want to harm them, etc. The work of repairing or changing old assumptions about the world or developing new assumptions cannot be accomplished through quick and easy techniques. In this work the therapist must first try to understand the world as seen by the children and dare to accompany them in the process of addressing the facts, misunderstandings, assumptions, fantasies and expectations that they have.

Throughout childhood the cognitive schemas or assumptions about the world (such as safe/unsafe), what others are like (such as nice/bad) and what one is like personally (such as invulnerable/vulnerable) are developed. A crisis often has the effect of disturbing this structure and development. Established assumptions break down or are subjected to necessary and extensive revisions. The experience of vulnerability and negative expectations about future events and loss, such as 'mummy can also die', 'something else terrible is surely going to happen', is believed to lead to anxiety and depression (Mireault and Bond 1992). Denes-Raj and Ehrichman (1991) have shown that adults who experience that one of their parents died when they were young, personally expect to have a shorter life span than those whose parents are both still alive. Concrete information about why we think the way we do, conversation about and assurances that can reduce such negative, destructive expectations and the stimulation of optimism about the future through adequate facts and self-instruction can reduce such vulnerability.

Some children struggle with guilt and shame about their own thoughts or actions. A review of the crisis event or loss with a focus on clarification of the facts and any misunderstandings, accompanied by assurances about things that they are not responsible for, can help. The same holds true for the use of symbolic forgiveness and therapeutic rituals. It is important that one does not just focus on the negative elements that children are criticizing themselves about, but also that one continues to cultivate the awareness of what they managed to do or the constructive aspects found in what they did not do. Many children overlook the fact that they may have made important and correct choices in dramatic situations. If they did not dare to do something, the situation can be discussed so that they understand that this was how the brain evaluated this in the midst of the dangerous situation, and that it probably was more correct than the way they are thinking about this after the event. To reverse the feeling of helplessness, one can develop a 'preparedness plan' for children in which one plans what they can do if they should find themselves in a similar type of situation again.

The fact that they neglected to do something can have contributed to saving their life and their actions can be a reflection of constructive thinking in a situation that was extremely chaotic for them. Children who criticize themselves often make the mistake in their thinking that they bring the knowledge that they only acquired after the event into the time when the event started or took place, even though they did not have this knowledge at the time. Simultaneously, it is important to emphasize that, after the event, we have a mechanism that attempts to collect information for better future coping. In order to expand our experience base every stone is turned and we reflect on what we should have done or thought. While this also involves a self-critical process in that we dwell on choices we missed, we can reinforce a positive focus by consciously carrying out a review of what we did well, which choices were made in order to survive, or other constructive thoughts and actions we managed to have or carry out in the situation. However, in order to take part in a discussion about this, the age of a child must be close to adolescence.

Many children will overlook how many important and correct choices they did make on the basis of life experiences that the brain utilized without there being any time to notice this. In a very short period of time our brain will use accumulated experience to produce a solution that we follow. There is often no time to think out what one shall do, so the brain's handling of this information often takes place without our being aware of it. This also means that we act in the best possible manner, even though we may question our actions afterwards. Together with the therapist, children can create a new review of the positive or constructive thoughts they had and the actions they carried out, and perhaps acquire another view of their actions. If they did not dare to do anything at all, the therapist can emphasize the possibility that any action could have made the situation even more dangerous. In particular, an 'analysis' of what the children thought in the situation itself – and afterwards – can create the basis for a new way of thinking about what took place. The fact that we think about what we should have done afterwards does not mean that it would always have been smart to do these things; also we can forget afterwards how frightened we were and that our fear gave us a clear message that it was dangerous to try to do something. Our feelings help us sometimes to remain calm in a situation where doing something could have made the situation even more dangerous.

The following questions can be used in the conversation about self-reproach and guilt with a child:

- How easy was it for you to influence what happened?

- If you are afterwards criticizing yourself for something, how did you experience this in the middle of the situation?

- What did you have time to think about then?

- What was the reason that you did what you did?

- Did you think that you should have done or said some of the things that you are so angry with yourself about now when you were in the middle of the situation?

- How could you know what was going to happen? Are you psychic?

- How much time did you have to decide what you should do?

- Can you describe three things that you thought or said that were good?

- What would you have thought if somebody else had done what you did? Would you have criticized him or her for this?

- Can you explain to me in detail why you believe it is your fault?

- What speaks for that?

- What speaks against it?

- What other explanations are there?

- If it had been someone other than you who was there when it happened, what do you think that person would have done?

Such questions, which are also called Socratic questions, can break negative thought cycles. They are best suited for older children. Younger children need adult support in reaching an understanding that there was nothing that they could have done.

Some people believe that, because a feeling is very strong, it must be true. Of course this is not the case. The use of simple examples can make this understandable for children, such as if one asks whether they have ever argued with a friend about something and been completely certain that they were right and then it turned out that they were wrong? Most have had such an experience and it can therefore be used as an example of the fact that even though they were convinced that they were right, the conviction was not proof of this being the case. This is how it works with guilt as well.

If children are criticizing themselves for something they initially thought or learned about afterwards, they can be asked if they know what it means to be psychic. If they do, they can be told that it would only be possible to know what was going to happen if they were psychic. It is also possible to challenge such 'psychic ability' through so-called behavioural experiments. 'Because you think that you could have known what was going to happen, perhaps you can guess which card I will pull out of this deck of cards? Shall we have a go?' A few repetitions of this will probably make the children fully aware of the fact that they cannot know about things that will happen in advance.

The psycho-educational information that upholds adult responsibility – in other words, that it is adults who are to protect children from traumatic events and that this is not the child's responsibility – is of course important. Meet children halfway and confirm that it is normal to feel guilt or blame oneself, even though they have no reason to do so. Repeat this. Guilt is often about a lack of perspective about one's own role and our job as therapists is to create a more flexible understanding of the situation. The children must be helped to understand that it is adults who are responsible for children not being subjected to traumatic situations and that they cannot blame themselves for things that have happened.

Allocation of responsibility is another important procedure in connection with guilt. This can be done in different ways. One way is to take a concrete incident that children feel guilty about and ask them how much guilt they felt. Younger children can demonstrate how much guilt they feel by using their arms, as when one demonstrates the size of a fish that can be very large or small, while older children can give percentages. Then one can ask how much guilt mother, father, a sibling, grandparent and other relevant individuals have. One can also ask how much guilt other adults, who could have stopped the traumatic event from happening, have. By introducing others into the situation, children can see that they are not alone in terms of responsibility. If they are old enough to understand percentages, they will after such a session hopefully have arrived at a more even distribution of guilt.

Children who are actually responsible for a traumatic event

It happens that children feel a sense of guilt about a traumatic event that is based on actual responsibility, if they, for example, were playing with matches and caused a fire, or brought a sibling out onto ice that was not safe, etc. The objective then is not to absolve the children of all responsibility, but that they nonetheless manage to live with their actions without this being destructive for them. It can be helpful to:

- make it clear that everyone can make mistakes

- emphasize that there is a difference between something that is planned and done on purpose and something that just happens (unforeseen mishap or accident)

- distribute the guilt among several people – for example, that the parents should have taken better care, adults are responsible in such situations, the person who was affected should have been more careful, etc.

- allow the child to take responsibility, admit mistakes, ask for forgiveness from the person or persons who were affected

- use rituals, letters or drawings to symbolically show regret and to apologize or ask for forgiveness (e.g. a child has caused a fatal accident)

If children are struggling with imagined guilt, it can help to:

- refrain from starting by telling children 'you mustn't think like that', or 'you know that it wasn't your fault', (even if this is to be communicated, it can shut down a conversation about the thoughts and feelings that are disturbing the children if this is said too early)

- think strong thoughts and use thought-stopping procedures

- express thoughts and feelings through letters, a diary, reading into a tape recorder, or talking with adults about them

- gradually redefine the guilt, assign it to the place where it more justifiably belongs, or ask others to help out in bearing it

- to explain to children in a simple fashion that feelings of guilt are important, because they force us to think through our actions so that we can learn from our mistakes. At the same time, such thoughts become even more unfair when we have not done anything wrong

- make sure that children know that it was not their fault, even if the conversation does not start out with one saying this (acquire the greatest amount of factual information possible that can counteract these thoughts in the children).

For children who have experienced repetitive traumas, this requires of course a more long-term therapeutic programme, because they must often learn to handle feelings virtually from the ground up. This is a gradual process, during which they must first learn to identify, distinguish between and feel different emotions. They must also practise handling or moderating the intensity of different types of feelings, feelings that before may have been heavily suppressed or that only meant danger and discomfort.

It can be even more difficult to build up trust in other people because the violations of trust have been so profound and so repeated that the child has learned that adults are not to be trusted. James (1994) has described different methods that are helpful in the context of this difficult task.

This gradual integration of the event into children's emotional life takes time. It occurs with assistance from the therapist but just as much in interaction with the friends and adults that the children have around them on a daily basis. This does not only take time, but it is also the case that such processing can continue or be resumed in different periods throughout childhood. This means that the therapist should be available over time, so that the door is open for the children to return if new difficulties should arise or, even more feasibly, at such time when material must be processed in light of the children's increased maturity, understanding or experience. Through the therapeutic contact the children and parents must also be prepared for the future and for problems that can arise. Such preparations must be given with caution so as not to frighten the children or parents, but are at the same time necessary in order for the children to be able to meet possible difficulties with constructive coping.

Therapy for young children

Many of the methods described here are best suited for children who have reached school age. Some can be used at late preschool age, but for most preschool-age children a lot of work is done with the connection or relationship between parents and children. Psychologist Alicia F. Lieberman and her colleagues have developed two treatment manuals, one for young children who have witnessed violence (Lieberman and Van Horn 2005) and one for those who at this age lose parents (Lieberman *et al.* 2003). Such child–parent psychotherapy entails joint meetings between the child and parents that are structured around the child's free play and interaction with the parents. Playthings are used that have relevance to the type of trauma situation that the child has experienced, such as an ambulance, 'doctor's bag' and figures representing health personnel and the police. Separate consultations with the parents are held as needed during the therapeutic process. To increase parents' understanding and promote good parenting, the therapist explains the child's behaviour and what it means in a developmental framework, or the meaning it has in relation to the trauma that the child has experienced.

The mode of treatment is directed towards inappropriate behaviour in the child and parenting styles that are punitive or not adapted to the child's developmental level, and interactive patterns that reflect distrust or misunderstandings. Good interactive patterns are supported through a series of different methods such as play, conversation, physical activity, counselling about development, role-play, emphasizing traumatic reminders, interpretations, crisis interventions and concrete assistance with common life problems, etc. A detailed description of the background and treatment is found in Lieberman and Van Horn (2008) and the results from use of the method are positive (Lieberman, van Horn and Ippen 2005).

The methods of Lieberman and her group (Lieberman and van Horn 2008) are based on classic psychotherapy with children. Direct approaches that use EMDR can sometimes have rapid effects on young children, particularly following individual traumas. While the parents are present, one can first bring the trauma up in the child's consciousness before giving bilateral stimulation while the child is focused on what has happened. A short case history illustrates this:

> Stephen, a five-year-old boy, had been attacked by a dog
> that bit him so badly that he had to go to the emergency

room to have stitches. Both he and his seven-year-old brother were attacked. Their father witnessed what happened from a distance and managed to chase the dog away when he reached them, but the damage was already done. Little brother first observed big brother receiving bilateral stimulation while he and father told of what had occurred during the attack. He was then asked about the 'hot-spots' (what were the worst parts) before these were targeted for repeated bilateral stimulation. Then it was little brother's turn. While father related in detail what happened and little brother added small details, he was given bilateral stimulation in the form of so-called tapping. What tapping implies is that the therapist uses the fingertips to alternately touch the client's right and left palm. Stephen was then asked to say what the worst thing was that had happened and indicate with his hands just how bad it was (as when one demonstrates the size of a fish that can be very large or small — a kind of SUD for preschool children). The 'hot-spot' moment was when he looked into the jaws of the dog before it bit him the first time. This revelation was cause for more tapping. Through this procedure his phobic fear of dogs was greatly reduced. The parents and children learned a system through which dogs could be gradually approached, a system to be practised as homework until the next session.

In the work with young children, the counselling of parents on how they can help the children has a central role. Parents must understand children's avoidance of situations so that they can help them find a gradual approach to the traumatic reminders that trigger the fearful reactions in them. This is of course extremely complicated if the children experience or have experienced violence in the family, where the assailant is a part of their daily life. As a rule, it is not advisable to diminish children's fear in relation to individuals who can again put them in danger. Before children can be helped, secure frames must be established around them. Gaensbauer has in a number of articles illustrated in an excellent manner how post-traumatic problems are exhibited in preschool children and how one can help through therapy (Gaensbauer 1994, 2000; Gaensbauer *et al.* 1995).

Therapy after cumulative traumas

The many methods described previously here can also be used in connection with work with children who have experienced living under extreme life conditions over a long period of time, such as is the case of domestic violence. Because their security in existence, trust in others and a series of other developmental areas may have been seriously affected by these life conditions, the therapy can require far more than the use of more trauma-specific methods. Before therapeutic work can be undertaken, an appraisal of the child's safety and home situation must be carried out. Work with collaborating bodies to secure better caregiving conditions for the child may have to be implemented before painful experiences can be approached at a pace that the child can tolerate.

For many children who have lived with cumulative trauma, their trust in others and ability to form relationships may have been damaged. A therapeutic relationship must be built up. Trust and confidence are developed starting in the first meeting with the children. This takes place through an interaction in which both verbal and non-verbal communication give the children or young people an image of what we as therapists are like as people, of our expertise, our humanity and our understanding. Much of the impression formation occurs at an early stage, even spontaneously. In the first meeting the children receive a confirmation or validation of their assumptions about the person and the 'system' they are encountering.

Those who have been victims of violence are particularly sensitive in relation to the initial contact. An observant adult who says little can be experienced in an extremely negative manner. Because many children who have been exposed to violence have a disorganized attachment where adults have not been trustworthy, the therapist's presence, predictability and ability to be there constantly and over time is an important aspect of the therapy. Due to such children's sensitivity, a therapist who says little will cause them to feel observed and evaluated and they will easily feel ill at ease. If they are also asked to fill out a questionnaire or take part in a structured interview, before the relationship has been soundly established, this can serve to emphasize an instrumental relationship. The result can be that the children will not come back for another session.

Children who live with a lot of violence in the family often have had their ability to absorb, evaluate and express feelings, use feelings actively for cognitive processing and regulate their own intense feelings (emotion regulation) inhibited (Diamond and Aspinwall 2003; Steele,

Steele and Croft 2008). Children who have been maltreated have problems differentiating between plausible and non-plausible reasons for being angry or sad (Perlman, Kalish and Pollak 2008). Although they can identify negative feelings, they have difficulties predicting and explaining them. Because many of the children who have been exposed to violence have had the development of their emotional regulation undermined or have 'survived' by pushing away or diminishing their feelings, the therapeutic work will include work in recognizing feelings. There are a number of different procedures for improving their capacity in this area. By speaking about everyday feelings with one another in therapy, the therapist can gain an understanding of the children's verbal and emotional ability with respect to recognizing with precision and expressing a range of emotions, while the children at an early stage can get to know the therapist and thereby come to understand that the therapist too has both bad and good feelings and is open to sharing these with them. Here the therapist becomes a role model for the children while the relationship-building is taking place.

If children have experienced living with long-term traumatization within or outside the home, the help will have to include parents or caregivers. In a study of children who had been sexually abused, the children were divided up in treatment with trauma-focused CBT with different degrees of parental involvement: therapy for children only, therapy for parents only, therapy with both parents and children, and a control group that received the type of treatment that was usual in the location where the study was done (Deblinger, Lippman and Steer 1996). The study showed that, when parents received treatment, it resulted in a significant improvement in the children's depressive and acting-out symptoms, even when the children did not take part in the therapy. Also the parent group treated showed a significant improvement in appropriate parenting skills. Another study, also of children who had been sexually abused, showed that by including a parental component the children exhibited less anxiety three months after the treatment stopped (King et al. 2000). Cohen and Mannarino (1996b) indirectly showed the significance of the parents by demonstrating that the parents' emotional reactions were a strong predictor of the children's treatment response immediately after treatment. This indicates that we have a greater chance of succeeding in helping children with such repetitive traumas if we simultaneously help their parents. At the same time, as mentioned earlier, the focus on the parents does not always have the added effect (Stallard 2006).

Often the help for the child and parent takes place in tandem. Some of the same themes are addressed in relation to both generations. It is also the case that many of the methods described earlier for use with children can also be used for parents.

In families where children live at great risk of psychological or physical violence, preventive activities are extremely important. Here programmes that emphasize interactive processes have proven effective. By increasing the parents' understanding of the child's emotions, behaviour and signals, by improving their response to the child's emotional needs, and by creating a predictable, coherent and warm atmosphere around the child, future problems can be prevented (Tarabulsy *et al.* 2008). By developing a relationship of trust with the parents, through feedback in the form of video recordings of interaction sequences between the parents and their children, combined with home visits, it has been possible to create good preventive programmes.

References

Aduriz, M.E., Bluthgen, C. and Knopfler, C. (2009) 'Helping child flood victims using group EMDR intervention in Argentina: treatment outcome and gender differences.' *International Journal of Stress Management 16*, 138–153.

Ahmad, A., Larsson, B. and Sundelin-Wahlsten, V. (2007) 'EMDR treatment for children with PTSD: results of a randomized controlled trial.' *Nordic Journal of Psychiatry 61*, 349–354.

Aubert-Khalfa, S., Roques, J. and Blin, O. (2008) 'Evidence of a decrease in heart rate skin conductance responses in PTSD patients after a single EMDR session.' *Journal of EMDR Practice and Research 2*, 51–56.

Borkovec, T.D., Roemer, L. and Kinyon, J. (1995) 'Disclosure and Worry: Opposite Sides of the Emotional Processing Coin.' In J.W. Pennebaker (ed.) *Emotion, Disclosure and Health.* Washington: American Psychological Association.

Cautela, J.R. and Wisocki, P.A. (1977) 'The thought stopping procedure: description, application, and learning theory interpretations.' *Psychological Record 2*, 225–264.

Chemtob, C.M., Nakashima, J. and Carlson, J.G. (2002) 'Brief treatment for elementary school children with disaster-related posttraumatic stress disorder: a field study.' *Journal of Clinical Psychology 58*, 99–112.

Chemtob, C.M., Nakashima, J. and Hamada, R.S. (2002) 'Psychosocial intervention for postdistaster trauma symptoms in elementary school children. A controlled community field study.' *Archives of Pediatric and Adolescent Medicine 156*, 211–216.

Cohen, J.A. and Mannarino, A.P. (1996a) 'A treatment outcome study for sexually abused preschooler children: initial findings.' *Journal of the American Academy of Child and Adolescent Psychiatry 35*, 42–50.

Cohen, J.A. and Mannarino, A.P. (1996b) 'Factors that mediate treatment outcome of sexually abused preschool children.' *Journal of the American Academy of Child and Adolescent Psychiatry 35*, 1402–1410.

Cohen, J.A., Deblinger, E., Mannarino, A.P. and Steer, R.A. (2004) 'A multisite, randomized controlled trial for children with sexual abuse-related symptoms.' *Journal of the American Academy of Child and Adolescent Psychiatry 43*, 393–402.

Cohen, J.A., Mannarino, A.P., Perel, J.M. and Staron, V. (2007) 'A pilot randomized controlled trial of combined trauma-focused CBT and sertraline for childhood PTSD symptoms.' *Journal of the American Academy of Child and Adolescent Psychiatry 46*, 811–819.

Deblinger, E., Lippman, J. and Steer, R.A. (1996) 'Sexually abused children suffering posttraumatic stress symptoms: initial treatment outcome findings.' *Child Maltreatment 1*, 310–321.

Deblinger, E., Steer, R.A. and Lippman, J. (1999) 'Two-year follow-up study of cognitive behavioral therapy for sexually abused children suffering posttraumatic stress symptoms.' *Child Abuse and Neglect 23*, 1371–1378.

Denes-Raj, V. and Ehrichman, H. (1991) 'Effects of premature parental death on subjective life expectancy, death anxiety, and health behavior.' *Omega 23*, 309–321.

de Roos, C., Greenwald, R., de Jongh, A. and Noorthoorn, E.O. (2004) 'EMDR versus CBT.' Poster presented at 20th Annual Meeting of the International Society for Traumatic Stress Studies, New Orleans, November.

Diamond, L.M. and Aspinwall, L.G. (2003) 'Emotion regulation across the life span: an integrative perspective emphasizing self-regulation, positive affect, and dyadic processes.' *Motivation and Emotion 27*, 125–156.

Diego, M.A., Field, T., Hernandez-Reif, M., Shaw, I.A. *et al.* (2002) 'Aggressive adolescents benefit from massage therapy.' *Adolescence 37*, 597–607.

Dyregrov, K. (2004) 'Bereaved parents' experience of research participation.' *Social Science and Medicine 58*, 391–400.

Dyregrov, K., Dyregrov, A. and Raundalen, M. (2000) 'Refugee families' experience of research participation.' *Journal of Traumatic Stress 13*, 413–426.

Ehlers, A., Mayou, R.A. and Bryant, B. (2003) 'Cognitive predictors of posttraumatic stress disorder in children: results of a prospective longitudinal study.' *Behaviour Research and Therapy 41*, 1–10.

El-Helou, M.W. and Johnson, P.R. (1994) 'The effects of the Palestinian Intifada on the behaviour of teenagers in the Gaza strip.' *Journal of Child and Youth Care 9*, 63–70.

Elofsson, U.O.E., von Scheele, B., Theorell, T. and Söndergard, H.P. (2008) 'Physiological correlates of eye movement desensitization and reprocessing.' *Journal of Anxiety Disorders 22*, 622–634.

Fernandez, I., Gallinari, E. and Lorenzetti, A. (2003) 'A school-based eye movement desensitization and reprocessing intervention for children who witnessed the Pirelli building airplane crash in Milan, Italy.' *Journal of Brief Therapy 2*, 129–136.

Field, T., Seligman, S. and Scafidi, F. (1996a) 'Alleviating post-traumatic stress in children following hurricane Andrew.' *Journal of Applied Developmental Psychology 17*, 37–50.

Field, T., Kilmer, T., Hernandez-Reif, M. and Burman, I. (1996b) 'Preschool children's sleep and wake behavior: effects of massage therapy.' *Early Child Development and Care 120*, 39–44.

Fivush, R., Marin, K., Crawford, M., Reynolds, M. and Brewin, C.R. (2007) 'Children's narratives and well-being.' *Cognition and Emotion 21*, 1414–1434.

Gaensbauer, T.J. (1994) 'Therapeutic work with a traumatized toddler.' *Psychoanalytic Study of the Child 49*, 412–433.

Gaensbauer, T.J. (2000) 'Psychotherapeutic treatment of traumatized infants and toddlers. A case report.' *Clinical Child Psychology and Psychiatry 5*, 373–385.

Gaensbauer, T., Chatoor, I., Drell, M., Siegel, D. and Zeanah C.H. (1995) 'Traumatic loss in a one-year-old girl.' *Journal of the American Academy of Child and Adolescent Psychiatry 34*, 520–528.

Giannopoulou, J., Dikaiakou, A. and Yule, W. (2006) 'Cognitive-behavioural group intervention for PTSD symptoms in children following the Athens 1999 earthquake: a pilot study.' *Clinical Child Psychology and Psychiatry 11*, 543–553.

Goenjian, A.K., Karayan, I., Pynoos, R.S., Minassian, D. *et al.* (1997) 'Outcome of psychotherapy among early adolescents after trauma.' *American Journal of Psychiatry 154*, 536–542.

Goenjian, A.K., Waling, D., Steinberg, A.M., Karayan, I., Najarian, L.M. and Pynoos, R. (2005) 'A prospective study of posttraumatic stress and depressive reactions among treated and untreated adolescents 5 years after a catastrophic disaster.' *American Journal of Psychiatry 162*, 2302–2308.

Greenwald, R. (1999) *Eye Movement Desensitization Reprocessing (EMDR) in Child and Adolescent Psychotherapy.* New Jersey: Jason Aronson Inc.

Hundeide, K. (1995) 'A critical note: balancing trauma therapy with some realities.' *Linjer nr. 1–2*, 12–14. Magazine published by the Psychosocial Center for Refugees, Oslo, Norway.

James, B. (ed.) (1994) *Handbook for Treatment of Attachment Trauma Problems in Children.* New York: Lexington Books.

Kataoka, S.H., Stein, B.D., Jaycox, L.H., Wong, M. *et al.* (2003) 'A school-based mental health program for traumatized Latino immigrant children.' *Journal of the American Academy of Child and Adolescent Psychiatry 42*, 311–318.

Kellner, R., Neidhardt, J., Krakow, B. and Pathak, D. (1992) 'Changes in chronic nightmares after one session of desensitization or rehearsed instructions.' *American Journal of Psychiatry 149*, 659–663.

King, N.J., Tonge, B.J., Mullen, P., Myerson, N. *et al.* (2000) 'Preventive intervention for maltreated preschool children: impact on children's behavior, neuroendocrine activity, and foster parent functioning.' *Journal of the American Academy of Child and Adolescent Psychiatry 39*, 1347–1355.

Krakow, B. and Zadra, A. (2006) 'Clinical management of chronic nightmares: imagery rehearsal therapy.' *Behavioral Sleep Medicine 4*, 45–70.

Krakow, B., Kellner, R., Neidhardt, J., Pathak, D. and Lambert, L. (1993) 'Imagery rehearsal treatment of chronic nightmares: with a thirty month follow–up.' *Journal of Behavior Therapy and Experimental Psychiatry 24*, 325–330.

Layne, C.M., Pynoos, R.S., Salzman, W.R., Arslanagi, B. *et al.* (2001) 'Trauma/grief-focused group psychotherapy school-based postwar intervention with traumatized Bosnian adolescents.' *Group Dynamics: Theory, Research and Practice 5*, 277–290.

Lieberman, A.F. and Van Horn, P. (2005) *Don't Hit my Mummy! A Manual for Child-Parent Psychotherapy with Young Witnesses of Family Violence.* Washington, DC: Zero to Three Press.

Lieberman, A.F. and van Horn, P. (2008) *Psychotherapy With Infants And Young Children.* New York: The Guilford Press.

Lieberman, A.F., van Horn, P. and Ippen, C.G. (2005) 'Toward evidence-based treatment: child–parent psychotherapy with preschoolers exposed to marital violence.' *Journal of the American Academy of Child and Adolescent Psychiatry 44*, 1241–1248.

Lieberman, A.F., Compton, N.C., Van Horn, P. and Ippen, C.G. (2003) *Losing a Parent to Death in the Early Years. Guidelines for the Treatment of Traumatic Bereavement in Infancy and Early Childhood.* Washingdon, DC: Zero to Three Press.

Miller, E. (1994) *Letting Go of Stress.* Menlo Park, CA: Source Cassette Tapes.

Mireault, G.C. and Bond, L.A. (1992) 'Parental death in childhood: perceived vulnerability, and adult depression and anxiety.' *American Journal of Orthopsychiatry 62*, 516–524.

National Institute for Health and Clinical Excellence (NICE) (2005) *The Management of Post Traumatic Stress Disorder in Primary and Secondary Care.* London: NICE.

Neuner, F., Catani, C., Ruf, M., Schauer, E., Schauer, M. and Elbert, T. (2008) 'Narrative exposure therapy for the treatment of traumatized children and adolescents.' *Child and Adolescent Psychiatric Clinics of North America 17*, 641–664.

Ollendick, T.H. and Davis, T.E. (2004) 'Empirically supported treatments for children and adolescents: where to from here?' *Clinical Psychology: Science and Practice 11*, 289–294.

Paunovic, N. (2003) 'Prolonged exposure counterconditioning as a treatment for chronic posttraumatic stress disorder.' *Anxiety Disorders 17*, 749–499.

Pennebaker, J.W. (1997) *Opening Up: The Healing Power of Expressing Emotions*, revised edition. New York: Guilford Press.

Pennebaker, J.W. (2004) *Writing to Heal. A Guided Journal for Recovering from Trauma and Emotional Upheaval.* Oakland, CA: New Harbinger Publications.

Pennebaker, J.W., Kiecolt-Glaser, J.K. and Glaser, R. (1988) 'Disclosure of traumas and immune function: health implications for psychotherapy.' *Journal of Consulting and Clinical Psychology 56*, 239–245.

Perlman, S.B., Kalish, C.W. and Pollak, S.D. (2008) 'The role of maltreatment experience in children's understanding of the antecedents of emotion.' *Cognition and Emotion 22*, 651–670.

Reich, W. and Kaplan, L. (1994) 'The effects of psychiatric and psychosocial interviews on children.' *Comprehensive Psychiatry 1*, 50–53.

Ribchester, T., Yule, W. and Duncan, A. (2010) 'EMDR for childhood PTSD after road traffic accidents: attentional, memory and attributional processes.' *Journal of EMDR Practice and Research.* Manuscript accepted for publication.

Rothschild, B. (2000) *The Body Remembers.* New York: W.W. Norton.

Shooshtary, M.H., Panaghi, L. and Moghadam, J. (2008) 'Outcome of cognitive behavioral therapy in adolescents after natural disaster.' *Journal of Adolescent Health 42*, 466–472.

Silverman, W.K., Ortiz, C.D., Viswesvaran, C., Burns, B.J. *et al.* (2008) 'Evidence-based psychosocial treatments for children and adolescents exposed to traumatic events.' *Journal of Clinical Child and Adolescent Psychology 37*, 156–183.

Smith, P., Dyregrov, A. and Yule, W. (1998) *Children and War. Teaching Recovery Techniques.* Bergen: Children and War Foundation.

Smith, P., Dyregrov, A. and Yule, W. (1999) *Children and Disaster. Teaching Recovery Techniques.* Bergen: Children and War Foundation.

Smith, P., Perrin, S., Yule, W. and Clark, D.M. (2007) *Cognitive Behavioural Therapy for PTSD in Children and Adolescents. Treatment Manual.* London: Institute of Psychiatry.

Spoormaker, V.I., Schredl, M. and van den Bout, J. (2006) 'Nightmares: from anxiety symptom to sleep disorder.' *Sleep Medicine Reviews 10*, 19–31.

Stallard, P. (2002) *Think Good – Feel Good. A Cognitive Behaviour Therapy Workbook for Children and Young People.* West Sussex: John Wiley & Sons Ltd.

Stallard, P. (2006) 'Psychological interventions for post-traumatic reactions in children and young people: a review of randomised controlled trials.' *Clinical Psychology Review 26*, 895–911.

Stanton, H.E. (1993a) 'Submodalities I: Adolescent happiness. A submodalities approach.' *International Journal of Psychosomatics 40*, 86–89.

Stanton, H.E. (1993b) 'Submodalities II: Theatre technique in the treatment of post-traumatic stress disorder.' *International Journal of Psychosomatics 40*, 90–91

Steele, H., Steele, M. and Croft, C. (2008) 'Early attachment predicts emotion recognition at 6 and 11 years old.' *Attachment and Human Development 10*, 379–393.

Stein, B.D., Jaycox, L.H., Kataoka, S.H., Wong, M. *et al.* (2003) 'A mental health intervention for schoolchildren exposed to violence.' *Journal of the American Medical Association 290*, 603–611.

Tarabulsy, G, M., St-Laurent, D., Cyr, C., Pascuzzo, K. *et al.* (2008) 'Attachment-based intervention for maltreating families.' *American Journal of Orthopsychiatry 78*, 322–332.

Task Force on Community Preventive Services (2008) 'Recommendations to reduce psychological harm from traumatic events among children and adolescents.' *American Journal of Preventive Medicine 35*, 314–316.

Taylor, T.L. and Chemtob, C.M. (2004) 'Efficacy of treatment for child and adolescent traumatic stress.' *Archives of Pediatric and Adolescent Medicine 158*, 786–791.

Thayer, R.E., Newman, J.R. and McClain, T.M. (1994) 'Self-regulation of mood: strategies for changing a bad mood, raising energy, and reducing tension.' *Journal of Personality and Social Psychology 67*, 910–925.

Tinker, R.H. and Wilson, S.A. (1999) *Through the Eyes of a Child. EMDR with Children.* Northvale, NJ: W.W. Norton & Company.

Weinman, J., Ebrecht, M., Scott, S., Walburn, J. and Dyson, M. (2008) 'Enhanced wound healing after emotional disclosure intervention.' *British Journal of Health Psychology 13*, 95–102.

Wells, A. and Sembi, S. (2004) 'Metacognitive therapy for PTSD: a preliminary investigation of a new brief treatment.' *Journal of Behavior Therapy and Experimental Psychiatry 35*, 307–318.

Wethington, H.R., Hahn, R.A., Fuqua-Whitley, D.S., Sipe, T.A. *et al.* (2008) 'The effectiveness of interventions to reduce psychological harm from traumatic events among children and adolescents.' *American Journal of Preventive Medicine 35*, 287–313.

Yule, W., Dyregrov, A., Neuner, F., Pennebaker, J., Raundalen, M. and van Emmerik, A. (2005) *Writing for Recovery. A Manual for Structured Writing after Disaster and War.* Bergen: Children and War Foundation.

Yule, W. and Gold, A. (1993) *Wise Before the Event. Coping with Crises in Schools.* London: Calouste Gulbenkian Foundation.

10

Traumas and the School

At any given time, a large number of children who have experienced trauma will be found in the school system. It is therefore important for teachers to have a good understanding of the kinds of reactions that children experience both immediately after the event and later, and what they can do to help. But at the same time it is important for parents and other caregivers to understand the type of impact that trauma can have on a child's school situation.

I have in other contexts described how the school can prepare itself to handle crisis and disaster situations (Dyregrov 2008). In this context, therefore, only aspects in connection with handling traumatized children in the school will be discussed.

Traumas and school performance

A list of studies done on the subject of trauma and school performance can be found in Dyregrov (2004). Yule and Gold (1993) have shown the important impact a traumatic event has on a child's schooling. They followed a group of English adolescents (girls) who survived a dramatic shipwreck in the Mediterranean. One girl and a teacher perished when the cruise ship they were on sank after a collision, and several of the surviving girls witnessed the tragic deaths, including two members of the rescue party being killed when they were caught between the sinking shipwreck and one of the rescue vessels. In addition to this, everyone's life was in danger for a period of time.

Yule and Gold (1993) showed that the school marks of these girls, which in the years before the accident were well above average, dropped to the average level compared with a control group, in the year following the accident. It has now been well documented that traumas have an impact on the ability to learn, due to disturbances in attention and memory. It is not the exposure to a trauma in itself that creates the difficulties but rather the presence of trauma symptoms that follow the event (Elbert *et al.* 2009; Schoeman, Carey and Seedat 2009; Scrimin *et al.* 2009).

In a large-scale study done after a discotheque fire in Gothenburg, around 25 per cent of the adolescents who survived said that they had either dropped out of school, had thoughts about this, or had been obliged to repeat a year (Broberg, Dyregrov and Lilled 2005). A large majority of the young people reported that their schoolwork had become more difficult, particularly in areas requiring concentration such as mathematics, physics and grammar. Around 60 per cent reported a drop in school marks. It was also shown that the more post-traumatic reactions the pupils demonstrated, the more school problems they struggled with. This means that a school must ensure that pupils struggling with such problems receive the help they need. The young people who considered the school's follow-up to be inadequate demonstrated more of both self-reported and interview-assessed post-traumatic symptoms one and a half years after the discotheque fire (Broberg *et al.* 2005). The problems that such children experience with learning show that it is important to reach a better understanding of what we can do to help them so that negative educational or social development can be avoided.

The problems with schooling that children report having developed are often accompanied by reports that the teachers' understanding of their situation is inadequate. For many children it can take time for them to absorb what has happened, particularly after a death, so the problems with schooling do not become apparent until some time has passed. Under the pressure of a hectic work schedule, teachers can forget that a child has experienced a loss or trauma. While pupils relate that teachers are extremely understanding in the period immediately after a loss or trauma, many pupils complain that they are not 'seen' or understood over time. The impaired learning capacity combined with less understanding on the part of teachers can result in considerable problems with schooling for some pupils.

In the last decade a number of programmes have been developed that can be implemented in a school when many pupils have been involved in a traumatic situation. Through so-called trauma-focused programmes, it has been shown not only that complex grief reactions and post-traumatic symptoms are reduced, but also that pupils' school performance is improved (Saltzman *et al.* 2001).

As one might expect, children who are subjected to repetitive violence in connection with sexual abuse, physical maltreatment, domestic violence and bullying also experience a clear reduction in their learning abilities with a corresponding negative impact on school performance. Such cumulative traumas have an impact on many aspects of a child's development and often result in problems far beyond the scope of purely post-traumatic problems, such as behavioural disorders, depression, substance abuse problems, etc. Children who experience such situations will almost always need a greater amount of support from the school. Here the school must collaborate with the family (or other caregivers) and the professional apparatus that is involved in order to help. Children who experience long-term traumatization will often constantly monitor their surroundings for signs of danger. Many develop a hypersensitivity that continues into adulthood, even though the danger has passed. Such danger monitoring requires the constant use of enormous emotional resources, which are then not available for learning and development. An experience of security and safety is a condition for exploration and learning, a 'luxury experience' few of these children will have been fortunate enough to enjoy, in that they are constantly scanning their surroundings for new dangers.

However, it is not only long-term traumatization that disturbs learning abilities – the loss of loved ones, divorce, etc. can lead to reduced motivation and impaired performance. In a number of studies done at our centre we have shown how sudden death, such as suicide, can have a large impact on motivation and schoolwork (Dyregrov 2009; Dyregrov and Dyregrov 2005). In a study that we carried out back in 1999, we showed how a classmate's death resulted in considerable after-effects among approximately one-fifth of the friends in the class as many as nine months after the death (Dyregrov, Bie Wikander and Vigerust 1999). Moreover, the effects were not of course limited to the class but also included close friends outside the class.

The reasons for such problems can be many. Yule and Gold (1993) report that the most common reason for school problems among the survivors after a shipwreck was a loss of motivation for schoolwork. Their thoughts can be summarized simply as such: 'What is the point of doing schoolwork when I might be dead tomorrow anyway?' Traumatic events have an impact on children's faith in the future as explained earlier in this book; many lose the belief in a good future for themselves or in any future whatsoever. Such a loss of motivation can of course also arise if one has lost a close friend or relative.

If one is sad and dejected, this can slow down the speed of one's thinking so that schoolwork and homework take longer than usual. Also intrusive images and memories that follow a traumatic situation, and arise in the thoughts spontaneously, disrupt the ability to concentrate and reduce learning capacity. Children state that these thoughts arise first and foremost when it is quiet all around them, but they can also arise in the middle of a class where there is a large amount of activity and discussion. This implies that disturbing and intrusive memories or fantasies can impair the capacity to maintain concentration on school assignments or homework. The impact on memory functions has also been explained previously as something that can create added difficulties in learning, both when a child is to learn new material and to remember old.

The state of constant vigilance (activation) that appears in the nervous system to pick up on new danger signals will also make children more distracted because they are in a constant state of preparedness. Some also distract themselves constantly to avoid thinking about what they have experienced. Others use cognitive mechanisms (thought strategies) to maintain a distance from or avoid the intrusive memories. When thoughts are characterized by such suppression and evasion mechanisms, this can also have an impact on spontaneity, inhibit creativity and decrease mental capacity.

The last possible reason for the school problems that are being addressed here is that traumatic situations that involve the family can result in role changes in the home. Sometimes children assume the responsibilities of adults so that they have reduced time and energy for schoolwork.

Regardless of the cause, an impaired learning capacity can have ramifications for the child at school. Particularly at risk are those children who have just started attending school and are to learn to read, write and do arithmetic, pupils who advance to a new school level (elementary school or high school) and those pupils who are to complete their schooling and therefore have their chances of carrying out the education that they wish to pursue undermined.

Schools and preparedness for traumas

It is the school's responsibility to produce guidelines for what is to be done if the school is involved in a traumatic incident. Some aspects of handling traumas in the school are outlined here.

Preparedness plans address the identification of potentially critical situations, decide on who does what and when, outline priority groups and propose the use of resources for helping the pupils. The school coordinates meetings with the police and collaborative resources before any such events; meetings of the school's crisis group are held on a regular basis and contact is established with those external people and resources to be summoned in the event of a crisis situation.

In order to ensure that the school's or other institution's management is able to handle traumatic events in the best possible manner, they should have knowledge about:

- crisis reactions and crisis management
- crisis leadership, management responsibility
- organizational reactions in a crisis
- grief hierarchy
- stress in the manager's role
- the importance of preparedness and training
- commemorative rituals
- handling of the press and media
- psychological first aid
- traumatic reminders
- internal and external help resources.

The development of such experience takes place gradually but calls for an effective management that actively seeks to expand its knowledge within this area. Some aspects of traumatic events are particularly easy to overlook. This applies to:

- events that occur in the school holidays
- hospitalized pupils

- reactions that persist over time
- traumatic reminders that the pupil(s) must manage.

Systematic crisis-related work means that the organization (the school, kindergarten, etc.) is aware of such factors and makes plans to take care of the children and young people in the long term, including those who are less prominent or more frequently absent.

Early contact with the school

As parents of children who have been exposed to a traumatic event outside school hours or during a holiday, it is important to inform the school. Give the class teacher, headteacher or guidance counsellor information about:

- what has happened
- how your children have been involved
- their exposure to sensory impressions
- the degree of threat to life
- any losses
- how the children are doing now
- any thoughts that you and the children have about the school days ahead.

The return to school is planned in collaboration with the teacher. Speak to the children about how they would like to be met upon returning to school. Form an agreement with the teacher about how classmates and close friends can be informed. The school probably has a procedure for this but ensure that the wishes of the children are heard. Make an agreement with the teacher to maintain close contact during the period after the incident, so that additional measures can be implemented if necessary.

Handling trauma and grief in the school

Although schools have gradually developed good preparedness for handling grief and trauma in the school setting and do this with the best intentions, we receive on a regular basis information about children and young people who either fall through the cracks of such help programmes or who experience that the manner in which help is given becomes an added strain. The school's strong class-based focus has caused problems for a number of students. This implies that when a pupil in a class experiences a traumatic situation or passes away, the follow-up work is concentrated to a very large extent on the particular class. We have shown how best friends outside the class are overlooked after a pupil's death in a traumatic accident (Dyregrov *et al.* 1995, Dyregrov *et al.* 1999). Not only are they overlooked, but some are inflicted with additional problems in that they are denied the chance for participation in ritual activities, or left to their own devices while they are experiencing difficulties with intrusive memories and thoughts. Unfortunately, a number of studies indicate that teachers to a certain extent seriously underestimate the scope of children's problems (Dyregrov 2009; Yule and Gold 1993).

Older children have felt 'persecuted' by teachers, not immediately after the traumatic event but over time.

> Robert lost his father suddenly and dramatically. His teacher initially had been extremely friendly, but in the following months for no apparent reason he began blaming Robert for negative things that happened in the class. Robert changed places in the classroom to see if it was his strategic seating in the middle of the teacher's line of vision that resulted in his being blamed for what happened, but this did not change anything. He addressed the matter with the guidance counsellor, which improved the situation somewhat. In a bereavement group he was attending, a number of the other young people who had experienced traumatic loss reported similar, irrational persecution by teachers. One girl had complained to the headteacher twice before things got better.

It is difficult to understand the basis for such behaviour on the part of teachers and it has been with scepticism and doubt that I (and others) have listened to these stories. With time, however, they have been confirmed, and with such an extensive amount of factual information that there is little reason to doubt them. We must instead attempt to understand why. Perhaps the lack of motivation that the pupils experience and demonstrate is understood as 'scorn' or an attack on the values of the school? Perhaps the sight of a grieving pupil triggers a guilty conscience on the part of the teacher in the context of a hectic school schedule where the pace and number of pupils offers little opportunity for individual follow-up and care? Regardless of the cause, it is important that teachers and parents are aware of this. Perhaps increased knowledge about the long-term effects of trauma, in relation to motivation for school and school performance, can contribute to creating a climate of caring that is more long-term in nature.

If pupils are constantly in conflict with their surroundings, it can be useful to give them a clear description of the problems, with an explanation as to why one believes these are associated with the event. After this a counsellor (or another teacher) can, together with the pupils, outline expectations regarding what is acceptable behaviour and the boundaries that must be respected. The transgression of boundaries must have clear consequences and the counsellor makes an agreement with the pupils for how to work towards changing the behaviour that is now causing problems, such as through participation in a group with other pupils in a similar situation, regular meetings with a counsellor, a referral to child psychiatric services or the school psychologist, extra classes in certain subjects, etc.

Fellow pupils can also impose added strain after traumatic situations. Some children are teased at school afterwards. Classmates understand that they are vulnerable after the traumatic event and use it against them.

> Lise had experienced an attempted violation by a man who was well known in the neighbourhood. At recess a girlfriend from her class repeated several times: 'There he is', and pointed across the schoolyard. Lise grew so frightened that she did not want to go out at recess. In this case it was necessary to address the situation in class for a change to occur. Another pupil was told after the death of his grandfather: 'I wish that your mother was dead, too.'

Older pupils can object to having parents or others intervene and are best helped by receiving advice and tips on how they can go about creating a change themselves. Such advice can be to suggest speaking to a teacher, whom they trust, a counsellor, the school nurse or headteacher.

In that preparedness plans have been developed at many schools, there is now a 'formula' that schools can follow after a traumatic event. Nonetheless, good follow-up means more than carrying out rituals, assemblies and practical arrangements. It is necessary to have an understanding of how traumatic events affect children or adolescents over time, how they think and feel in the months that follow the initial period when everyone is attentive and supportive. Here both sensitive and knowledgeable adults are required, who are able to recognize when there is a need for professional follow-up and who do not view it as a personal failure if someone needs help beyond what they can offer personally. The school management must get involved and ensure that the children who need it receive long-term follow-up. It is far too easy to step back and think, 'I am sure they will be fine.' Our experience is that many suffer alone.

In the school situation, support from friends is often more important than support from teachers. In the study mentioned earlier, which two students did for our centre (Antonsen and Pilø 1995, see Chapter 5), it was found that young people wanted personal support from teachers in a crisis situation only to a limited extent. This can be a reflection of the fact that pupils most frequently encounter a teacher in a group situation and thereby expect the greatest investment from the teacher in the form of help with what is taking place in the class (i.e. for the group) rather than for the individual. Nonetheless, the teacher's role is important as one that contributes to ensuring good support from friends. This can be done by making it possible for friends and classmates to spend time together, but also through information about common reactions and how one can help in such a situation.

The school and sensitive themes in teaching situations

A traumatized child will inevitably find that a theme similar to what they have experienced is addressed or mentioned in class. It can be that there is a discussion about losing somebody, about rape, alcohol abuse, divorce, or sexuality. If large-scale accidents occur that receive media coverage, this can trigger thoughts in the mind of a child or young person who has previously experienced a similar type of trauma.

Teachers should be attentive to the particular difficulties traumatized pupils can have when such topics are brought up or when special events stir up a child's personal traumas. Teachers, who speak ahead of time with pupils whom they know will feel particularly upset, can both prepare the pupils for this and find a sensitive way of talking about the subject in a group setting. It is more difficult if the subject arises spontaneously, such as when one of the pupils brings it up. It is easy to forget that this can perhaps affect some of the students in a particular manner. Young people, especially, can express dogmatic opinions that can be painful for traumatized classmates to listen to. A teacher, who then 'modifies' this and offers nuances in a sensitive manner, can be a good form of support for the 'vulnerable' pupils.

The school and the family at home

The home will usually be the most important source of support for children who experience traumatic situations. But the home can also be the place where children are inflicted with traumas, or parents can be incapable of giving the children the support they need. The latter can be because the parents are so traumatized themselves that they are not able to support their children, or they can have alcohol abuse problems, psychological problems or for other reasons be insensitive to their children's needs.

Regardless of the cause, staff from kindergarten and school become important support resources in such situations. These people will usually have good knowledge about the type of resources found in the family. If this is not the case, one should find out by asking, 'Do your mother and father live together?' 'Can you speak to your mother or father about what happened?' A meeting with family members increases understanding of what the child can count on in the way of support.

When one suspects that the home is producing traumatic situations, one should proceed with caution so that one does not create additional problems for the child.

Schools and violence

Violence is a problem on the increase in school systems throughout the western world. While bullying has been recognized as a problem for many years, the use of weapons in the classroom and schoolyard is a new phenomenon. In recent years there have been several school shootings and murders in European countries, and stabbings and other episodes involving brutal violence are no longer unusual, particularly in large cities.

When children and young people meet with increasing violence outside school and many experience domestic violence, it is particularly important to preserve the school as a violence-free zone. In crisis and trauma situations, the school and the kindergarten are of great significance for the stability, continuity and security they represent. If nothing else in the child's life is stable, the school is. This makes it important to prioritize the task of working to maintain the school as an area free from violence and conflict.

Violence nonetheless happens and necessary measures must be taken. The incidence of violence in a school does not only underline the importance of a good system for following up the children when something has happened, but also requires the development of good internal communication channels with an eye towards the possibility that something can happen. In practical terms this implies that the need exists for communication between and within buildings, and that one has both first-aid equipment and training, and clear emergency signals. A close collaboration with the local police authorities and a greater emphasis on violence prevention work in the school can reduce the frequency of violence and improve preparedness if something should happen.

School shootings – multiple homicides at school

In recent years there have been more than 50 school shootings in the USA, Canada and Europe, with many fatalities as a result. Even with an inclusive school environment where a focus on the prevention of bullying is a priority, it is not possible to maintain that nothing will happen here. Violence in the school can be seen as a breakdown of feelings of belonging and identification with the school. By creating the best possible school affiliation, the chances of violence are reduced. Such a perspective does not claim that the school is responsible for the violence, rather that certain circumstances within the school community and environment can to varying degrees be violence-promoting factors. When pupils find themselves at odds with the school, this imposes serious requirements on how the school should address this and 'see' the pupils. By increasing the pupils' connection to the school and preventing estrangement, exclusion or 'stigmatization' of the pupils can be prevented. They must experience caring from the school and be helped to make a meaningful contribution. This is no simple task but a number of pupils who do not fit in or who are problem pupils experience both teachers' and classmates' irritation and, at times, contempt, and little compassion that can give them the experience of having significance. Through an investment in the development of a protective, caring school culture, through the promotion of pupils' development of social skills with good conflict management abilities, by having fair disciplinary strategies and classroom interaction that develops collaboration and compassion, and with a school structure and organization that encourages input and influence from the pupils, the best foundation is perhaps laid for a school environment that minimizes the risk of our being faced with homicide in the school.

Prevention

In connection with school shootings in Finland in 2008 we produced guidelines for school administrators for such situations (Dyregrov, Raundalen and Schultz 2008). Here there was an emphasis on the school administrators having an important role in the planning and coordination of prevention. They are both to demonstrate compassion and vigilance for lonely pupils who are particularly interested in bizarre ideas about violence, terrorism and well-known perpetrators, and simultaneously to work towards the creation of an active and inclusive environment, which ensures that few will feel left out. At the same time, there must be a systematic dialogue with the student body so that pupils quickly report violence-inspired presentations on the internet and attitudes that glorify violence.

Preparedness for violence and threats of violence

It is difficult to give advice on the basis of psychological knowledge about perpetrators and their thought processes. This is both because there is little knowledge available on this subject and because it is difficult in its own right to predict violence. Below some of the advice that we have developed is summarized.

All threats, including those that can be perceived as vague or are spread as rumours, must be taken seriously. That does not mean that one always starts with action, but that one quickly discusses a means of handling the situation with the police, who are best equipped to assess a situation involving a threat. Before any threats have occurred, the school administration can discuss with the police and justice authorities how to address allegations and rumours that someone has a weapon at school. The contents of the preparedness folder should clearly state who is responsible for contact with the police and which telephone number is to be used. Here the school administration's strategy for handling such situations is to be found but not made public.

In the event of an evacuation of the school, well-rehearsed procedures should be used. If the school's PA system is used, one should be careful in formulating instructions so that all unnecessary panic is avoided – for example, through code words that either signal evacuation or securing (barricades, down on the floor, etc.) of the classroom. In some situations involving threats, there will be time to discuss strategies with the police.

Real-life situations are best handled if school personnel have discussed and rehearsed the procedure, so that they conduct themselves calmly, with certainty and without panicking, in order to avoid misunderstandings. Given the low level of risk that such events will occur, a thorough assessment should be made as to whether drills are to include full-scale ones in which the students participate. This can upset students, while any pupils representing a possible risk will gain knowledge of the procedures. There is a big difference between a school in a large urban area and a small school in the countryside, and both planning and measures must therefore be adapted to local conditions.

We have collected some concrete items for good preparedness and crisis management.

- Discussion and review of the school's emergency preparedness contributes to emotional preparation and makes both administrators and staff better equipped to handle any crisis situations.

- At each school a 'table-top exercise' should be held where the school personnel go through how they are to proceed if an actual situation involving violence arises.

- The school personnel must physically walk through evacuation routes that can be used.

- The conduct of administrators gives signals to the pupils. A calm voice on the PA system can help to ensure a calm response on the part of the pupils.

- All the school personnel must know how to secure, block and lock pupils' and staff's day rooms and lounges to keep out or reduce access for any perpetrators.

- Pupils are asked to report internet activity in which classmates speak of plans for violent episodes, or thoughts and attitudes that are extremely fixated on violence.

- Teachers make a note of pupils displaying extremely deviant attitudes towards violence and aggression, both pupils who have a provocative and aggressive style, and those who are loners and have withdrawn from the community.

Handling threats

- All threats that have been called in or notices or videos on websites are immediately reported to the police. At large schools, someone on the staff can be assigned the task of making a daily check of any mention of the school on the internet.

- Serious threats that are communicated orally are to be reported to the school administration, which in turn contacts the police and possibly confers with parents and school authorities. If any of the risk factors mentioned later exist, extreme vigilance should be exercised.

- Teachers' knowledge about pupils constitutes a resource for the evaluation of the degree of severity and a pupil's potential for carrying out the threat.

- Threats are noted in a logbook and any escalation of threats from pupils shall result in contact with the school's emergency system and possibly with the police.

- Threats that become known among the pupils require good management. This implies calm, clear, precise information to pupils about what has happened and about what is now being done.

- Serious threats are communicated to the pupils' guardians, either in writing and/or orally at a parent–teacher conference.

Handling a real-life situation

- Personnel must be aware of what they can do in a room to maximize the possibility of survival – that is, lie down, stay away from windows and doors, seek out safe places, do not attract attention.

- Personnel must usually wait for a signal that the danger has passed.

- Calm conduct on the part of the administration calms down pupils and others.

- If you notice that your anxiety and fear are increasing, focus your attention outside yourself. If the situation calls for a long period of quiet and waiting, concentrate on calming down the students and keeping their morale up.

Risk factors

There is not enough precise knowledge about who commits homicides but the pattern that presents itself indicates a combination of many risk factors. Some are easy to spot and are typical of relatively many young people. It is only when several, and particularly when many such factors exist at the same time, that the risk of violent acts increases. Preti (2008) claims that more than 50 per cent of school shootings were preceded by an action that gave notice of imminent violence – particularly when it was a matter of suicidal thoughts.

- Some signs of immediate danger:
    - clear, specific threats (signals) put out on the internet or orally and/or in writing
    - bragging about what one will do
    - access to weapons
    - glorification of violence, great interest in previous school shootings
- Other factors
    - individual circumstances
        ▷ history of violations, exposure to bullying and/or personal involvement in violent episodes
        ▷ explicit suicidal behaviour (thoughts, plans, attempts, etc.)
        ▷ substance abuse
        ▷ antisocial attitudes and behaviour, uncontrollable rage
        ▷ excessive interest in violent video games and violent movies
        ▷ poor or diminished school performance
        ▷ abrupt mood swings, often sad
        ▷ highly motivated to carry out homicide
    - family factors
        ▷ low level of parental involvement
        ▷ abuse or neglect
        ▷ difficult home life situation – family conflicts – poor financial situation

- school and network factors
  - ▷ spends free time with deviant friends
  - ▷ rejection by friends, often bullied
  - ▷ feels persecuted or tormented by others.

Schools must be equipped to address violent episodes if they should occur. Work that ensures a good, inclusive environment, involving collaboration between teachers and pupils but also collaboration with the home, the police and institutions, associations and clubs in the local community can help prevent such violence from occurring. The same holds true for the reduction of bullying and good follow-up of smaller conflicts. Involving young people as well in this work through active participation contributes to consciousness-raising in relation to the problems, and this can also give them a greater sense of ownership in relation to the process leading to a safe school. By emphasizing such factors, violent episodes can be prevented. Such work is contingent upon systematic work carried out over time, where the development of experience and communication within and between schools is crucial to success.

Less media attention on school shootings will also reduce the chance of copycat events. There should also be a mechanism for anonymous reporting of concerns about pupils with extreme attitudes. A low threshold for seeking help when someone is struggling psychologically, and easy access to qualified professionals, will also contribute to reducing the risk.

Follow-up of school shootings

When a place where children and young people spend a great deal of their time on a daily basis suddenly becomes an unsafe place, the return to this place after an event is a considerable challenge. Follow-up of the pupils will involve both meetings in groups and individual follow-up for those in need of this. In addition, the initial return to school and the encounter with the places where fellow students and others have been killed requires a systematic approach. This is also the case for the re-commencement of teaching in rooms where others have been killed. After school shootings in both Finland and Germany, a programme was implemented for the pupils to address such concerns: before class started again the students spent time 'taking back' the building and approaching the areas where they had been and where fellow students had died.

Conversation and ritual commemorations were used in this process, along with support from teachers and mental health personnel. Before this took place, the teachers were given the opportunity to do the same.

Schools and suicide

If pupils take their own life, this is of course a traumatic event for their guardians, but also for their closest friends, classmates and others who are directly affected (e.g. the one or those who were witnesses or found the deceased). A suicide allows no time for preparation; it is often entangled in dramatic events, rumours, strong sensory impressions and fantasies. Also the perception of what others are capable of doing is torn down and thoughts about whether one could do such a thing personally are activated. Last, but not least, suicide can sometimes lead to extreme self-reproach, such as if a pupil who has been bullied commits suicide.

In some situations, parents can wish not to make public the fact that their child committed suicide, or they can be extremely reserved about allowing friends and classmates to receive information. This normally results in many speculations and the starting of rumours that distort the situation for the circle of friends.

> In one situation the parents did not want what had happened to be made public. They only wanted people to know that their son had been found dead. In a meeting with his closest friends (to talk through the situation), it was obvious that they did not want to believe that their friend had committed suicide. They believed that something criminal had to lie behind it. Only after the parents permitted them to be informed of how he had died and that he had used an object that he had brought from his own home, could the friends' speculations be moderated and the rumours stopped.

Usually parents are receptive if someone with authority explains why it is so important to give precise information to fellow pupils that can hinder the spreading of rumours. If one makes an appeal to them that this would help the friends, most parents will understand and want to cooperate.

In such a situation, good contact between the group of friends and the parents is helpful for both parties. Many parents greatly appreciate the friends coming home to them. Often teachers will serve as a natural contact between the friends and the home. Teachers can contact the home and ask when the family wants friends and fellow pupils to come and visit.

If the suicide is extremely incomprehensible, such as if there were few warnings before it happened, no suicide note, etc., friends are of even greater significance for the parents, because they can provide key facts and information that can make the incomprehensible comprehensible.

> In a situation where nobody understood why an adolescent had committed suicide, the teachers and psychologist made a request to friends and classmates that, if they should know of anything that could help explain what happened, they should communicate this, either to them or directly to the parents.

The school is often reluctant to take enough time to address what happened out of the fear that this will lead to further suicides. But suicide will affect the pupils, regardless of what the school does. By abdicating its responsibility for the students, they are left to their own devices, own thoughts, own potential glorification of what happened, and, in the worst cases, experimentation with thoughts and actions about what would happen to them if they were to try to do the same. We have shown that good school management reduces the risk of further suicides (Poijula, Wahlberg and Dyregrov 2001).

In conversations with pupils after a suicide it can be extremely useful to speak directly about it:

> Some of you perhaps think that it is 'cool' to do something like this, that it requires courage. Actually it is only sad, sad that someone tries to solve their problems by taking their life, when these problems without a doubt could have been solved by speaking to someone who has experience in helping people who have such problems. What George failed to give adequate consideration was the amount of pain that this would cause everyone who loved him. Just think of how you are feeling now and how it must be for his parents. When someone becomes so desperate or confused in their thoughts as George must have been to do this, they often view their situation in a completely unique way. They think, 'It is best for everyone if I do this.' It is as if a kind of solar eclipse occurs in the mind. If any of you ever should think about taking your own life, just

remember two things: first of all, the problems that right now, at this moment, appear to be great will seem like trivialities to you later and, even more important: nothing is worse than the pain, grief, longing and despair that your mother and father and others who love you will feel. The grief after a suicide is extremely heavy to bear.

Sometimes I have told groups of young people about clients I have had contact with after a suicide attempt. As a part of the help I have said that in a few years when you are an adult and you have perhaps had children, you will think back on this time as having been difficult and heavy going, but you will certainly think: 'Imagine that I could have considered taking my own life.' A number of former clients I have met with later, when they are eagerly pursuing an education, or are proud new parents with their entire future before them, have shaken their heads when thinking back on what they tried to do back then. It is important that young people understand the kind of pain a suicide causes and that it will always be possible to solve problems if they seek help. An appeal can also be made that they take such good care of one another that they tell adults and be sure to help a friend whom they fear is going to commit suicide.

The factors indicating that friends are more at risk for the development of post-traumatic problems after a friend's suicide are summarized in Box 10.1.

Box 10.1 Risk signs of PTSD among friends after a suicide

- Close friendship with the deceased.
- Found or witnessed the suicide, saw the site.
- Mentioned in the suicide note.
- Knew that it would happen (was warned) but failed to do anything.
- Spoke with the deceased on the day of the death.
- Argument or estrangement, or the break-up of a 'couple' just before the suicide.
- Problems in own family. Conflicts with siblings and friends.
- Previous death in the family or among friends.
- Simultaneous depression (Brent et al. 1993).

If teachers or other adults know of a friend who meets a number of these criteria, this person should receive close follow-up and a referral should be considered.

Among factors of significance for assessing the risk of suicide are:

- biological risk factors
    - familial strain
- social risk factors
    - divorce and family problems
    - bullying and tormenting from friends
    - sexual abuse, maltreatment
    - school problems of a disciplinary nature, fear of the reaction of parents
    - media coverage of suicide methods
    - alcohol and drug abuse
    - role models that can be imitated
- psychological risk factors
    - serious suicidal thoughts
    - former attempts, particularly serious attempts
    - isolation and withdrawal
    - depression and feelings of hopelessness
    - lack of reflexive ability – cognitive immaturity
    - aggression and impulsiveness
    - low emotional regulation ability
    - previous psychological problems (Bridge, Goldstein and Brent 2006; Bursztein and Apter 2008; Dervic, Brent and Oquendo 2008).

On the basis of my own experience and a review of the research literature on children, adolescents and suicide, I would also highlight the following risk signs or factors:

- over-preoccupation with the death or the suicides of others
- planning: gives away possessions, plays with knives, takes unnecessary chances (risk taking), etc.

- radical personality changes; changes in performance, behaviour and attitudes.

It is usually recommended to ask directly if one suspects the risk of suicide, such as in response to hints or insinuations: 'Are you thinking about taking your own life?', 'Have you planned how you will do it?', 'What is it you have thought to do?', 'Have you lost the desire to live?', 'Do you feel that you have nothing to live for?'

In the event of affirmative answers, the person deemed to be at risk of committing suicide must immediately be put in contact with the assistance network. I have elsewhere given an account of how to go about explaining what has taken place to a child who has lost a loved one by suicide (Dyregrov 2008).

References

Antonsen, N.E. and Pilø, A.B. (1995) *Forebyggende arbeid i skolen. Ungdommers tanker om ulike typer støtte ved en venns død.* Hovedoppgave Det Psykologiske Fakultet, Universitetet i Bergen.

Brent, D.A., Perper, J.A., Moritz, G., Allman, C. *et al.* (1993) 'Psychiatric sequelae to the loss of an adolescent peer to suicide.' *Journal of the American Academy of Child and Adolescent Psychiatry 32,* 509–517.

Bridge, J.A., Goldstein, T.R. and Brent, D.A. (2006) 'Adolescent suicide and suicidal behavior.' *Journal of Child Psychology and Psychiatry 47,* 372–394.

Broberg, A.O., Dyregrov, A. and Lilled, L. (2005) 'The Göteborg discotheque fire – posttraumatic stress, and school adjustment as reported by the primary victims 18 months later.' *Journal of Child Psychology and Psychiatry 46,* 1279–1286.

Bursztein, C. and Apter, A. (2008) 'Adolescent suicide.' *Current Opinion in Psychiatry 22,* 1–6.

Dervic, K., Brent, D.A. and Oquendo, M.A. (2008) 'Completed suicide in childhood.' *Psychiatric Clinics of North America 31,* 271–291.

Dyregrov, A. (2004) 'Educational consequences of loss and trauma.' *Educational and Child Psychology 21,* 77–84.

Dyregrov, A. (2008) *Grief in Children. A Handbook for Adults.* 2nd edition. London: Jessica Kingsley Publishers.

Dyregrov, A., Bie Wikander, A.M. and Vigerust, S. (1999) 'Sudden death of a classmate and friend. Adolescents' perception of support from their school.' *School Psychology International 20,* 191–208.

Dyregrov, A., Raundalen, M. and Schultz, J-H. (2008) Veileder for skolens møte med trusler om vold. Oslo: Utdanningsdirektoratet, available from: www.udir.no/Artikler/_ Satsingsomrader/_Laringsmiljo/_Krise/Skolens-mote-med-trusler-om-vold-etter-det-andre-skoledrapet-i-Finland (accessed 6 Feb 2010).

Dyregrov, A., Gjestad, R., Bie Wikander, A.M. and Vigerust, S. (1995) 'Traumatic grief following the death of a classmate.' Paper presented at the Fourth European Conference on Traumatic Stress, Paris, 7–11 May.

Dyregrov, K. (2009) 'The important role of the school following suicide. New research about the help and support wishes of the young bereaved.' *OMEGA – Journal of Death and Dying 59,* 2, 147–161.

Dyregrov, K. and Dyregrov, A. (2005) 'Siblings after suicide – "the forgotten bereaved".' *Suicide and Life Threatening Behaviour 35*, 714–724.

Elbert, T., Schauer, M., Schauer, E., Huschka, B., Hirth, M. and Neuner, F. (2009) 'Trauma-related impairment in children – a survey in Sri Lankan provinces affected by armed conflict.' *Child Abuse and Neglect 33*, 238–246.

Poijula, S., Wahlberg, K-E. and Dyregrov, A. (2001) 'Adolescent suicide and suicide contagion in three secondary schools.' *International Journal of Emergency Mental Health 3*, 169–175.

Preti, P. (2008) 'School shootings as a culturally informed way of expressing suicidal hostile intentions.' *Journal of the American Academy of Psychiatry and Law 36*, 544–550.

Saltzman, W.R., Pynoos, R.S., Steinberg, A.M., Eisenberg, E. and Layne, C.M. (2001) 'Trauma and grief-focused intervention for adolescents exposed to community violence.' *Group Dynamics: Theory, Research and Practice 5*, 291–303.

Schoeman, R., Carey, P. and Seedat, S. (2009) 'Trauma and posttraumatic stress disorder in South African adolescents.' *The Journal of Nervous and Mental Disease 197*, 244–250.

Scrimin, S., Moscardino, U., Capello, F. and Axia, G. (2009) 'Attention and memory in school-age children surviving the terrorist attack in Beslan, Russia.' *Journal of Clinical Child and Adolescent Psychology 38*, 402–414.

Yule, W. and Gold, A. (1993) *Wise before the Event. Coping with Crises in Schools.* London: Calouste Gulbenkian Foundation.

11

Being a Helper

Why is work with traumatized children so exhausting?

When healthcare personnel all over the world are asked which experiences in connection with their work are the worst, the answer is unanimous: the death of a child or work with extremely traumatized children (Mitchell 1984; Vachon 1987). Why are such situations so stressful for helpers?

Many of those who help traumatized children are characterized by a large capacity for compassion, empathy and a sense of obligation to help others. They are frequently driven by an intense personal commitment. Such motivational factors become especially intense when one works with children, because they are viewed as being innocent and helpless. Under such circumstances the level of personal involvement can be extremely high.

Adults who work with children have also been children themselves once upon a time, and they can remember feelings of fear and vulnerability, often associated with the fear of separation and loss. When something happens to a child, this former anxiety and fear can be reactivated.

When children are the victims of dramatic events, this also makes us aware of how meaningless and unfair life can be. It threatens our perception of a just world. Because children cannot protect themselves, such situations are perceived as being unreal and unfair. If a child dies, the normal sequence of life events is turned upside down: the child is supposed to survive the parents. Such events therefore upset fundamental life perceptions.

Usually helpers employ different methods to distance themselves and regulate their feelings in trauma work. When children are involved, it appears to be more difficult to achieve such emotional distancing. In many ways, the natural mental defence system is broken down.

As helpers we find that we strongly identify with children and their families when children are affected. We are all in different relationships to children, as parents, siblings, grandparents, uncles, aunts, etc. It is easy to imagine that the event could have happened to someone we love, and many helpers therefore experience that they worry about something happening to their own children.

Reactions among those who help traumatized children

If one works with traumatized children, one can personally experience different reactions that reflect how difficult such work can be. Some common reactions are described here.

Helplessness

Helpers are eager to help: we want to provide assistance and comfort those in need. In many traumatic situations there is nothing we can do except be present for the child or family affected. Many helpers describe feelings of complete helplessness in such situations, where they know that there is nothing they can do to redress the situation. It is easy to feel overwhelmed and quickly become tired.

Fear and anxiety

Perhaps the most important consequence of work with traumatized children is the change that takes place in the helper's own experience of vulnerability. Many experience fear for their own children or children who are close to them. Most of us are protected by our tendency to think that terrible things happen to others, but not to us. This illusion of invulnerability (Janoff-Bulman and Frieze 1983) is a protective strategy that prevents anxiety in daily life. When one encounters traumatized children, this illusion falls apart and the feelings of vulnerability and fear that something terrible will happen to one's loved ones, or oneself, increase.

Such fear can be accompanied by the need to monitor and overprotect one's own children: 'I catch myself all the time telling my children that they must be careful in traffic, when they are swimming, etc.' Others say directly: 'I have become more afraid for my children.' Helpers relate how they often feel compelled to go in to check on their children after bedtime, and often feel a great need just to be close to them and hug them.

Existential insecurity

Some helpers ask themselves about the meaning of life. A child's trauma makes it difficult to find a suitable frame of reference or structure to fit the event into. McCann and Pearlman (1990) claim that a trauma can destroy the helper's faith in and expectations about the world and human nature. Confidence and security in the world and one's faith in one's own abilities can also be affected, and some find that they become more cynical and pessimistic.

Anger and irritability

Some experience increased irritation in relation to others or they feel rage and anger, particularly when others have been the cause of injury to children. When others speak of relatively trivial things such as a cold, insomnia or stress, after having worked with a traumatized child one can feel irritation about the fact that others are caught up in such insignificant concerns. Unfortunately, this type of irritation is often taken out on those closest to the helper.

Grief and pain

It is perhaps possible to grow accustomed to adults dying, but with the death of a child one frequently experiences feelings of grief, frustration, helplessness and pain. But sadness can also be experienced when one feels the desperation and grief of a child.

It is not uncommon for helpers to cry when they come home from a critical situation where children are involved, often when they see their own children: 'It was only when I came home to my wife and children that I understood how heavy a burden the experience was to bear. Then I began to cry.' Sometimes helpers cry openly at an accident site if children are victims.

Intrusive images

For helpers who are present at an accident site, memories can of course become imprinted by way of all sensory channels, as is the case for children. But we also know that listening to the painful accounts of traumatized children can be followed by intrusive fantasies or reliving of the events based on the accounts they have heard. The danger of such secondary traumatization (as it is called) is particularly large in connection with work with children.

Self-reproach, shame and guilt

Such reactions can occur when helpers feel that there was little they could do, or they ponder over what more they could have done or what they could have done differently.

Positive experiences

Those who help traumatized children will also experience positive consequences, which often correspond to those described by children and young people in Chapter 2. Many helpers experience that they appreciate their loved ones, particularly the children much more, value life more, do not take things for granted, feel that life is more intense, sense their own growth and maturation, and feel respect for the strength of other human beings.

Help for helpers

When helpers are directly involved in rescue work they often use emotional distancing and activities to keep their feelings at bay so as to avoid being overwhelmed by their own reactions. Accordingly, at an accident site it is necessary to maintain a certain distance, emotionally speaking. If this distance is reduced, helpers can find that their capacity to help is correspondingly reduced. As long as they remain active, have concrete tasks to carry out and are able to control their emotions, they can work efficiently.

After such work most helpers feel that it is best to talk with others. Colleagues are mentioned as being the most important source of support in the context of follow-up measures; with colleagues one can speak about thoughts, impressions and reactions (Dyregrov and Mitchell 1992). By actively confronting impressions and reactions through meetings that provide the opportunity to speak with colleagues and others, helpers are best equipped to handle the after-effects.

The group review that was described for use with children in Chapter 8, in professional terminology called 'Critical Incident Stress Debriefing (CISD)', is taken from a model developed for helpers (Mitchell 1983; Dyregrov 1989, 2002). This type of group meeting addresses in detail facts in connection with a critical event, but also thoughts, sensory impressions and reactions. Such a meeting is a good idea when several helpers have worked in the same situation. However, it is not to be commenced on the day of the event. It is part of a comprehensive follow-up that also includes good management and colleague support systems. Such a debriefing is recommended for those who have helped children following type I traumas, particularly those who have worked at an accident site or at a hospital. But such a debriefing can also be advantageous if carried out for teachers, preschool staff or others who have worked with helping children following a traumatic situation.

Some helpers will need trauma-specific help to counter intrusive images, fantasies or lingering thoughts. For some, post-traumatic therapy can be necessary to process experiences. But helpers can also use different self-help techniques to reduce or prevent unnecessary post-traumatic reactions. The following suggestions can be helpful:

- Speak with others about what happened (seek support from friends, colleagues and family). Professional secrecy does not prevent you from speaking about your own experiences, although there are many factors that cannot be mentioned. Seek out others who were there as helpers; then it is possible to speak about everything.

- Write down events in a diary, letter, on a computer or in other ways. It is just as important to write down thoughts and feelings as the actual events.

- Reduce or take care not to increase consumption of caffeine and sugar so as to prevent an unnecessary activation of the nervous system.

- Avoid using alcohol to relax; music or a massage can have the same effect.

- Do relaxation exercises to loosen up tensions in the neck and shoulders.

- Seek out more factual information to try and understand what happened.
- Maintain daily routines.

Cumulative stress reactions in helpers

Those who primarily work with children often become deeply involved, and sometimes too involved, in their work. They often have the feeling that they are not doing enough, or develop feelings of inadequacy. Constant work with traumatized children can overwhelm helpers over time.

Listening to traumatized people, children as well as adults, can often cause stress in the listener. Shortt and Pennebaker (1992) have shown that those who have the chance to speak about a trauma, and the thoughts and feelings it caused, experience a reduction in tension, while those who listen to accounts of the traumas of others experience an increase in bodily tension. In a way, the listener absorbs the victim's trauma. Helpers should therefore be aware that they should not spend too much of their time exclusively on trauma work; the work should be varied so that the desire to work is not broken down over time. Rothschild and Rand (2006) have in greater detail made suggestions for different support strategies for helpers.

What if one has been traumatized personally?

Personal experience can contribute to making a helper better prepared to understand and help others. Simultaneously, personal traumas can have a negative effect on health work. Many of the professional helpers who work in the fields of medicine or counselling have consciously or subconsciously chosen their profession in an attempt to fight illness, reverse feelings of helplessness or to master or control an unpredictable world (Elliott and Guy 1993). Doctors and mental health personnel show a relatively high incidence of illness, trauma and family problems in childhood (Elliott and Guy 1993; Fussell and Bonney 1990; Johnson 1991). Many appear through their choice of profession to be seeking to repair parts of their childhood and therefore choose a role as a professional helper.

This can make it easier to become involved, but it can also contribute to some 'dark patches' that can prevent one from being a good source of help. The expression 'counter transference' refers to a helper's unresolved or subconscious conflicts or worries. Those who have personally experienced a trauma can identify so strongly with a traumatized child or the child's parents that they have problems distinguishing between their own and the traumatized person's wishes and choices. In the worst cases, a helper with this type of background can 'force' a child to remain in the role as client or patient, so that the helper can continue as a helper indefinitely. The helper can also take part in denying pain because they cannot bear to confront their own pain.

McCann and Pearlman (1990) observe that listening to accounts of traumas can lead to one taking on the memories of the traumatized person. If the helpers, on the basis of their own traumas, protect themselves from the child's experience or needs, this can hinder the child from receiving adequate help. Without the opportunity to understand and work through such experiences, helpers can also be at greater risk of feeling overwhelmed, numb, emotionally distanced or incapable of giving warmth or showing empathy in relation to children or their parents. To be able to provide support, helpers must understand what is happening to them. If this does not occur, the helper will often ruminate or relive personal losses when listening to a traumatized child (see McCann and Pearlman 1990 for a more comprehensive discussion of this theme).

The professional helper role leads to greater expertise and for many this also provides a means of helping oneself. We know, however, too little about the impact such a background has on the capacity for empathy and clarity in the helper role over time.

Taking care of oneself over time

If one works with traumatized children over a long period of time, the result can be a relatively constant stress load. Here are some suggestions for counteracting such cumulative stress.

Leave the situation

At an individual level it is possible for helpers to either leave the stressful situation or change their reactions. There are a number of ways to change the situation. One course of action is to discontinue the helper role completely. This is a drastic decision, but can sometimes be necessary. If one has taken on too much of this type of work over a long period of time, a change is perhaps what is required in order to 'recharge the batteries'.

Relaxation techniques

A number of techniques can be used to reduce tension after stressful work. Many people have previous knowledge and experience of such techniques. Relaxation exercises are effective for counteracting stress and pressure from exhausting work.

Monitoring of own stress situation

It is also important to keep an eye on how one's workload affect one's:

- sleep
- family
- recreational activities
- consumption of alcohol, nicotine and coffee
- physical health
- frequency and severity of mistakes and the quality of one's decisions
- attitudes (e.g. if one becomes cynical, negative or far too critical in relation to one's work)
- behaviour (e.g. more easily irritated, explosive or more withdrawn)
- feelings (e.g. helplessness, sadness or anxiety).

Set limits

It can be important to set limits for one's level of involvement. This can be done by:

- imposing realistic requirements on oneself: is it realistic that I will be able to manage everything that I am now taking on?
- promising oneself not to work too much overtime and not to work every weekend, etc.
- learning to say no and not promise too much.

Seek out social support from family and friends

Having someone to share one's worries and frustrations with is an important buffer against work-related stress. To prevent tension between one's private and professional life, it is a good idea to allow loved ones to acquire a clear understanding of what the work involves. Family and friends can be important sources of support in terms of reducing stress, but can also contribute to added stress if they do not have an understanding of one's situation.

Regular group meetings

Among helpers working with traumatized children over time, one should hold regular meetings to talk about how the work affects the group. This can be the most important factor for keeping helpers healthy and functioning well in a long-term perspective. Unfortunately, such activities appear to have low priority in many institutions and organizations.

At such meetings the impact of the work on the group and individual members should be addressed. Here stress factors involved in the work can be discussed and ways of solving problems and conflicts addressed. What does meeting so many children in difficulty do to us? What happens to our relationship to our own children? How the group functions should also be discussed. How do we function together as helpers? What can we do to improve wellbeing? Is the stress, behaviour and/or attitudes of one of the group members a problem for other members of the group?

Guidance and recognition

Helpers who work with traumatized children should receive regular follow-up to maintain the quality of their work. The establishment of a guidance system for personnel involved in help for children is good policy. Discussions and feedback on practical aspects of one's work, as well as recognition and praise from others, helps to raise morale and promote enthusiasm. While such formal recognition and feedback often exist for health personnel, often teachers, preschool staff and others receive less support and recognition for their work with traumatized children. Although it is perhaps more difficult to implement fixed guidance routines for these groups in connection with trauma work, they can receive recognition in the form of offers of further education and participation in seminars and conferences that address the theme.

Realistic expectations

When working long-term with traumatized children it is necessary to have an understanding of one's own vulnerability in relation to traumas and loss, and correspondingly realistic expectations about one's role. It is also important to find a balance between empathy on the one hand and over-involvement on the other. Realistic goals must be set for what one can achieve in the work with children, particularly those who have experienced cumulative traumas. The helper cannot take on the child's pain but they can be present by listening, giving information and establishing a kind of contact and atmosphere that helps the child to process experiences. Often the demands helpers make on themselves are those that are the most difficult to meet.

Encouraging activities

Although courses and seminars are not intended as encouraging activities, they can function in this way. Helpers should set aside time for 'charging their batteries'. Helpers have an unfortunate tendency to put the needs of others before their own.

To ensure that helpers do not over-extend themselves completely, organizations must both set limits for involvement and invest resources in personal development. This can be done by:

- not permitting an excessive number of working hours

- giving information to personnel so that they manage to make a separation between work and free time a priority

- encouraging personnel to take part in activities outside working hours (e.g. hobbies, art, family gatherings and sports), and to go for walks and get outdoors

- emphasizing professional stimulation in the form of courses and conferences that provide a refill in the way of new knowledge, and simultaneously give new stimulus and energy

- understanding that humour and laughter can be important means of reducing strain and tension. Humour is often necessary for survival in the demanding work of helping traumatized children.

Taking care of new colleagues

For those who are 'beginners' in the field of trauma it is particularly important that they receive information and advice from those with greater experience on how they have protected themselves against stress overload and how they have taken care of themselves.

Conclusion

It is important for individuals and organizations to have routines that are designed to reduce stress levels and to disclose when expectations exceed the capacity of the helper, or when personal experiences have a negative impact on the helper, so that the helper suffers. An important task for health institutions, schools, kindergartens and other organizations lies in the establishment of effective routines that ensure a satisfactory quality in the help children receive after traumas. But individual helpers also have a responsibility to take care of themselves, so that new traumatized children who come into contact with them also benefit from a sensitive and understanding adult helper.

References

Dyregrov, A. (1989) 'Caring for helpers in disaster situations: psychological debriefing.' *Disaster Management 2*, 25–30.

Dyregrov, A. (2002) *Psykologisk debriefing. Hvordan lede gruppeprosesser etter kritiske hendelser.* Bergen: Fagbokforlaget.

Dyregrov, A. and Mitchell, J.T. (1992) 'Work with traumatized children – psychological effects and coping strategies.' *Journal of Traumatic Stress 5*, 5–17.

Elliott, D.M. and Guy, J.D. (1993) 'Mental health professionals versus non-mental-health professionals: childhood trauma and adult functioning.' *Professional Psychology: Research and Practice 24*, 83–90.

Fussell, F.W. and Bonney, W.C. (1990) 'A comparative study of childhood experiences of psychotherapists and physicists: implications for clinical practice.' *Psychotherapy 27*, 505–512.

Janoff-Bulman, R. and Frieze, I.H. (1983) 'A theoretical perspective for understanding reactions to victimization.' *Journal of Social Issues 39*, 1–17.

Johnson, W.D.K. (1991) 'Predisposition to emotional distress and psychiatric illness amongst doctors: the role of unconscious and experiential factors.' *British Journal of Medical Psychology 64*, 317–329.

McCann, L. and Pearlman, L.A. (1990) 'Vicarious traumatization: a framework for understanding the psychological effects of working with victims.' *Journal of Traumatic Stress 3*, 131–149.

Mitchell, J.T. (1983) 'When disaster strikes… the critical incident stress debriefing process.' *Journal of Emergency Medical Services 8*, 36–39.

Mitchell, J.T. (1984) 'The 660-run limit.' *Journal of Emergency Medical Services 9*, 52–54.

Rothschild, B. and Rand, M. (2006) *Help for the Helper, Self-care Strategies for Managing Burnout and Stress.* New York: W.W. Norton & Company.

Shortt, J.W. and Pennebaker, J.W. (1992) 'Talking versus hearing about Holocaust experiences.' *Basic and Applied Social Psychology 13*, 165–179.

Vachon, M.L.S. (1987) *Occupational Stress in the Care of the Critically Ill, the Dying, and the Bereaved.* New York: Hemisphere Publishing Corporation.

Appendix 1

Post-Traumatic Problems: Help for Preschool and Early School-Age Children (4 – 7 Years)

PROBLEMS	HELP
Increased anxiety	Stability in the home. Fixed routines. Assurances of presence or proximity. Physical contact, massage.
Incomplete understanding of the event or the death	Explain in a concrete manner. Use drawings, attend rituals, give the children the facts.
Confusion	Provide repeated explanations.
Anxious attachment reactions	Stable routines. Assure children that they will be picked up at kindergarten, etc.
Regressive behaviour	Expect this for a period. Start gradually with age-appropriate expectations.
Anger	Help the child find words and a focus for reactions.
Sleep disturbances	Regular bedtimes, gradual reduction of adult presence, soft music at bedtime.

PROBLEMS	HELP
Nightmares	Allow the child to speak about and draw what happened in detail. Sit by the bed and gently stroke the child's back.
Somatic reactions	If persistent, check with a doctor. Check for similarity to the reaction during the traumatic event.
Avoidance reactions	Careful, gradual confrontation of the subject or object of fear. Adult support. Assurances, calm conversation and reassuring physical contact (patting, stroking as the fearful material is approached).
Repetition and constant replaying of the events of the trauma situation	Help the child to express 'new' aspects of the event through play. Ask simple questions; suggest a new ending for the game.
Specific fears	Identify the source (traumatic reminder); teach the child control methods; systematic approach of the threatening situation.

Appendix 2

Post-Traumatic Problems: Help for School-Age Children

PROBLEMS	HELP
Sleep disturbances – falling asleep	Regular bedtimes. Thought control, music at bedtime, relaxation exercises.
Sleep disturbances – waking up or nightmares	Create a new dream. Rehearse it. Sit beside the bed and gently stroke the child's back.
Intrusive memories and thoughts	Imagery techniques – take control of the memories. Allow the child to relate, write or draw in detail what happened (all sensory impressions). Thought control.
Concentration problems	Check what is disrupting concentration. Choose method according to cause. Adjust schoolwork; be prepared that it can take time for concentration to return to normal.
Feelings of guilt and self-reproach	Explain cause–effect, go back in time, normalize, ritualized forgiveness.
Avoidance reactions	Gradual exposure to the feared situation, combined with relaxation and cognitive restructuring.

PROBLEMS	HELP
Somatic afflictions	If persistent, check with a doctor. Compare with what they were feeling during the traumatic event.
Anger and aggression	Use expressive methods. Put the reaction into words. If necessary, provide assistance in practising anger control and putting feelings into words.
Assumption of an 'adult role'	Let the adult system take responsibility, stimulate contact with peers. Discuss the situation in a family meeting.
Sadness	Set aside a specific time to think about sad things. When sad thoughts arise outside of this time period, children are to tell themselves that they will think about this in the allocated time period.
Fear (reminders)	Identify the source (traumatic reminder); teach the child control methods; systematic approach of the threatening material.
Difficulties with social contact	Stimulate contact with friends, inform friends to prevent rumours, give advice about breaking out of isolation. Make necessary arrangements so friends can meet.
Ruminating about the event	Help the child or young person to put the event in perspective. Talk about the deeper meaning of the event. Search for a personal meaning that is attributed to what happened. Set aside time for rumination.

Subject Index

Page numbers in *italics* refer to figures and boxes.

acceptance 111, 121–2
action-oriented responses
    69–70, *71*, 72
activities for helpers 229
adolescents *see* school children/
    adolescents
adults
    advice for 110–12
    management of traumatic
        reactions 20–1
    see also helpers; parents
American Psychiatric
    Association (APA) 43
amnesia 62
anger and irritability 28–9
    of helpers 222
anxiety *see* fear and anxiety
assessment
    early 91
    of need for help 83–9, 90–2
    of post-trauma recovery 92
    of post-traumatic stress
        disorder (PTSD) 44–5
attachment
    disorganized 60
    insecure 55, 60
    secure 55, 89
auditory memories 156–7
avoidance reactions 27–8, 43,
    118
    therapeutic approaches
        118–26, 167–9

behavioural memories 25, 63
belonging, sense of 36–7
bereavement groups 132, 139,
    171, 204

bilateral stimulation 146–7,
    158, 189–90
bodily reactions and memory
    30, 36, 54, 63, 160
books 118, 171
brain
    effects of stress on
        development 37–8, 59,
        61–2
    immediate responses *15*
    information processing
        16–17, 18–19, 20
break-taking in discussion
    123–4
breathing methods 174–5
'butterfly-hug' 147

CDs/DVDs 155–7, 167,
    174–5
child abuse *see* domestic
    violence; sexual abuse
classroom interventions 108
cognitive behavioural therapy
    (CBT) 143–4
cognitive restructuring 180–2
cognitive schemas 32–3, 183
common reactions, information
    about 104–6
communication
    of facts 102–3
    non-verbal 96–7
    parent–child relationship
        57–8
    see also discussion; groups
complex grief reactions 88–9
compulsive behaviour, thought
    control method for 163
computer(s) 69, 72, 164, 172
    mixing board 157
concentration, reduced 28, 40

confirmation 121–2
confrontation 169
control, sense of 119–20, 169
coping ability 39–40, 79–80
coping images 161, 168
cortisol 37, 61–2, 110
counter-conditioning 160–1
'creative text writing' 171–2
'crisis' 11
'Critical Incident Stress
    Debriefing' (CISD) 224
cumulative traumas *see*
    repetitive/cumulative
    traumas

debriefing groups 132–42
    for helpers 224
defence mechanisms 13–14
depression, mother–child
    relationship 55–6
developmental perspective *see*
    life stages
Diagnostic and Statistical
    Manual of Mental
    Disorders (DSM IV) 43
diaries 69, 72, 117, 170, 172
discussion
    active and direct approach
        120–1
    emphasize 'positive' aspects
        125–6
    'follow' the child 122
    follow up 122–3
    listening, acceptance and
        confirmation 121–2
    rhythm and respect 124–5
    sharing feelings 124
    take breaks 123–4
    timing and content of
        118–20

discussion *cont.*
  turn taking 124
  worst memories 121
  see also groups
disorganized attachment 60
dissociation 13–14, 19–20,
  38–9, 80, 86–7
distraction method 161–2
domestic violence 58–61, 100,
  132
double attention task method
  158
drawing
  and groups 135, 140
  and play 112–17
DVDs/CDs 155–7, 167,
  174–5

early assessment 91
early contact with school 203
early intervention 95–101
emotional reactions 16–17, 18,
  19, 20
emotional repression 72,
  170–1
emotionally unavailable parents
  38–9, 55–6
emotions
  dissociation 13–14, 19–20,
    38–9, 80, 86–7
  group stimulation of 130–1
  identification of 112
  regulation of 38–9
  sharing 124
empathy 124
epilepsy 30
exhaustion in helpers 220–1
existential insecurity of helpers
  222
expectations of helpers 228–9
'experience bank' 16
exposure factors *84*, 85
exposure methods 167–9
  return to scene of event
    106–8
exposure prevention 98
Eye Movement Desensitization
  and Reprocessing (EMDR)
  146–7, 158, 189–90

facts, communication of 102–3
family
  support for helpers 227–8
  see also parent–child
    relationship; parents

fantasies 99–100, 114–15,
  146–7
  rescue 114, 115
  revenge 29, 70, 114, 115
fear and anxiety 22–3, 80
  of helpers 221–2
  time setting for 165–7
feelings
  sharing 124
  see also emotions
friends
  difficulties in contact with
    74–6
  encouraging contact with
    77–8
  gender differences 68–9, 70,
    74, 75, 76–7
  network of 36–7, 76, 78,
    111, 128–9, 214–15
  risk signs of PTSD after
    suicide of 216–17
  significance of 73–4
  and social withdrawal 31,
    36
  support for helpers 227–8
  and teacher support 206
  type of support 76–7
future, lack of faith in 35, 44,
  201

gender differences 67–72
  therapeutic methods 172
grief
  complex reactions 88–9
  handling of in school
    203–6
  of helpers 222
groups
  debriefing 132–42, 224
  experiences of traumatized
    children 129–32
  Eye Movement
    Desensitization and
    Reprocessing (EMDR)
    147
  for helpers 223–4, 228
  post-traumatic stress
    disorder (PTSD) 144–5
  purpose of 128–32
  small 108
    for school children/
      adolescents 136–42
    for young children 134–6
  start-up 130

stimulation of mental and
  emotional processes
  130–1
  topics 131–2
guidance for helpers 228
guilt 26–7, 80
  actual responsibility for
    traumatic event 187
  of helpers 223
  parental 109–10
  therapeutic approach 183–8

helpers
  cumulative reactions in 225
  exhaustion 220–1
  help for 223–5
  personal experience of
    trauma 225–6
  reactions of 221–3
  taking care
    of new colleagues 229
    of oneself 226–9
helping images 161
helplessness of helpers 221
hospitalization 96–7
'hot spot' moments 181, 190

imagined actions 63
imaginery methods 152–60,
  161
Imaginery Rehearsal Technique
  176–8
'imaginery rescripting' 176
immediate reactions 15–21
information
  interventions 100–1, 102–6
  processing 16–17, 18–19,
    20
insecure attachment 55, 60
insomnia *see* sleep disturbances
intervention
  early 95–101
  methods 101–18
intrusive images 24
  of helpers 223
'irrational' actions 20
irritability *see* anger and
  irritability

learning abilities 28, 40,
  198–202
letter-writing 171

life stages 50–3
  and increasing maturity 26
  regression 30
  stress and brain development
    37–8, 59, 61–2
  writing 170
  see also school children/
    adolescents; young
    children
limit setting for helpers 227
listening 121–2
'log' method of writing 165,
  172
long-term effects of traumas
  34–42
loss
  bereavement groups 132,
    139, 171, 204
  of motivation 200–1,
    204–5
  of parent 39, 41
  responses to 29–30
'lucid dreaming' 178

massage 56, 110, 147, 179
meaning, search for 31–3, 111
memory 17–18, 24–6, 61–4,
  80
  auditory 156–7
  behavioural 25, 63
  bodily reactions and 30, 36,
    54, 63, 160
  displacements and omissions
    62
  imagined actions 63
  sense 139, 154–60
  and traumatic reminders
    53–5
  visual 154–6
  worst, discussion of 121
moral development 37
mothers see parents
motivation, loss of 200–1,
  204–5
music 176

narrative approach/storytelling
  63–4, 115, 117, 147–8
'near miss' situations 23
new colleagues, taking care
  of 229
nightmares see sleep
  disturbances
normalization 112, 122–3

olfactory impressions 158–9
omens/warnings 32, 62

parent–child relationship 55–6
  communication 31, 57–8
  role reversal 57, 60–1, 83
parents
  advice and information for
    98–9, 100–1
  and child suicide 214–15
  and commencement of child
    therapy 148–9
  emotionally unavailable
    38–9, 55–6
  and groups 130, 132
  guilt 109–10
  loss of 39, 41
  reactions to trauma 81–2,
    83, 106
  reduced capacity 41, 178–9
  and school contact 203
  and school support 207
  therapy 108–10, 150, 190,
    192–3
permission to react 111
personality development 34–5
personality factors 82
pharmacological therapy 180
phobias 86, 168–9
physical contact 178–80
  massage 56, 110, 147, 179
physical reactions 15, 16
physiological hyperarousal,
  post-traumatic therapy
  173–80
play
  and drawing 112–17
  and other forms of
    expression 117–18
  pre-school children 31, 36
  repetitive 25, 112–13
poly-victimization 59, 91
'positive' emphasis in
  discussion 125–6
post-traumatic reactions 13,
  21–33
post-traumatic stress disorder
  (PTSD) 42–4
  assessment 44–5
  prevalence of 45–6
  risk signs among friends
    after suicide 216–17
  screening instruments 91

post-traumatic therapy
  commencement 148–52
    pace and approach 151–2
    relationship building
      149–51
  for cumulative traumas 188,
    191–3
  for guilt 183–8
  methods 152–82
    cognitive behavioural
      therapy (CBT) 143–4
    group 144–5
    other 146–8
  for school children
    233–4 appendix
  for young children 189–
    90, 231–2 appendix
'postponed worry exercise'
  166–7
prayer and ritual 117–18,
  172–3, 178
pre-verbal stage 25, 63
preschool children see young
  children
profession, choice of 40–1
protective factors 89–90
psychogenic attacks 30
psychological debriefing see
  debriefing
'psychological trauma' 11–12

re-experiencing of event,
  persistent 42–3
recognition of helpers 228
red letter days 54
regression 30
relationships see friends;
  parent–child relationship;
  therapeutic relationship
relaxation 168–9, 174
  for helpers 227
repetitive play 25, 112–13
repetitive/cumulative traumas
  13, 35–6, 37
  dissociation 13–14, 19–20,
    38–9, 80, 86–7
  in helpers 225
  reduced learning ability 200
  therapeutic approach 188,
    191–3
repression 72, 170–1
rescue fantasies 114, 115
resilience 89–90
respect 124–5
return to scene of event 106–8

revenge fantasies 29, 70, 114, 115
risk factors 81–3
  assessment of need for help 83–9, 90–2
  complex grief reactions 88–9
  post-traumatic stress disorder (PTSD) after suicide of friend 216–17
  school violence 212–13
risk profile 87–8
ritual and prayer 117–18, 172–3, 178
role reversal, parent–child relationship 57, 60–1, 83
routines, security of 99

sadness 29–30
'safe place' method 153–4
schemas 32–3, 183
school
  classroom interventions 108
  early contact with 203
  handling of trauma and grief in 203–6
  and home situation 207
  learning abilities 28, 40, 198–202
  preparedness 202–3
  and sensitive themes in teaching situations 206–7
  and suicide 214–18
  trauma-focused programmes 200
school children/adolescents 31–2, 33
  post-traumatic therapy for 233–4 appendix
  small event-related groups for 136–42
  see also life stages
school violence (shootings and multiple homicides) 207–9
  follow-up 213–14
  handling real-life situation 211
  handling threats 211
  preparedness 209–10
  prevention 209
  risk factors 212–13

'screening techniques' 154–6
secure attachment 55, 89
security of routines 99
self-care of helpers 226–9
self-confidence 39–40
self-help for helpers 224–5
self-instruction 164–5
self-reproach see guilt
sense memories
  therapeutic approaches 154–60
  verbalization of 139
sensory responses 16–17
sensory triggers 23–4
sexual abuse 27, 35, 36, 59, 61
  therapeutic approaches 144, 151–2, 192–3
sexual assault 46, 54–5, 70
shame see guilt
sharing feelings 124
shock 20
situational factors 81
sleep disturbances 25–6
  therapeutic methods 175–8
small groups see groups, small
smell 158–9
social withdrawal 31, 36
storytelling/narrative approach 63–4, 115, 117, 147–8
stress
  and brain development 37–8, 59, 61–2
  hormones 37, 61–2, 110
  monitoring for helpers 227
  see also post-traumatic stress disorder (PTSD)
strong thoughts 164–5
structured review of event 103–4
suicide 214–18
survival guilt 27
symbolic stimuli 54

tapping 146, 190
taste impressions 158, 159
therapeutic relationship 146, 191, 192
  building 124–5, 149–51
therapy see post-traumatic therapy
thought control methods 162–3

time
  and content of communication 118–20
  distortion of perception 18–19
  setting for anxiety and rumination 165–7
toys 116
trauma
  definition 11–14
  factors 12
  types 12
traumatic reminders 53–5
  information about 105
trust 188, 191, 193
turn-taking in discussion 124

violence
  domestic 58–61, 100, 132
  and post-traumatic stress disorder (PTSD) 46
  risk factors 81
  see also school violence (shootings and multiple homicides)
visual memory 154–6

warnings/omens 32, 62
witnessing traumatic events 13, 57–8, 70, 81
World Health Organization (WHO) 43
worst memory, discussion of 121
writing 169–72
  self-instruction 164–5

young children
  anger 29
  play 28, 31, 36
  post-traumatic stress disorder (PTSD) criteria 44
  post-traumatic therapy for 189–90, 231–2 appendix
  pre-verbal stage 25, 63
  small event-related groups for 134–6
  see also life stages

Author Index

Adúriz, M.E. 147
Ahmad, A. 147
Alexander, J. 46
Almqvist, K. 60
Amirkan, J.H. 82
Andersen, S.L. 59
Antonsen, N.E. 76–7, 206
Aspinwall, L.G. 191
Aubert-Khalfa, S. 146

Bandler, R. 159–60
Bassøe, C.F. 16, 125
Bauer, P.J. 64
Better, R.W. 82
Bie Wikander, A.M. 74, 200
Blin, O. 146
Bluthgen, C. 147
Bohanek, J.G. 64
Bokszczanin, A. 58
Bonanno, G.A. 118
Bond, L.A. 183
Bonney, W.C. 225
Branje, S.J.T. 73
Broberg, A. 60, 218
Bryant, B. 180
Bryant, R.A. 82, 85
Buckley, H. 41, 59

Carey, P. 199
Carlson, E. 89
Carlson, J.G. 147
Carrion, V.G. 61
Cautela, J.R. 162
Chemtob, C.M. 143, 145, 147
Cicchetti, D. 35, 59

Cohen, J.A. 60, 144, 151–2, 180, 192
Connolly, D.A. 61
Copeland, W.E. 46
Croft, C. 191–2
Cryder, C.H. 92

Davis, T.E. 143
De Bellis, M.D. 37, 59
de Goede, I.H.A. 73
de Roos, C. 147
Deblinger, E. 144, 192
Dekovic, M. 82
Denes-Raj, V. 183
Denholm, C.J. 17
DePrince, A.P. 59
DeSantis, L. 80
Diamond, L.M. 191
Diego, M.A. 110, 147
Dikaiakon, A. 145
Diseth, T.H. 14
Dockett, S. 113
Duncan, A. 147
Dutra, L. 38–9
Dyregrov, A. 16, 25, 30, 46, 67, 74, 78, 81, 96, 106, 120n, 125, 139, 142, 145, 151, 198, 200, 204, 209, 215, 218, 223, 224
Dyregrov, K. 78, 151, 200

Edleson, J.L. 132
Egeland, B. 89
Ehlers, A. 180

Ehrichman, H. 183
Einarsdottir, J. 113
El-Helou, M.W. 173
Elbert, T. 199
Elklit, A. 45
Elliot, D.M. 225
Elofsson, U.O.E. 146
Eth, S. 115
Evans, C.A. 55

Fairbank, J.A. 35, 59
Feijó, L. 56
Fernandez, I. 146
Field, T. 55–6, 110, 147, 179
Finkelhor, D. 81
Fivush, R. 170
Fowler, P.J. 81
Foyes, M.M. 59
Frederickson, B.L. 90
Freyd, J.J. 59
Frieze, I.H. 221
Fussell, F.W. 225

Gaensbauer, T.J. 190
Gallinari, E. 146
Giaconia, R.M. 45
Giannopoulou, J. 145
Giedd, J.N. 52
Gjestrad, R. 25
Glad, K.A. 96
Glaser, R. 170
Goenjian, A.K. 144, 145
Gold, A. 167, 198, 199, 200–1, 204
Goldstein, A. 46
Green, B. 58
Greenwald, R. 147

Gunnar, M. 37, 38
Guy, J.D. 225

Hamada, R.S. 145
Harley, K. 64
Harris, W.W. 35, 59
Harvey, M.R. 92
Heir, T. 107
Hernandez-Reif, M. 110
Hock, E. 58
Hogan, N.S. 80
Holmes, E.A. 96
Holt, S. 41, 59
Hundeide, K. 151

Iglebaek, T. 33
Ippen, C.G. 189
Irwin, C. 56

James, B. 188
Janoff-Bulman, R. 221
Jensen, T.K. 33
Johnson, P.R. 173
Johnson, W.D.K. 225
Joseph, S. 46

Kalish, C.W. 192
Kang, M.J. 58
Kaplan, L. 151
Kaplow, J.B. 63
Kataoka, S.H. 145
Kazak, A.E. 12
Kellner, R. 176
Kessler, R.C. 45
Kiecolt-Glaser, J.K. 170
Kilpatrick, D.G. 52

Kim, J. 35, 59
King, N.J. 144, 192
Kitzmann, K.M. 81
Knopfler, C. 147
Krakow, B. 176

La Greca, A.M. 45–6
Langeland, W. 84
Larsson, B. 146
Law, F. 31, 97, 141
Layne, C.M. 145
Lengua, L.J. 13
Lewis, M.D. 39
Lieberman, A.F. 189
Lilled, L. 199
Lindgaard, C.V. 33
Lippman, J. 144, 192
Lonigan, C.J. 82
Lorenzetti, A. 146
Luthar, S.S. 46
Lutz, W.J. 58

McCann, L. 222, 226
McClain, T.M. 161
MacDonald, H.Z. 60
McFarlane, A. 56
Mannarino, A.P. 151–2, 192
Martinez, P. 57
Massad, S. 83
Mayou, R.A. 180
Meeus, W.H.J. 73
Meiser-Stedman, R. 45, 56, 82
Mireault, G.C. 183
Misch, P. 116, 117
Mitchell, J.T. 220, 223, 224
Moghadam, J. 145
Murdoch, K. 23
Mynard, H. 46

Nader, K. 20, 25, 63, 64, 70, 113, 114
Nakashima, J. 145, 147
Naybar, N. 75
Neuner, F. 148
Newcombe, R. 101
Newman, J.R. 161
Nijenhuis, E.R.S. 38

Olff, M. 84
Ollendick, T.H. 143
Ormrod, R.K. 81

Panaghi, L. 145
Paunovic, N. 160
Pearlman, L.A. 222, 226
Peled, E. 132
Pennebaker, J.W. 75, 148, 169–70, 225
Pereda, N. 46
Perlman, S.B. 192
Perry, B. 113
Perry, B.D. 59
Pilø, A.B. 76–7, 206
Pine, D.S. 60
Poijula, S. 215
Policansky, S.K. 56
Pollak, S.D. 192
Pollard, R. 59
Porter, C.L. 55
Preti, P. 212
Price, H.L. 61
Prinstein, M.J. 45–6
Proctor, L.J. 56
Putnam, F.W. 35, 59
Pynoos, R.S. 20, 62, 63, 64, 70, 81, 113, 114, 115

Qouta, S. 29
Quevedo, K. 37, 38

Rand, M. 225
Raundalen, M. 25, 120n, 151, 209
Rawlins, W.K. 73
Reese, E. 64, 101
Reich, W. 151
Reiss, A.L. 61
Ribchester, T. 147
Richards, J.M. 118
Richters, J.E. 57
Risinger, R.T. 82
Rodway, M.R. 108
Roques, J. 146
Rose, A.J. 73
Rothschild, B. 225
Rueckert, L. 75
Rutter, M. 85, 89

Sack, W.H. 25
Saeger Wewerka, S. 64
Saigh, P.A. 13
Salmon, K. 82
Salter, E. 46, 92
Salzman, W.R. 200

Scafidi, F. 110, 147
Scheeringa, M.S. 44, 46
Schoeman, R. 199
Schredl, M. 178
Schultz, J.-H. 209
Scrimin, S. 199
Seedat, S. 199
Seligman, S. 110, 147
Sembi, S. 166
Shannon, M.P. 82
Shooshtary, M.H. 145
Shortt, J.W. 75, 225
Silverman, W.K. 143
Sinclair, E. 82
Smith, P. 145, 174, 182
Solomon, R.M. 16, 125
Spoormaker, V.I. 178
Sroufe, L.A. 89
Stallard, P. 31, 46, 92, 97, 141–2, 143, 162, 192–3
Stanton, H.E. 160
Steele, H. 191–2
Steele, K. 38
Steele, M. 191–2
Steer, R.A. 144, 192
Stein, B.D. 145
Stormyren, S. 33
Suliman, S. 46
Sundelin-Wahlsten, V. 146
Swickert, R.J. 82

Tannen, D. 70
Tarabulsy, G.M. 60, 193
Taylor, T.L. 143
Teicher, M.H. 59
Terr, L.C. 12, 19, 25, 44, 62
Thayer, R.E. 161
Tinker, R.H. 147
Tugade, M.M. 90
Turner, H.A. 91

Udwin, O. 23

Vachon, M.L.S. 176
Valentino, K. 35, 59
van den Bout, J. 178
van der Hart, O. 38
van der Kolk, B.A. 37

Van Horn, P. 189
Velleman, R. 46
Vigerust, S. 74, 200

Wagar, J.M. 108
Wahlberg, K.-E. 215
Ward-Begnoche, W.L. 91
Weems, C.F. 61
Weinman, J. 170
Weisæth, L. 107
Wells, A. 166
Wetherington, H.R. 143
Whelan, S. 41, 59
Williams, L.M. 61
Williams, R.M. 81
Wilson, S.A. 147
Wisocki, P.A. 162
Wraith, R. 134

Yule, W. 23, 81, 145, 147, 167, 171, 198, 199, 200–1, 204

Zadra, A. 176
Zeanah, C.H. 44